What Your Colleagues Are Saying

Often most curricular reforms start with asking *what* to change—resulting in recycled old ways to teach the "same"—garnished with activities that masquerade as agency. This book starts with the *why* and sets out to invite the *who* into designing the journey of change. What you get are simple, yet mature, frameworks and proven strategies to support educators in empowering their students with the tools to see the wondrous interconnectedness of life and their role to sustain and nourish this web. This book is a must for all those who want their children to graduate with optimism and skills to design a more compassionate, sustainable tomorrow, today!

—Kiran Bir Sethi, Founder
The Riverside School and Design for Change

Educating young people to be "worldwise" and to integrate heart, head, and hand to become the citizens the world so desperately needs has just become a whole lot easier. This brilliant and essential book provides the vision, blueprint, examples, and direction that teachers can utilize right now to ensure their students, and the world they will shape, are both able to thrive.

—Zoe Weil, President and Co-Founder
Institute for Humane Education

How can we, as teachers, create classrooms that tap students' innate desire and capability to shape a better world, and how can we use this as a catalyst to develop our students' knowledge, skills, understanding, and dispositions? *Worldwise Learning* delivers what it promises. Through a clear vision, an easy-to-follow framework, ready-to-use strategies, and real examples drawn from classrooms around the world, educators now have a guide to turn this aspiration into a reality. Transformative learning centered on local, global, and intercultural issues not only speak to students' passions and lived experiences, but it also cultivates the modern skill set needed for students to pursue their own dreams and to become a transforming influence in our world.

—Tiffanee Brown, Consultant, Co-Author
Concept-Based Literacy Lessons

Carla Marschall and Elizabeth O. Crawford, with *Worldwise Learning*, have delved deep into the complexity and multifaceted nature of providing learning journeys for children to become contributing global citizens, something the world needs desperately. I particularly love the emphasis and support around co-planning lessons.

—Emer Beamer, Founder and Learning Lead
Design-a-thon Works; Ashoka Fellow

Carla Marschall and Elizabeth O. Crawford have written a masterpiece that affords a guide for educators to build, alongside their students, a just and sustainable future. Not only do the authors present a vision for transformative education, but they also offer a dynamic learning cycle, practical strategies, and stories from diverse classrooms throughout the world to support the development of students' global competences. This book is a must-read for the 21st century educator.

—Jacob Sule, Executive Director
iRead To Live Initiative, Nigeria

Marschall and Crawford compel readers to see schooling in a different way, one that is focused more on worldwise learning. Using examples from their own lives and schools around the world, they illustrate how teaching and learning can be more globally minded. For any educator or community member who wants to critically reflect on their own practices and work to envision a more sustainable approach to education, this book is for you.

—Dr. Emily Liebtag, Co-Author
Difference Making at the Heart of Learning

Worldwise Learning opens a door to the kind of learning that David Perkins has memorably called "life worthy." This is a door that many teachers are looking for as the importance of connecting learners to local and global issues, and to their sense of passion and purpose, strains against more traditional models of learning that no longer serve our needs.

—Stuart MacAlpine, Senior Programme Specialist
LEGO Foundation

Collaborative Learning Network will make it a priority to share *Worldwise Learning* with each team of thoughtful educators we are fortunate to work with. The inspiring stories, spotlights, and strategies in each of the chapters will deepen the practice of educators around the world. This book illustrates many ways to meaningfully connect learners to their natural curiosity, to understand the world around them, and to extend their learning into harmonious action.

—Nick Salmon, Founder and CEO
Collaborative Learning Network

This book represents a message of hope for the future, calling on educators to honour each of our stories, passions, and concerns. Through a pedagogical framework designed to give students meaningful connection with their lived experiences; deep relational understanding through being seen, heard, and valued; and empowerment to take authentic action in their communities, *Worldwise Learning* demonstrates how educators can design learning for students of all ages to become positive contributors to the world. With inspiring spotlights, practical strategies for applying and transferring learning, and easy-to-follow ideas for co-planning with students, *Worldwise Learning* provides educational tools and frameworks that align with Globally Reconnect's vision: to co-create a harmonious world in which we can all flourish. This beautiful book is a must-read for all educators co-creating with us.

—Kavita Tanna, Founder
Globally Reconnect

We are living at a time when global competence is essential, not only for individuals but also for global stability, prosperity, and peace. And yet developing globally competent students is complicated. Luckily *Worldwise Learning* has provided a road map that recognizes the value of voice and agency, as well as the transformative power of storytelling to engage, illuminate, and, perhaps most important, connect young people across a diversity of cultures and geographies. In this very large world that is going to keep getting smaller and more interdependent, the message of *Worldwise Learning*—Connect, Understand, Act—has never seemed more relevant.

—Kayce Freed Jennings, Senior Advisor and Director
U.S. Educator Program, Girl Rising

Worldwise Learning offers a necessary pedagogical framework to advocate for students to push for global understanding and action. Building a co-created classroom that positions itself in global meaning-making is a profound need for maintaining our democracy, educating our youth, and allowing students to channel their inner curiosity. This work offers a clear outline for transforming one's classroom for worldwide change.

—Chris McNutt, Founder and Executive Director
Human Restoration Project

This book is an invitation, guidebook, and launchpad aimed at activating the Worldwise Learner in us all. Relevant, authentic, inspiring, and chock full of tools to reflect, grow, and synergize, *Worldwise Learning* truly empowers us to think for ourselves, explore alternative futures, and take action to ensure the well-being of our entire global ecosystem.

—Julia Fliss, Sixth-Grade Language Arts Teacher
Evergreen Middle School, Evergreen, CO

I am recommending *Worldwise Learning: A Teacher's Guide to Shaping a Just, Sustainable Future* because as a global educator and Black woman it is imperative for others to understand the ins and outs of being a global citizen. Our students need to be able to learn from those who are wanting to teach culturally relevant teaching and to be able to share their voice with others. We as educators need to be able to show our students, parents, and surrounding communities what diversity, equity, and inclusivity really looks like and how to stand up for the truth. This book takes the time to help others unlearn and dismantle oppressive systems within and beyond us.

—Marla Hunter, Founder and CEO of Live. Love. Teach!, LLC
Diversity, Equity, Inclusion, and Justice Specialist; Global Educator

There could be no better time to publish a book on transformative education for a better, fairer, world. May this thoughtfully crafted learning tool not only spark students and educators intellectually but also touch their hearts. This can bring about the much needed shifts from competition to compassion and from comparison to all children everywhere shining in their true potential; like stars on Earth.

—Charlotte Leech, Co-Founder
Loka School India

Worldwise Learning is a compelling and timely book that presents a powerful vision of transformative education for our times. Steeped in democratic values and a respect for student agency, the authors offer a framework for educating responsible and compassionate learners in a complex and interconnected world.

—Dr. Shari Tishman, Project Zero
Harvard Graduate School of Education

We can't afford to fail in our pursuit to raise citizens empowered to understand and take action on local and global challenges. While too many adults look the other way, educators like Marschall and Crawford inspire children and young people to be the force for change that this world needs. *Worldwise Learning: A Teacher's Guide to Shaping a Just, Sustainable Future* is grounded in research and filled with practical strategies inspiring students to engage critically, take responsibility, and produce change.

—Rachel French, Director of Professional Learning International
Co-Author, *Concept-Based Inquiry in Action*

WORLDWISE LEARNING

*To those who strive daily to create a more
peaceful, just, and sustainable future for all.*

WORLDWISE LEARNING

A Teacher's Guide to Shaping a Just, Sustainable Future

CARLA MARSCHALL
ELIZABETH O. CRAWFORD

Foreword by VERÓNICA BOIX MANSILLA

Illustrations by CHRIS GADBURY

CORWIN

FOR INFORMATION:

Corwin

A SAGE Company

2455 Teller Road

Thousand Oaks, California 91320

(800) 233-9936

www.corwin.com

SAGE Publications Ltd.

1 Oliver's Yard

55 City Road

London EC1Y 1SP

United Kingdom

SAGE Publications India Pvt. Ltd.

B 1/I 1 Mohan Cooperative Industrial Area

Mathura Road, New Delhi 110 044

India

SAGE Publications Asia-Pacific Pte. Ltd.

18 Cross Street #10-10/11/12

China Square Central

Singapore 048423

President: Mike Soules

Associate Vice President and
    Editorial Director: Monica Eckman

Executive Editor: Tori Mello Bachman

Associate Content
    Development Editor: Sharon Wu

Associate Editor: Eliza B. Erickson

Editorial Assistant: Nancy Chung

Project Editor: Amy Schroller

Copy Editor: Deanna Noga

Typesetter: C&M Digitals (P) Ltd.

Proofreader: Dennis W. Webb

Cover Designer: Gail Buschman

Marketing Manager: Margaret O'Connor

Printed in Great Britain by Ashford Colour Press Ltd.

Library of Congress Cataloging-in-Publication Data

Names: Marschall, Carla, author. | Crawford, Elizabeth O., author.

Title: Worldwise learning : a teacher's guide to shaping a just, sustainable future / Carla Marschall, Elizabeth O. Crawford.

Description: Thousand Oaks, California : Corwin, [2022] | Series: Corwin teaching essentials | Includes bibliographical references and index.

Identifiers: LCCN 2021018647 | ISBN 9781071835944 (paperback) | ISBN 9781071835937 (epub) | ISBN 9781071835920 (epub) | ISBN 9781071835913 (pdf)

Subjects: LCSH: Education and globalization. | Education—Environmental aspects.

Classification: LCC LC191 .M37 2022 | DDC 370.116—dc23
LC record available at https://lccn.loc.gov/2021018647

This book is printed on acid-free paper.

21 22 23 24 25 10 9 8 7 6 5 4 3 2 1

CONTENTS

For additional content related to
Worldwise Learning please visit
www.teachworldwise.com.

FOREWORD

We live in times of profound social, technological, cultural, and environmental transformations that call for new visions about the role of education in the construction of future societies. As this book goes to print, we peek into the future through the windows of our homes. COVID-19 continues to color our calendars with unfathomable loss and reshape daily patterns of human interaction. The pandemic has brought to light harrowing global inequities and systemic forms of exclusion that leave no one untouched. It has revealed democratic institutions in need of repair and collective vulnerabilities in need of attention. Without doubt, COVID-19 represents yet another chapter in the story of our global interdependence as a species, confirming that what happens on the other side of our small planet has direct impact on our lives and vice versa.

This is not the first, nor will it be the last, time a global phenomenon of this magnitude demands that we examine who we are, what values and principles we choose to live by, and who among our fellow human beings is within our realm of mutual obligation. Neither is this the first nor the last time a generation is moved to stop and rethink the education of their young. In tumultuous times, educators emerge as key players in the construction of better societies. Throughout the pandemic, we have witnessed educators' implacable dedication to our children. Professionalism took the form of accelerated efforts to learn to teach online, embrace children's well-being, and communicate with caregivers and cultural institutions in search of insight and resources. What is perhaps less visible is the fact that, day in and day out, in the intimacy of Zoom class discussions, or the adaptive, micro-decisions they make when planning lessons or assessments, these educators are quiet protagonist of an emerging paradigm shift in the world of education itself.

Enduring paradigm shifts in education rarely emerge from times of peace and prosperity. Much to the contrary, movements such as those inspired by

John Dewey in the United States, Loris Malaguzzi in Italy, or Paulo Freire in Brazil represent visionary educational responses to historic moments of reckoning. Dewey's progressive education placed the child and her adjustment to a changing world at the center of a hands-on and in-the-world educational experience, seeking to strengthen democracy at a time when rapid industrialization, urbanization, and immigration met the Great Depression. Decades later in Italy, Loris Malaguzzi responded to the wreckage of World War II and the Nationalist movements that fueled it with a vision of education centered on the image of a capable citizen-child, bearer of the right to education and able to make sense of the world in 100 languages. The result was in the long-standing tradition of Reggio Emilia schools we see today. Years later, in Brazil, Paulo Freire responded to the wave of dictatorships that swept Latin America with the pedagogy of the oppressed, as an effort to nurture social and political consciousness. The approach consisted in giving agency to the dispossessed and empowering them to "read and write" texts as well as the reality around them.

Today, as we reckon with a pandemics cascade, we may find hope in the fact that difficult times can breed enduring humanizing educational visions. These in turn, can reframe how we think about the purposes, principles, values, and tools with which we nurture our children's minds, hearts, and hands. But new educational paradigms like the ones the thinkers above proposed are never the result of a single book or a single mind. Rather paradigms change through the bottom-up emergence of ideas, practices, and tools that challenge the status quo, finding local zones of possibility and generativity. Eventually, conditions permitting, these eclectic developments reach a collective tipping point and restructure the field. In other words, a paradigm shift is the work of many.

It is therefore pertinent that, at a time of global reckoning with the multiple pandemics afflicting our children and our future, Carla Marschall and Elizabeth O. Crawford bring to us *Worldwise Learning: A Teacher's Guide to Shaping a Just, Sustainable Future.* This carefully researched book proposes a comprehensive and accessible synthesis of ideas, practices, and strategies that practitioners of global education working in a broad range of contexts have found useful over time. At the heart of the argument and recommendations for practice stands the Worldwise Learning Framework—an elegant and accessible pedagogical articulation featuring three learning phases: Connect, Understand, and Act. Marschall and Crawford do not tell teachers exactly what to teach or do in their classrooms. Rather, they offer principles that invite teachers to think for themselves and design suitable curricula. Equally relevant is the extensive collection of practical strategies the authors have compiled drawing from pedagogies that range from storytelling, to systems thinking and conceptual thinking, to using design thinking and change-making approaches to take action. The wealth of ideas and strategies here curated is leveraged by the authors' accessible language—which readers will find inviting.

I anticipate that *Worldwise Learning: A Teacher's Guide to Shaping a Just, Sustainable Future* will become a beloved resource for practitioners working with children in Grades K–8. Teachers, curriculum developers, teacher educators, and designers will find themselves coming back to their favorite chapters, revisiting and expanding their repertoire of strategies. Perhaps equally important, educators will find in these pages a timely reminder of the purpose of education for our times, which I would characterize as nurturing every child equitably to flourish in their full human potential (socio-emotional, cognitive, aesthetic, ethical, civic) and contributing to the construction of kinder, more inclusive, equitable, and sustainable societies. In this regard, Marschall and Crawford's work entails a significant contribution to the new human-centered global educational paradigm taking shape under our feet.

Verónica Boix Mansilla
Principal Investigator, Project Zero
Research Director, Re-Imagining Migration
Harvard Graduate School of Education

PREFACE

"The fact is that, given the challenges we face,

education doesn't need to be reformed—it needs to be transformed."

—Sir Ken Robinson, Author, Speaker, and Arts Education Advocate

On December 31, 2019, the Wuhan Municipal Health Commission reported a series of viral pneumonia cases in the People's Republic of China (World Health Organization, 2020). Soon after, the outbreak spread quickly to other countries, closing borders and eventually schools throughout the world. By April 2020, 1.6 billion students in 190 countries were not learning in their classrooms, exacerbating existing inequalities in lower-resourced communities and for marginalized learners (United Nations [UN], 2020). For those with access to remote learning, the lack of social interaction with peers and caring adults negatively affected students' social, emotional, and mental well-being. Indeed, school is much more than academic learning. Beyond education systems, the ripple effect of the pandemic has been felt in every facet of daily life for the nearly eight billion people who share our planet: social, economic, technological, political, and cultural. If we were to pause and listen deeply to the lessons of 2020, what would they tell us?

When the World Health Organization officially named the novel coronavirus disease COVID-19 in February 2020, we had just begun writing this book. Our aim as pedagogical leaders, educators, and authors was to support teachers in their critical work cultivating the minds and hearts of students in the context of our fast-paced, globalized world characterized by volatility, uncertainty, complexity, and ambiguity (Bennis & Nanus, 1986). Then we were suddenly living it. Without question, a nanometer-sized virus has revealed a web of interconnected global challenges that characterize the contemporary world, from poverty and health care to technology infrastructure and employment

stability. It has allowed us to reflect on our rapidly changing world and our preparedness for the future challenges our students will undoubtedly face. One year later, the pandemic continues to be a powerful presence in our lives today, underscoring the critical importance of preparing students for the challenges and opportunities of living in a global society.

With the backdrop of the coronavirus, other issues and questions also emerged, creating a tapestry of complexity: Black Lives Matter, natural disasters, climate change, elections, and technology. Our students were puzzled, often filled with worry and anxiety. We did our best to provide stability, although the swirl of current events threatened to take us with it. And in attempting to address our students' concerns, our own questions emerged as educators:

1. How can we meaningfully integrate the issues our students want to explore into our teaching?

2. How can we give students a sense of agency while uncertainty and ambiguity encircle us?

3. How can we ensure education is a humanizing force in a time characterized by detachment and isolation?

The Purpose of This Book

To address these questions, we designed a pedagogical framework for Grades K–8 and identified accompanying practices that support the creation of humane, democratic classrooms. In these learning spaces, students are seen, inspired, and empowered to act on interconnected global challenges, what we coin *Worldwise Learning*. We show you how to draw on students' strengths, passions, concerns, and experiences to choose issues as meaningful organizers for learning. We help you honor student questions and find the time for children to explore them within the constraints you may face. We walk you through a learning cycle that enables your students to form personal connections, develop deep understanding, and take informed action on issues in the world. Importantly, this book is not meant to be a how-to guide or step-by-step process for curriculum planning. Instead, we aim to support educators across myriad contexts to recognize and leverage students' concerns as powerful organizers for learning.

Throughout the chapters in this book, we outline flexible pathways, strategies, and stories from the classroom that, together, bring Worldwise Learning to life. Because each school is a unique sociocultural context with diverse needs, available resources, and pedagogical priorities, this book includes classroom examples from different countries and models of schooling. In some cases, teachers have full autonomy to design the curriculum. In others, educators must follow school- or district-level pacing guides and curriculum frameworks. Instead of calling for a radical revisioning of the school day or curriculum, we advocate for transforming education by centering pedagogy on students' lives and significant interdisciplinary issues. In essence, we propose creative use of the curriculum to allow learners to make sense of the world around them and their roles in it. We illustrate the many ways educators can approach this important work.

A nanometer-sized virus has revealed a web of interconnected global challenges that characterize the contemporary world, from poverty and health care to technology infrastructure and employment stability. It has allowed us to reflect on our rapidly changing world and our preparedness for the future challenges our students will undoubtedly face.

The Worldview and Beliefs That Frame This Book

This book reflects our thoughts, beliefs, and experiences. We are White, middle-class women who have been privileged to have had access to high-quality education and international experiences in a variety of school contexts. We understand that our backgrounds and life experiences have shaped our world-views and perspectives on education and that we communicate these through our writing. In essence, we write *who we are*. Although this may seem obvious, we feel it is vital to explicitly mention our awareness of potential limitations in writing this book from our perspectives. Likewise, we feel it is important to lay out some foundational beliefs we've used to put together this book and the choices we've made as a result:

1. *We believe that . . .* The idea of universality comes from a Western viewpoint that limits indigenous and non-Western perspectives. There is no singular truth or one way to educate learners to understand contemporary issues: It all comes down to context. *For this reason . . .* We've intentionally thought about the ways we can reflect a pluriversality of thoughts and opinions through the Spotlights, quotes, and examples of practice we've drawn together. These reflect Western, non-Western, and indigenous approaches and voices from diverse racial, cultural, and linguistic backgrounds.

2. *We believe that . . .* Worldwise Learning should apply to all learners, not just a small number of privileged students who have social, cultural, and financial capital. *For this reason . . .* We've worked with teachers in a variety of school contexts to collate examples: traditional and charter public schools, independent schools, and international schools. Likewise we've collaborated with nonprofit organizations that have a wide global reach and experiences both within schools and in other types of institutions.

3. *We believe that . . .* Global citizenship as a construct goes beyond responsibilities to human communities to include all species on Earth. We are but one living being on this expansive planet and have a duty to ensure that all organisms can thrive. *For this reason . . .* We've drawn from related fields such as sustainability education, humane education, and peace education to weave together a vision for global citizenship for K–8 learners. We've included connections to the idea of unity with the natural world across the book and included many examples related to life on land and in water as a way to support the ecoliteracy of our readers.

4. *We believe that . . .* teaching is an inherently political act. There is no such thing as being neutral in the classroom. From the curricular choices we make (or don't make), teachers influence how and what children think, including the lenses they use to view the world. Being political does not mean being partisan or talking about political parties and their viewpoints in the classroom. It means that by promoting democratic values, such as voice, participation, and perspective-taking, we teach children how to become active citizens. *For this reason . . .* We've included protocols and strategies that support the creation of democratic classrooms.

From co-planning with students to encouraging rigorous dialogue and the exchange of ideas, Worldwise Learners take part in a participatory process, where they develop values and dispositions through the act of learning.

An Invitation to the Reader

In a world characterized by daunting environmental and social challenges, it takes courage to be an educator who is conscious of the work that lies ahead. In 2005, Maxine Greene coined this a critical pedagogy of *wide-awakeness* whereby educators must be "awake, critical, open to the world. It is an honor and a responsibility to be a teacher in such dark times—and to imagine, and to act on what we imagine, what we believe ought to at last be" (p. 80). This is complemented by Brazilian educator and philosopher Paulo Freire's (1998) concept of *conscientization*, the process of developing a critical awareness of real problems through reflection and action. Both Greene and Freire call for committing ourselves to critical interrogation and the creation of more democratic classrooms. In the same way that small actions combine to create big impacts, each of our classrooms becomes an important part of a greater system, which we have the ability to transform. As you begin reading, we invite you to reflect on your power to leverage education as a positive force to shape and unite individuals, communities, and the world at large. It is no easy task, but surely with our collective might, we can do it together.

Carla Marschall and Elizabeth O. Crawford

ACKNOWLEDGMENTS

The vision for this book was shaped by the contributions of numerous educators, authors, and education leaders working in a variety of contexts with the shared goal of creating a better world through education.

We are especially grateful to the following educators for sharing their insights, as well as for opening up their classrooms, allowing us to showcase their practice as part of this book: Jim Bentley, Tiffanee Brown, Geraldine Brogden, Grant Burwash, Jon Butcher, Martina Croom-Schöfberger, Julia Fliss, Megan Gill, Donovan Hall, Shannon Hardy, Mike Hoare, Lorraine Jacobs-Hyde, Aisha Kristiansen, Charlotte Leech, Kris Leverton, Jerry Liu, Laura Montague, Andrea Morgen, Amelia O'Brien, Katelyn Patterson, Sally Petermann, Daniel Withington, and Daun Yorke.

We also thank the following generous colleagues whom we interviewed for their expertise and perspectives: Emer Beamer (Design-a-thon Works), Carol Bliese (Population Education), Melissa Daniels (High Tech High), Dr. Sheldon L. Eakins (Leading Equity Center), Michael Fauteux (GiveThx), Hanna Hjerppe (Taksvärkki ry), Mike Johnston (Compass Education), Shohei Kawakami (Soka Gakkai), Chris Lintott (Zooniverse), Stuart MacAlpine (New Zealand Green School), Keith Moore (Gapminder Foundation), Rachel Musson (ThoughtBox), Alejandra Peña Pous (Social Design), Mary Quinnan (Waters Center for Systems Thinking), Cleary Vaughan-Lee (Global Oneness Project), Harrison Wavell (Ellen MacArthur Foundation), and Zoe Weil (The Institute for Humane Education).

To the incredibly talented and humble artist and illustrator of this book, Chris Gadbury: It has been an honor to collaborate with you on this project. You have helped bring the text to life.

Finally, we are grateful to our families whose love and tireless support made this book possible.

Publisher's Acknowledgments

Corwin gratefully acknowledges the following individuals:

Nicholas Alchin
Head of Campus, UWC South East Asia, East Campus

Tiffanee Brown
Author and Educational Consultant

Julia Fliss
Educator, Evergreen Middle School, and TeachSDGs Ambassador

Rachel French
Director, Professional Learning International

Rick Hannah
Chair of Service and Sustainable Development,
    UWC South East Asia, East Campus

Emily Liebtag
Author and Educational Consultant

Jennifer McMahon
Director of Learning, Livonia Central School District (USA) and
Director of Education Initiatives and Teacher Development,
    Butterfly Pea Charitable Foundation (Cambodia)

Mary Quinnan
Vice President, Waters Center for Systems Thinking

Elaine Shobert
Literacy Coach and Lead Teacher, Rock Rest Elementary School

Faye Snodgress
Former Executive Director, Sustainability Advisor - Educational Leaders
    Without Borders

Jennifer Williams
Executive Director, Take Action Global

ABOUT THE AUTHORS

Carla Marschall is an experienced educator, curriculum developer, and pedagogical leader, who has worked in a variety of leadership roles in international schools in Switzerland, Germany, Hong Kong, and Singapore over the past 10 years. She currently works as the Director of Teaching & Learning at UWC South East Asia, with the mission to make "education a force to unite people, nations, and cultures for peace and a sustainable future." A certified Lynn Erickson Concept-Based Curriculum and Instruction Consultant, Carla is the co-author of *Concept-Based Inquiry in Action* (Corwin, 2018). Carla holds a Masters in Elementary Education from Teachers College, Columbia University, and a Masters in Applied Educational Leadership and Management from the Institute of Education, University of London.

Elizabeth O. Crawford is a teacher educator and curriculum designer specializing in global education. She has taught in a variety of school contexts, including elementary and middle schools in France and the United States. Currently an Associate Professor of Elementary Education at the University of North Carolina Wilmington, Elizabeth supports educators to address interconnected global challenges in the curriculum. She collaborates with other teacher educators, classroom teachers, and organizations globally to advance the Sustainable Development Goals. Elizabeth holds a Masters in Elementary Education from Florida State University, an Educational Specialist in Educational Leadership and Policy Studies from the University of Alabama, and a PhD in Educational Policy, Planning, and Leadership from the College of William & Mary.

ABOUT THE ILLUSTRATOR

Chris Gadbury is a visual arts teacher and illustrator in Hong Kong who is passionate about inquiry and visual learning. In 2019, Chris gave a TEDx talk about how he informs students about global issues through his series of illustrated storybooks whilst encouraging them to come up with solutions. Chris is perhaps best known for his quirky art videos on his popular website ArtLesson.blog, as well as for his PYP-themed posters that are used in IB schools around the world. Chris has designed resources for organizations such as The World's Largest Lesson and Managebac. He is a TeachSDGs Ambassador and has been commissioned as a sketchnote artist by the United Nations.

INTRODUCTION
The Imperative

"Before you finish eating breakfast this morning,
you've depended on more than half the world."
—Dr. Martin Luther King, Jr., Minister and Civil Rights Activist

Early each morning, before the sun rises above the horizon, our students unknowingly take part in multiple local and global systems. Whether they eat breakfast at home or at school, this meal is the outcome of a complex journey. From the oats in their cereal, to the apples in their juice, intricate stories exist behind each of these foods. The apples grew crisp and ripe with the help of millions of pollinators and a predictable temperate climate with warm days and cold nights. The fruit was likely harvested by migrant workers who sought to improve their economic prospects by leaving home. Placed on cargo ships that sailed across the ocean, the apples even played a role in the global economy, when they were bought and sold as goods in our neighborhood supermarkets. And that's just breakfast. Before they see us each morning, our students also get dressed, travel to school, and even use devices to communicate with family or friends, which are all connected to their own complex processes. Imagine zooming out to view the planet as a whole, seeing all those invisible threads of connection spread, linking each student to people and places all around the world. Our interconnectedness provides us with access to resources, people, and ideas from around the world, yet can also propel unintended consequences.

As the COVID-19 pandemic spread in 2020, educators saw firsthand the extent to which these global connections touch our lives. Flights were canceled, and loved ones were seen less frequently. With disruptions to manufacturing and trade, we bought up essentials whenever they were in stock. Navigating virtual learning environments, we grappled with meeting the social-emotional needs of young learners, who were physically removed from their classmates. And hearing our students' questions about the ripple effects the virus created in our lives, we were challenged to help them understand the world around them. How does the virus make people sick? How did it travel around the world? Why are essentials that were once readily available now unavailable? What role do politicians and public servants play in reducing the severity of the pandemic? When will it end? Answering such questions requires interdisciplinary thinking and comfort with ambiguity. They cause us to reflect on whether our curriculum, broken into discrete subject areas, adequately prepares students to think critically, act responsibly, and seek solutions to complex, interconnected issues.

Undeniably, the global challenges we face transcend the artificial boundaries societies have made, such as city, state, or national borders. They have no single cause and no simple solution. This idea is not new, of course. Fifty years ago, environmentalist Dr. Barry Commoner sounded an early alarm about environmental crises: from radioactive fallout and air pollution to pesticides and water contamination. He argued that these issues occur not in isolation but rather are connected to everything else, including war, poverty, racism, and social inequalities (Commoner, 1971). Today, globalization has furthered interconnectedness on our planet, often with catastrophic impacts: climate change, food and water insecurity, extreme poverty, and now a global pandemic. Warming oceans, shrinking ice sheets, sea level rise, and ocean acidification are leading to a whole host of issues such as flooding, extreme weather and biodiversity loss (National Aeronautics and Space Administration [NASA], 2021). By 2050, the world's population is expected to reach nearly 10 billion people, limiting the Earth's capacity to produce adequate food, space, and other resources (UN Environment Programme, 2020). Such far-reaching issues cannot be solved by a single individual, or even a single country. Global challenges can only be improved together, through communication, cooperation, and commitment. They also call for an innovative approach to education that prepares students as knowledgeable, compassionate, and engaged global citizens (United Nations Educational, Scientific, and Cultural Organization [UNESCO], 2014).

This book presents a vision for transformative education, one that allows us to collectively rise from the ashes of trauma and loss caused by recent events. It unpacks what it means to educate in the context of our complex world. While recognizing that globalization has in many cases increased levels of inequality, promoted consumption, and made dominant voices louder, our aim is to consider how we can co-construct humane, democratic classrooms within this context. Learning that encourages children to seek solutions to problems they face. Learning that fosters students' emotional connection, personal well-being, and reverence for the natural world. Learning that demands students participate

This book unpacks what it means to educate in the context of our complex world. While recognizing that globalization has in many cases increased levels of inequality, promoted consumption, and made dominant voices louder, our aim is to consider how we can co-construct humane, democratic classrooms within this context.

actively in their communities. Such learning *matters*. It is authentic, purposeful, relevant, and engaging. It builds and improves neighborhoods. It prepares learners to navigate an unknown future. Through such teaching, we communicate a key message: to learn is to hope. Learning is a light, which can guide us through times of darkness.

Global Competence: Transforming Learning to Action

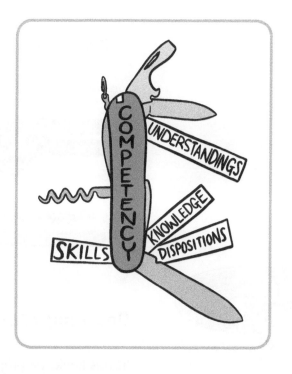

Despite the challenges communities face today, education can empower children and youth to find practical, scalable solutions that balance human needs with the needs of the environment. When we ask students to meaningfully apply their learning to complex issues, **global competence** emerges. The mobilization of learning to meet complex demands (Organisation for Economic Co-operation and Development [OECD], 2018b), **competency** bridges the gap between student learning and student action. We can think of a competency like a Swiss Army knife. Faced with a particular novel or complex context, we can draw from our knowledge, skills, understandings, and dispositions like a set of tools that can be combined for a purpose. Cooking dinner at the campsite? Get out your can opener, knife, and corkscrew. Fixing the tent? Use your screwdriver, pliers, and wood saw. And as we know from camping, they're very handy to have in your back pocket.

Global competence is the Swiss Army knife for facing situations in our volatile, uncertain, complex, and ambiguous world. By global, we mean *encompassing* and *inclusive*, not just applicable to issues relating to the whole world. Learners display their global competence at various scales, especially the local. Importantly, it emerges when students wrestle with novel or complex situations.

For example, imagine students are studying soil health and the specific issue of soil erosion. When teachers design learning experiences with global competence in mind, all learning domains are addressed. Students develop *knowledge* of soil and facts about soil erosion. They strengthen their information literacy *skills* as they locate relevant information and create infographics on soil health. Students develop *understandings* about how living organisms interact and the role of soil in the global food system. They display *dispositions*, such as questioning and thinking creatively. As students are driven to act on the issue of soil maintenance on campus, they grapple with complexity and demonstrate their global competence.

Importantly, unlike these four learning domains, global competence is not an outcome to be displayed and then mastered; rather, it is a lifelong endeavor that accompanies a global and intercultural outlook (Boix Mansilla & Jackson, 2011). Figure 0.1 shows the interaction between the four learning domains, their application to novel or complex situations as global competence, and the resulting action that occurs. Relationships between the four learning domains are explored further in Chapter 1.

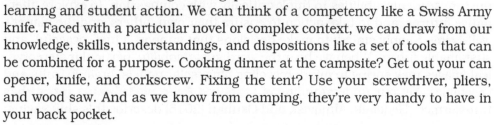

Through such teaching, we communicate a key message: to learn is to hope. Learning is a light, which can guide us through times of darkness.

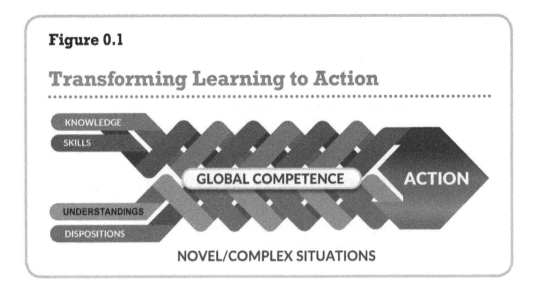

Figure 0.1

Transforming Learning to Action

KNOWLEDGE

SKILLS

GLOBAL COMPETENCE → ACTION

UNDERSTANDINGS

DISPOSITIONS

NOVEL/COMPLEX SITUATIONS

We want learners to feel genuine concern and love for the world around them. We want learners to view themselves as capable and competent in affecting positive, long-lasting change. We want them to live their learning with intention and purpose.

Pedagogy for People, Planet, and Prosperity

In this book, we propose a **Pedagogy for People, Planet, and Prosperity** to nurture students' abilities to think critically with compassion, to explore alternative futures, and to take action to ensure their own, others' and the planet's well-being. Simply stated: to make decisions that support a just, peaceful, and sustainable future. When we hear the word *sustainability*, particular stereotypical images may spring to mind: recycling bins, solar panels, organic fruits and vegetables. Yet our understanding of **teaching for a sustainable future** has transformed. Hedefalk, Almqvist, and Östman (2015) describe this shift saying:

> [It] has evolved from teaching children facts about the environment and sustainability issues to educating children to act for change. This new approach reveals a more competent child who can think for him- or herself and make well-considered decisions. The decisions are made by investigating and participating in critical discussions about alternative ways of acting for change. (Extract from Abstract)

When engaged as critical thinkers and conscientious citizens, students engage in **sustainable development** to "[meet] the needs of the present without compromising the ability of future generations to meet their own needs" (World Commission on Environment and Development, 1987, p. 15). Economic prosperity is necessary for communities to thrive. However, our students must understand that growth must balance planetary impacts, the protection of human rights, and individual and collective well-being. It is only by bringing together these three pillars—people, planet and prosperity—that we can create a sustainable future that benefits all.

Achieving such a vision requires *a different kind of learning*. If global competence is the versatile application of learning to navigate complex issues, students need to be presented with rich learning experiences that require them to problem-solve. They need to be nudged into that territory, where they feel challenged to use their learning with adaptability. Such learning nurtures students' holistic well-being, peaceful relationships with others, and appreciation for nature. In other words, simply understanding an issue is not enough. We want learners to feel genuine concern and love for the world around them. We want learners to view themselves as capable and competent in affecting positive, long-lasting change. We want them to *live their learning* with intention and purpose. Such students are hopeful, instead of despondent. They understand that individual actions do indeed make a difference. We call these students **Worldwise Learners**.

For students to foster self, community, and ecosystem well-being, Worldwise Learners require the ability to connect, understand deeply, *and* take purposeful action on issues. To do so, the heart, the head, and the hand must work in tandem. When we do not integrate the heart, the head, and the hand in our instruction, learning remains passive or becomes disjointed. For instance, let's say students learn about energy use in the classroom, yet do not apply their understanding to their interactions in the world. This creates passive citizens who are overwhelmed by the immensity of problems or believe they are unable to affect change: "The problem is so big, and I'm just one individual. What significant change could I possibly make?" Likewise, when students act without deep understanding, they produce surface-level actions that do not address root causes or, even worse, contribute to the problem. Figure 0.2 shows what occurs when we do not bring together the heart, head, and hand in our curriculum design.

Figure 0.2

Integrating the Heart, Head, and Hand

Heart	Head	Hand	Outcome
 X	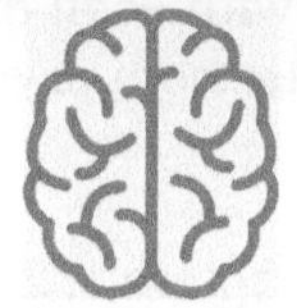 (brain)	 (hand)	Students lack a moral compass to guide their actions, making decisions using reasoning that does not consider connection to humans or nature.
 (heart)	 X	 (hand)	Students oversimplify issues and engage in surface-level actions that address symptoms instead of root causes, potentially making issues worse.
 (heart)	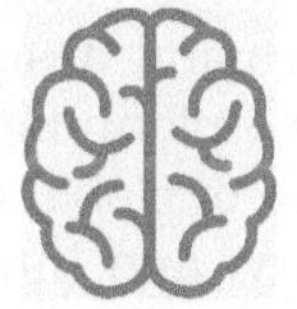 (brain)	 X	Students lack a sense of personal responsibility and the will to act. They do not view themselves as agents of change and remain passive recipients of learning.
 (heart)	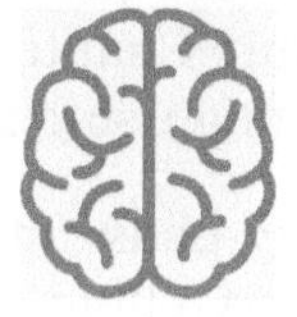 (brain)	 (hand)	Students use their identities, prior knowledge, and deep understanding to engage critically with problems in communities at various scales. They view themselves as able to produce positive change.

Book Features and Structure

The aim of this book is to support K–8 educators as they nurture Worldwise Learners, students who make connections, deeply understand, and purposefully act when learning about global challenges. To do so, we provide a framework to enact meaningful interdisciplinary learning that uses issues as curricular organizers. We couple theory and practice to build educators' understanding of why local, global, and intercultural issues represent significant classroom learning, as well as pedagogy to make them come alive.

Throughout the chapters of this book, we provide:

- **Practical classroom strategies:** Classroom strategies show what Worldwise Learning looks like at the lesson level. These strategies, generally placed at the end of each chapter, help educators easily implement the ideas in each chapter and provide tips for scaffolding students' thinking.

- **Images of student work and learning activities:** Images often accompany classroom strategies or Spotlights to help educators visualize meaningful Worldwise Learning moments.

- **Spotlights:** Spotlights tell stories about learning from diverse student, teacher, and organization perspectives.

- **Sample lessons and units:** Sample lessons and units help educators understand how the planning process links to and can support teaching and learning about global challenges. Many of these you'll find on our companion website.

- **A companion website:** The learning doesn't stop with this book. In addition to adding resources over time, our companion website allows teachers to discuss topics and share ideas with each other. Come on over to our website at http://www.teachworldwise.com or engage in dialogue on Twitter using #teachworldwise.

This book is organized into four parts. Part I (Chapters 1, 2, and 3) describes the conditions required for Worldwise Learning to flourish. Chapter 1 explores the challenges and opportunities of our global interconnectedness. It outlines the Worldwise Learning Framework and accompanying tenets for a Pedagogy for People, Planet, and Prosperity, which frame the rest of the book. Chapter 2 outlines what we mean by taking an integrated approach in the classroom, exploring how we can create inclusive, democratic classrooms. The chapter considers how we can instill democratic values and design authentic opportunities for participation, such as through co-planning with our learners. Chapter 3 looks at the interdisciplinary nature of global challenges. It differentiates between disciplinary, multidisciplinary, and interdisciplinary learning as well as provides a continuum to explore ways to integrate opportunities for interdisciplinary thinking into the curriculum. Chapter 3 considers how we can plan for meaningful interdisciplinary learning using issues as organizers.

Part II (Chapters 4 and 5) unpacks the Connect phase of Worldwise Learning into chapters about perspective-taking and storytelling. Chapter 4 discusses the importance of self-awareness and perspective-taking to make sense of a multicultural, globally connected world. Chapter 5 focuses on the power of story as a way to build empathy, develop intercultural understanding, and establish a sense of place. Each of these chapters is made up of two sections: an introduction providing the theoretical background for the focus of the chapter and a practical section sharing a number of strategies that can be easily implemented in the classroom.

Part III (Chapters 6 and 7) considers the Understand phase of Worldwise Learning. Chapter 6 explores how "systems thinking" can allow students to see the interconnected nature of people, places, and systems in local, global, or intercultural issues. Chapter 7 explores the role of conceptual thinking to help students construct "big ideas" that transfer across time, place, and situation. Again, each of these chapters is made up of an introduction and a practical strategy-focused section for bringing these types of thinking to life in the classroom.

Part IV (Chapters 8 and 9) focuses on the Act phase of Worldwise Learning and concludes the book. Chapter 8 looks at how we can develop global citizens who identify as changemakers, read information critically, and think in entrepreneurial ways to develop solutions and take purposeful action. Chapter 9 brings these ideas to the life of educators: It is our call to action. How can we, as teachers, create classrooms that tap students' innate desire and capability to shape a better world?

At its core, this book provides a vision for transformative education. Using the Worldwise Learning Cycle, you will be able to support students in applying critical thinking at different scales: personal, local, national, regional, and global. As our students become Worldwise Learners, they will be able to bring together ideas with action and emotion with reason. They will be able to unravel the everyday complexity they encounter to identify leverage points for positive change. Throughout, you play a critical role in nurturing the heart, head, and hand of each student. It is our hope that this book contributes to a more just, prosperous, and sustainable world through education.

PAUSE AND REFLECT

As you begin to explore these chapters, we invite you to reflect on these questions:

- How have you experienced our VUCA (volatility, uncertainty, complexity, and ambiguity) world recently as an educator? How have your students experienced it?

- What might learning that develops global competence look like in your classroom?

- What does teaching for a sustainable future mean to you?

- Imagine one of your students as a Worldwise Learner, who lives their learning with intention and purpose. What is this learner thinking, feeling, saying, and doing?

PART I

CREATING THE CONDITIONS FOR TRANSFORMATIVE EDUCATION

Conditions Explored

- Curriculum design that supports deep understanding and active learning.

- A Pedagogy for People, Planet, and Prosperity that builds student awareness of our local and global interconnectedness.

- A democratic classroom approach that sees, hears, and values students through authentic participation.

- Relevant and purposeful interdisciplinary learning that uses local and global issues as organizers.

CHAPTER ONE
THE WORLDWISE LEARNING FRAMEWORK

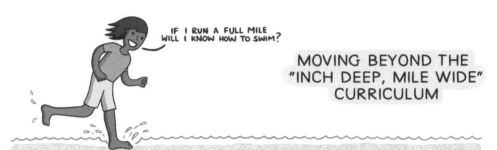

MOVING BEYOND THE "INCH DEEP, MILE WIDE" CURRICULUM

PEDAGOGY FOR PEOPLE, PLANET, AND PROSPERITY

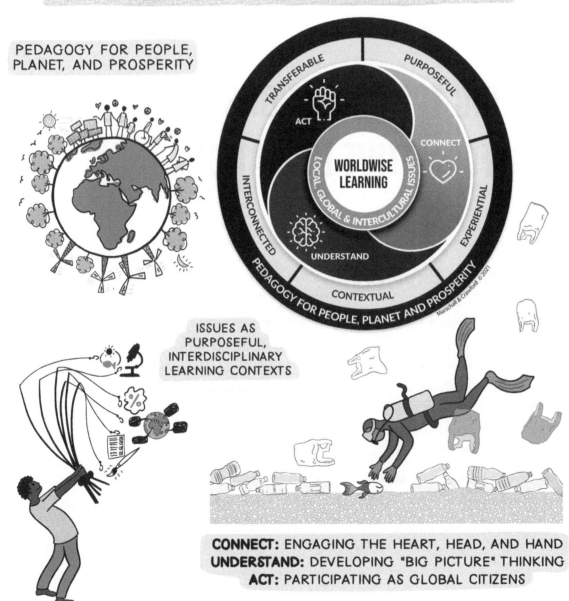

ISSUES AS PURPOSEFUL, INTERDISCIPLINARY LEARNING CONTEXTS

CONNECT: ENGAGING THE HEART, HEAD, AND HAND
UNDERSTAND: DEVELOPING "BIG PICTURE" THINKING
ACT: PARTICIPATING AS GLOBAL CITIZENS

THE WORLDWISE LEARNING FRAMEWORK

"Children are the living messages we send to a time we will not see."

—Neil Postman, Author, Educator, and Cultural Critic

Throughout the world, youth express that they care about global challenges and feel a responsibility to act on them. Yet many feel ill-prepared to do so. In a 2019 survey of 9,500 adolescents in 20 countries, students stated that school should help them understand the world and prepare for the future. Of those surveyed, less than half reported that they understand the most significant societal issues or know how to find solutions to them (World Innovation Summit for Education, 2020). These are the students who will need to solve problems that don't yet exist. As educators, we must reverse this trend. We need to create meaningful learning experiences that allow K–8 students to connect to the world and develop as citizens of it. In this chapter, we consider the challenges that emerge from our global interconnectedness and the opportunities that these present educators. Specifically, we explore a learning framework designed for the purpose of connecting curricular standards with relevant issues that speak directly to our students' lived experiences.

Learning in a Globalized World

Purposefully transforming education means to look outward. Does learning serve the current and future needs of our students? To answer this question, we must first consider what the world is like today and the forces that shape it. The prevailing conditions of our world have been described as **VUCA**: volatility, uncertainty, complexity, and ambiguity (Bennis & Nanus, 1986). We saw this firsthand during COVID-19 global lockdowns, virus mutations, and vaccine rollouts, where the complexity of the issue resulted in increased uncertainty. Change in a VUCA world may be rapid or unpredictable, necessitating agile and flexible responses. Looking at this acronym, we may initially experience a sense of powerlessness: How can we expect students to be competent in the face of so much change? However, knowing that the world exhibits these attributes is merely a starting point: We *can* prepare students for it. Once we acknowledge the dynamic nature of the world today, we can help students adapt to and confront complex challenges with dexterity and grace.

Globalization, the increased interaction and interdependence of people and places across borders, brings with it high levels of change that show these VUCA attributes in real time. Globalization has brought about a number of major changes that students need to navigate to thrive as individuals and community members. For example, we've experienced the trend toward digital transformation during the pandemic, heightening inequalities in society. We've also seen how increased trade interactions have led to exploitative labor and resource extraction practices around the globe. Yet how do such effects of globalization necessitate change within our classrooms? Focusing on three changes—increasingly diverse societies, a changing jobs landscape, and complex global challenges—we draw connections between the outcomes of globalization and our responsibilities as educators to help students grapple with them.

INCREASINGLY DIVERSE SOCIETIES

Due to migration, cultural diffusion, and thought exchange, societies are becoming increasingly diverse. In fact, as a whole, international migrants made up approximately 3.5% of the world's population in 2019, up from 2.8% in the year 2000 (United Nations Department of Economic and Social Affairs, 2019). In some countries like the United States, immigrants constitute a significant proportion of the population. In 2018, 13.7% of the U.S. population were immigrants (Migration Policy Institute, 2020), and "almost one out of four (23 percent) public school students in the United States came from an immigrant household in 2015" (Camarota, Griffith, & Zeigler, 2017, para. 4). Add to this the 79.5 million people who were forcibly displaced by the end of 2019 (United Nations High Commission for Refugees, 2020), and we can begin to see the extent of human movement across the planet.

This diversity brings with it a wealth of backgrounds and experiences, with the concept of *home* being one that often spans across borders. However, interactions between racially, culturally, and linguistically diverse individuals can also be a source of conflict. Misunderstandings can occur, and prejudice can form. To successfully navigate a diverse world, learners need to recognize their own perspectives as well as understand the perspectives of others. They need to be able to identify bias, dominant worldviews, and voices that might be silenced in society. Students need to know what it means to be an active citizen in a diverse society and how to participate effectively in local, national, and global communities. To this end, we must design culturally sustaining, inclusive learning environments. By *culturally sustaining*, we refer to the ability of pedagogy "to perpetuate and foster—to sustain—linguistic, literate, and cultural pluralism as part of schooling for positive social transformation" (Alim & Paris, 2017, p. 1). To build on the diversity of our student populations, we must intentionally connect learning to students' identities and promote **student agency**, each child's capacity and motivation to influence their own learning processes.

A CHANGING JOBS LANDSCAPE

Technological, socioeconomic, and geopolitical shifts are transforming the world of work. Although machine learning is leading to the automation of jobs and disrupting industries, completely new industries are being created as well, such as 3D printing, tissue engineering, and saltwater agriculture. These changes are not all bad, and many support increased quality of life. For instance, an algorithm has been developed to detect tumors in mammograms as accurately as radiologists, improving breast cancer detection.

However, coupled with evolving global risks such as climate action failure, extreme weather, and natural disasters (World Economic Forum, 2020b), such shifts to the jobs landscape require new skill sets and mindsets from young people. In fact, it's often said that we're preparing students for jobs that don't yet exist (International Society for Technology in Education, 2020). To remain agile as industries shift and develop, students need to be able to use their creativity to locate possibilities and think in innovative ways about issues. They need to be able to think *in systems* to develop and test solutions. Engaging children's natural playfulness to prototype ideas, while asking them to critically reflect on our behaviors and their effects on the planet, allows us to shape learners who can adapt to change with resilience.

COMPLEX GLOBAL CHALLENGES

As discussed in the Introduction, global challenges are a powerful, unintended outcome of globalization. Billions of individuals act independently around the globe, yet collectively their small actions cascade to create impact at scale. Global challenges such as climate change can quite literally shape the physical and cultural landscape of our planet. By **global challenges**, we refer to situations where multiple factors interrelate to produce intended and unintended consequences, often at various scales. They are:

- Persistent
- Borderless
- Large in scale
- Complex and connected to multiple **local, global, and intercultural issues**.

Note: The term *global challenge* is replaced by local, global, and intercultural issues in the following chapters, because challenges need to be broken down into smaller, bite-sized issues in the classroom, often within local contexts. Example global challenges include the COVID-19 pandemic, plastic pollution, or wealth inequality.

To understand contemporary global challenges, we can look to the UN Sustainable Development Goals (SDGs). Adopted in 2015, they provide a 15-year blueprint for achieving a better world for all people, everywhere (United Nations General Assembly, 2015). The SDGs and their targets frame the most urgent contemporary issues, and though each goal is articulated separately, they are heavily interdependent. Holistically, these issues reflect connections between three key areas and aims:

1. **People:** *Ensure dignity, equality, and well-being for all people.*

2. **Planet:** *Protect our planet's natural resources and climate for future generations.*

3. **Prosperity:** *Ensure prosperous and fulfilling lives in harmony with nature.*

Example global issues relating to these areas can be found in Figure 1.1. These are illustrative rather than exhaustive.

Figure 1.1

Example Global Challenges

People	Planet	Prosperity
Ensure dignity, equality, and well-being for all people.	*Protect our planet's natural resources and climate for future generations.*	*Ensure prosperous and fulfilling lives in harmony with nature.*
Advertising and media	Air, water, and soil pollution	Adequate housing
Bullying, discrimination, and prejudice (e.g., racism, ablism, etc.)	Animal rights	Consumerism
Colonization	Biodiversity loss, including endangered species	Consumption and production patterns
Conflict and violence	Climate change and global warming	Corruption in society and governments
Education	Coral reefs and low oxygen "dead zones"	Economic growth
Equity and inclusion	Ecological footprint	Employment and economic ethics
Food processing and waste	Food production	Energy production and consumption
Forced labor, slavery, human trafficking, and working conditions	Human population	Equal pay
Health and well-being	Pollinator die-out	Inclusive, safe, resilient, and sustainable cities and communities
Human rights and needs	Sea-level rise	
Hunger, food insecurity, and malnutrition	Soil erosion	Infrastructure
Migration and refugeeism	Ocean and land resource use	Industrialization
Misinformation	Waste generation and management	Innovation and entrepreneurship
Natural disasters	Water security and sanitation	Governance and political systems
Poverty	Wildlife trafficking and poaching	Tourism
Privilege		Wealth inequality
Technological disasters		
White supremacy		

A significant change stemming from globalization, global challenges represent an authentic and rigorous learning context for our students. By learning *about* global challenges, we can make improvements to current issues today, while also preparing our students for unknown challenges they will encounter in the future. Just as multiple independent actions can create negative impacts for people and the planet, they can also combine to be a force for *positive change*. By identifying as **changemakers**, our students can remain curious and hopeful in the face of such challenges.

Curriculum Design for Understanding and Action

Recognizing that globalization has produced increasingly diverse societies, a changing jobs landscape, and the complex global challenges we face, we must reflect on how well our curriculum design speaks to these trends. Traditionally, teaching is organized using disciplinary, verb-driven standards derived from school-based, state, or national curricula. For example, a Grade 1 Common Core English Language Arts standard is: "Identify the main topic and retell key details of a text." Standards are often isolated from the big ideas and dispositions that help students integrate and unify their learning. We need to consider what kind of curriculum has the potential to liberate our students and allow them to become productive, thriving citizens. We need our curriculum design to promote deep *understanding* about the world, as well as the will to take *action* on issues in it. Regardless of school context, we can make this a reality.

Knowledge and skill learning is integral, yet it is not sufficient to create Worldwise Learners who *understand* the world deeply. Knowledge, acquired as a series of **facts** related to a **topic**, is locked in time, place, and situation. Likewise, skills, when taught discretely, become disconnected from broader processes like the reading or writing process. For this reason, authors Lynn Erickson and Lois Lanning (2014) describe this model as *two-dimensional*: "The two-dimensional model driving traditional curriculum design focuses on facts and skills and generally *assumes* deeper, conceptual understanding. This model can produce the often quoted 'inch-deep, mile-wide' approach to curriculum design" (p. 22). If we want to promote coherence, connection-making, and deep learning, we must create opportunities for intellectual engagement by teaching beyond the factual level. We must employ a *three-dimensional* model by including **concepts**, abstract mental organizers that transfer *across* time, place, and situation. We must also support our students to articulate **conceptual understandings**.

Drawn from a topic or process, a conceptual understanding is a big idea that describes the relationship between two or more concepts (Erickson, Lanning, & French, 2017). These are also called **generalizations**. Because they are meant to be true statements that transfer to new situations and contexts, they may use qualifiers such as *sometimes, often, can,* or *may.* For example, <u>*Misinformation*</u> *can change people's* <u>*opinions*</u> *and* <u>*perspectives*</u> *on an* <u>*issue*</u>. Note that the concepts in this understanding are underlined.

Why are conceptual understandings so powerful? Developing conceptual understandings enables students to recognize patterns and make connections between past and current events, as well as make predictions about those that may come in the future. For example, students learning about natural disasters are introduced to the 2011 tsunami and subsequent damage to the Fukushima nuclear reactor in Japan. The teacher wants her learners to go beyond the facts of the case study to understand that *Urban planning can reduce the impact of natural disasters by minimizing risks to a community.* By scaffolding students' thinking to the conceptual level, the teacher has now created the conditions where authentic **transfer** can occur. Here students can "stress-test" their understandings (Marschall & French, 2018) by applying them to other contexts, for instance to the building of sea walls in many communities to reduce flood risk.

The ability to analyze events, see underlying ideas, and make connections is vital for our learners who are inundated with information from news platforms and social media. Concepts give information *meaning.* Developing students' conceptual understanding, in addition to knowledge and skills, allows them to face new, uncertain situations with cognitive flexibility. An exploration of how to support conceptual thinking is addressed in Chapter 7. To read more on how to construct and scaffold conceptual understandings with students, see *Concept-Based Inquiry in Action: Strategies to Promote Transferable Understanding* by Carla Marschall and Rachel French (2018).

While it is clear that knowledge, skills, and conceptual understandings together produce learning that transfers, these three learning domains alone will not end in conscientious student *action.* We need to get *four-dimensional* by also developing students' **dispositions.** By dispositions, we refer to characteristic patterns of behavior and ways of thinking that are relatively enduring, meaning that students display them in different contexts and situations. Because they are acquired and not innate, we can influence them through our instruction and teach them explicitly. They include thinking dispositions, such as open-mindedness, imagination, and metacognition, and other more affective dimensions, such as empathy and curiosity. In addition, dispositions comprise students' beliefs about learning and their self-efficacy, or the belief that they "can produce desired effects by their actions" (Bandura, 1997, p. 3). Seldom enacted individually, dispositions are interlinked and used in different configurations depending on the situation. So why is the development of dispositions crucial for promoting purposeful student action? As Arthur Costa, author and founder of the Institute for Habits of Mind, states:

> We are interested in enhancing the ways students *produce* knowledge rather than how they merely *reproduce* it. We want students to learn how to develop a critical stance with their work: inquiring, editing, thinking flexibly, and learning from another person's perspective. The critical attribute of intelligent human beings is not only having information but also knowing how to act on it. (Costa & Kallick, 2008, p. 16, emphasis in original)

Dispositions frame students' relationship to their learning, leading them to either associate it with responsibility and action or with dependence and passivity. Students' self-stories are integral as they form their identities as changemakers and are just as important as the knowledge, skills, and understandings they gain. Dispositions play a vital role in empowering our learners, giving them a mindset that wants to engage with issues instead of ignore them. An overview of these four learning domains and how they relate to Worldwise Learning can be found in Figure 1.2. Please visit our companion website for examples of the learning domains in sample unit plans.

Figure 1.2

The Four Learning Domains in Worldwise Learning

Learning Domain	What Does This Look Like in Worldwise Learning?
Knowledge *"Students will know . . ."*	Learners acquire knowledge connected to particular issues as illustrative case studies. For instance, middle school students may learn about coral bleaching at the Great Barrier Reef or the Paradise, California, wildfires as consequences of climate change. Knowledge, made of facts, comes from a topic of study and is locked in time, place, and situation (Erickson, Lanning, & French, 2017). Students develop conceptual understandings as they draw patterns from the knowledge they acquire.
Skills *"Students will be able to . . ."*	Learners build disciplinary and interdisciplinary skills, such as the ability to produce persuasive arguments or locate relevant information, to make sense of an issue. Skills are drawn from and connected to broader processes, such as the writing process or the research process (Erickson, Lanning, & French, 2017). Skill learning enables students to create, analyze, plan, and communicate possible solutions to challenges. As students develop conceptual understandings about skills and strategies, they become adept at applying their learning with intention.
Conceptual Understanding *"Students will understand that . . ."*	Learners form conceptual understandings, statements of relationship between two or more concepts, allowing them to make connections to new case studies they encounter. For instance, let's take the conceptual understanding *Access to quality education can increase the opportunities available to individuals in society.* This links the concepts of *access, quality education, opportunity,* and *society.* Also called generalizations, conceptual understandings transfer across time, place, or situation (Erickson, Lanning, & French, 2017). These understandings may emerge from knowledge or skill learning.
Dispositions *"Students will show . . ."*	Learners develop dispositions, characteristic patterns of behavior and ways of thinking that are relatively enduring, describing the "kind of person" the student has become (Boix Mansilla, Miller, & Gardner, 2000). These shape their character and allow them to view themselves as changemakers. Although acquired and not innate, dispositions represent both what a child brings to learning experiences (e.g., a child's sense of fairness) as well as how engagements develop and deepen their attitudes and values about the world. The child's identity influences their openness and receptiveness to learning about particular issues.

If knowledge, skills, conceptual understandings, and dispositions are our pedagogical *ingredients*, how can we combine these in creative ways to enable our learners to engage purposefully with the world around them? A number of frameworks exist outlining core competencies students need to thrive in a rapidly changing world (Asia Society, 2005; Campbell-Patton & Mortenson, 2011; Organisation for Economic Co-operation and Development, 2018a; OXFAM, 2008; United Nations General Assembly, 2015). Helping students learn to contribute positively to a global, interconnected world has never been more urgent. Because of current trends such as political polarization, geographic and racial division, the unwillingness to accept opposing views, and the spread of false information, Tina Lane Heafner (2020), President of the National Council for the Social Studies, goes so far as to call our current situation a "Sputnik moment . . . an event that makes people collectively say that they need to do something, and set a course in a new direction" (p. 5).

While we have drawn from various frameworks to construct our Worldwise Learning Cycle, what differentiates our model is the development of transferable conceptual understanding as central to making sense of complex issues. As previously explored, unless learners gain deep understanding while building the knowledge, skills, and dispositions to take action, they can engage in tokenistic or shallow activities that do not address root causes. Our Worldwise Learning Cycle is made up of three distinct, yet interwoven, components: the learning context, the learning process, and the Pedagogy for People, Planet, and Prosperity, which guides our instructional decisions (Figure 1.3). A color version of this cycle is available for download on our companion website.

ISSUES AS PURPOSEFUL LEARNING CONTEXTS

At the center of the Worldwise Learning Cycle is our learning context: local, global, and intercultural issues. These are relevant and meaningful case studies that resonate with our students. These can be investigated locally, regionally, or globally, as well as in the past or the present. These issues can be chosen in collaboration with our students through co-planning strategies such as those shared in Chapter 2. Issues can also be linked to broader themes, such as the transdisciplinary themes from the International Baccalaureate's Primary Years Programme or the global contexts from the Middle Years Programme.

Using issues as organizers for learning provides us with flexible ways to address curricular outcomes, while giving our students opportunities to make tangible real-world connections. Thinking about global challenges as examples of transferable conceptual understandings is key. A school in Michigan may explore the effects of elevated lead blood levels in Flint's children caused by

Figure 1.3

Worldwise Learning Cycle

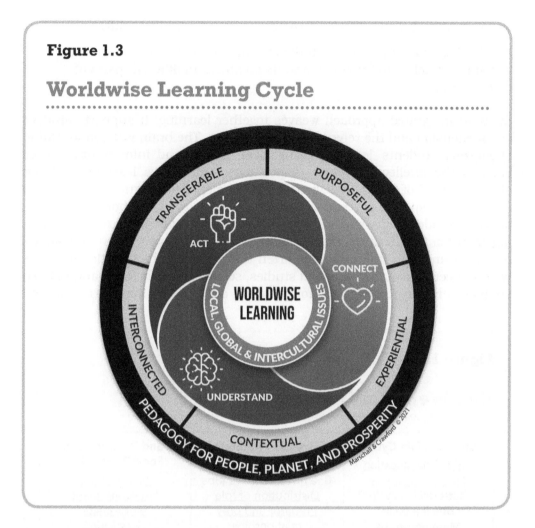

water pollution. Another in California may inquire into how the state's air pollution causes childhood asthma. Yet at the same time, these two classrooms may uncover the same conceptual understanding, *Pollution can harm body systems, impairing function, or leading to disease.*

Issues act as *authentic organizers.* They can engage our students in powerful interdisciplinary learning that mirrors the wider world. Here learning from across the disciplines is meaningfully drawn together, bringing curricular outcomes into a coherent narrative. Learning about overfishing, for instance, would require learning in the following disciplines:

- *Science,* because students investigate marine life cycles, ecosystems, and fishing impacts on animal populations, water and soil quality, and natural systems.

- *Social Studies,* because students uncover how and why humans fish, including how these behaviors connect to education, culture, human health, government, and employment and labor.

- *Mathematics,* because students inquire into proportions and percentages of fish being lost through overfishing.

- *English Language Arts,* because students produce questions, research, take notes, and present their findings.

- *Visual Arts*, because students represent their learning visually.

- *World Languages*, because students come to understand the cultural values attached to the ocean and its creatures in different parts of the world.

For a step-by-step overview of how to create a unit web access the video using this QR code, or visit **teachworldwise.com/ resources**.

Such an integrated approach weaves together learning. It supports student comprehension and the retention of information. The brain is wired for unity: Organizing students' learning using local, global, and intercultural issues engages the intellect, develops dispositions, and allows learners to think about the kind of future they want for the planet. Using issues as organizers for discipline-specific curricular standards also allows us to honor and make space for student passions and concerns. What does it look like to draw learning from across the disciplines together using an issue? Figure 1.4 shows a sample unit web from a kindergarten unit on pollinators. Notice how this web connects learning from social studies, science, mathematics, and English language arts. In this strategy for planning designed by Lynn Erickson and

Figure 1.4

Unit Web (Pollinators)

Strand 1: Life Cycles
Animal classification
Needs and wants
Butterfly life cycle
Bee life cycle
Metamorphosis
Host plant

Strand 2: Habitats
Shelter
Bee hives and hive jobs
Distribution of role
Predator and prey
relationships
Pollination
Germination
Symbiosis
Balance within a habitat

Strand 3: Farming and Food Production
Monoculture
Flowering plant
Biodiversity
Pesticide
Organic farming
Bee and butterfly nutrition

Pollinator Power!

Conceptual Lens:
Interactions

Strand 4: Pattern
Regular and Irregular
Shapes
Hexagons
Repeating Pattern
Tessellation
Patterns in nature (e.g.,
honeycomb)
Shapes in garden design
(e.g., plots)

Strand 5: Information Texts
Explanation
Information Text
Text Features
Table of Contents
Titles
Photographs
Captions
Labels

Strand 6: Stewardship
Yards and Gardens
Bee and butterfly
identification
Pollinator-friendly plants
(e.g., wildflowers)
Natural pesticides (e.g.,
ladybugs and neem oil)

Lois Lanning (2014), concepts related to each of the strands, or areas of the unit, are underlined. Factual knowledge such as bee and butterfly nutrition is not. A conceptual lens is articulated in the middle of the web with the unit title, supporting the integration of the disciplines and design of unit questions. The corresponding kindergarten unit plan relating to this web is available in Appendix A. Other planners can be found on our companion site.

EXPLORING ISSUES WITH K–8 LEARNERS

Some educators may question if learning about complex issues is appropriate for K–8 learners. Learning about the world is not about exploring some abstract reality that exists halfway around the planet. As mentioned, global challenges occur at various spatial scales. This means that they often present themselves locally, regionally, and globally *simultaneously*. For this reason, depending on students' ages and developmental stages, we may begin an investigation at the local level. For instance, current research has uncovered that the Earth's land insect populations shrunk 27% in 30 years (van Klink, Bowler, Gongalsky, Swengel, Gentile, & Chase, 2020), leading to global biodiversity loss. How might this global issue be explored meaningfully by young children? To learn more about insect loss and their effect on ecosystems, Grade 1 students in Iowa inquire into the monarch butterfly: its life cycle, needs, and migration. They plant milkweed on school grounds and report sightings of the butterfly on their migration route using Journey North (https://journeynorth.org/monarchs). Analyzing data from prior years to determine whether there are fewer or greater numbers of monarchs during that season, students make recommendations to their families and friends about how to create and protect habitats for the butterfly. During this process, the teacher then shares information on global patterns related to insect loss, reiterating to these young learners why their actions are so vitally important. Their local actions make a global impact. By placing emphasis on the unique location where students live, we can help them form a connection to place and take their learning beyond the four walls of the classroom. At the same time, we can use local information to make sense of and interpret global patterns.

This said, only some issues will be appropriate for the youngest of learners, such as kindergarten to Grade 3 students. To choose developmentally appropriate challenges for young children, our role as educators is to listen closely as our learners share their passions and concerns and consider what issues enable the development of actionable, local solutions. For example, although young children love animals, learning about animal endangerment may tacitly encourage students to be passive (e.g., "This issue is too big and too far from my sphere of influence"). By studying local pond health instead, young learners could gather data, help clean a pond polluted by waste, or recommend specific actions to policy makers. As a general rule, we go by David Sobel's (2004) recommendation of "no catastrophes" before fourth grade. This means we choose small-scale, local issues, where students can form connections to a place and see the direct impact of their actions on their communities. A shorter table including a number of age-appropriate issues for younger children can be found in Figure 1.5. This list is illustrative rather than exhaustive.

Figure 1.5

Example Global Challenges for K–3 Students

People *Ensure dignity, equality, and well-being for all people.*	Planet *Protect our planet's natural resources and climate for future generations.*	Prosperity *Ensure prosperous and fulfilling lives in harmony with nature.*
Advertising to children	Animal and plant needs	Access to green spaces and areas for play
Bias, prejudice, and stereotypes	Decomposers (e.g., worms)	Access to healthy food
Cultural traditions and celebrations	Environmental stewardship	Access to transportation
Education	Local biodiversity and habitats	Being a changemaker
Fairness and equality	Local water sources	Child-friendly cities
Families	Types of farming (e.g., monoculture, biodynamic)	Creativity, innovation, and solution development
Food production system	Nature reserves and parks	Energy use
Gender norms (e.g., colors, toys, clothes)	Pollinators (e.g., butterflies, bees)	Goods and services
Identity, representation, and self-love	Pesticides	Local homelessness
Healthy choices (e.g., diet, exercise)	Single-use plastics	Materialism
Human rights and needs	Soil health	Natural resource use (e.g., water)
Media consumption (e.g., TV, tablets)	Stray and homeless animals	Neighborhood gardens
Migration	Waste practices (e.g., composting, littering)	
Mindfulness		

Although we have categorized issues as being more related to one column, no issue exists in isolation. In fact, global challenges are like a huge rubber band ball with each issue twisted, wrapped, and intertwined with others. Even though they're perceived as separate challenges, once viewed in context, they're highly interconnected. For this reason, it is useful to consider connections that exist across the categories, even if we're focusing on one.

Try it yourself: pick two issues, from across the People, Planet, and Prosperity columns (from either of the two tables in this chapter). How do these issues connect? For instance, imagine we wanted to connect *inequality* with *natural disasters*. Consider the multiple causes and consequences of these issues and how they might be linked. Although we might initially view these as disconnected issues, on closer analysis we can see how they relate to each other. For instance, research published in Scientific American shows that urban flooding disproportionately impacts minority and low-income city residents (Frank, 2020). These neighborhoods are often in low-lying areas, lack the green space to absorb flood waters, and have deteriorating stormwater infrastructure. Flooding in these neighborhoods then perpetuates inequality, as locals manage economic losses or instable housing conditions. Such natural disasters exacerbate racial, gender, and socioeconomic inequalities over time (Vidili, 2018). This strategy, which we call *Linking Ps*, can also be used with students. Inviting students to see relationships across different types of issues is vital, promoting out-of-the-box thinking and an awareness of the interdependence of challenges. It can be used across the K–8 spectrum to support learners in making connections across issues. Younger learners can engage in this strategy using picture cards for age-appropriate issues found across the columns. This is a great culminating strategy, which nudges students to draw connections across all issues explored in a year! Subsequent chapters of this book include a number of strategies teachers can use to help students understand complex, interconnected issues.

The Learning Process: Inquiring Into People, the Planet, and Prosperity

Once we have identified a relevant issue to explore with our students, we guide them through an inquiry process, where they develop learning across the four domains, apply it in creative and critical ways, and take action. The learning process is the second component of the Worldwise Learning Cycle, represented by the concentric ring labeled Connect, Understand, and Act. This ring outlines a three-part inquiry cycle that teaches to the heart, head, and hand of the student. It promotes student agency and action. When we say "inquiry cycle," we mean that learning engagements are structured using teacher or student questions. For example, in the unit about overfishing, students might explore teacher questions like, "How do marine organisms rely on each other in the coastal ecosystem?" or "At what point does fishing become overfishing?" As we explain this learning process in more detail, we illustrate each of the three phases of the Worldwise Learning Cycle with a sample learning experience that relates to the pollinator unit described earlier in this chapter using the unit web.

CONNECT: ENGAGING THE HEART, HEAD, AND HAND

The Connect phase of inquiry engages the heart, head, and hand by activating students' prior knowledge, sparking an emotional and intellectual connection to the learning, and widening students' awareness. Students are introduced

Connect

to unit questions as well as encouraged to develop their own. To build issue-awareness, where students become familiar with issues, they acquire and apply disciplinary knowledge and skills. For example, they may use a range of comprehension strategies to read for meaning about an issue. Learners also develop their self-awareness and ability to listen to and understand diverse perspectives. Through dialogue and storytelling, students build their empathy and understanding of others, including non-human beings. Outdoor learning provides hands-on opportunities, through which students can develop an understanding of place and a connection to nature. Chapters 4 and 5, exploring perspective-taking and storytelling, further elaborate on the Connect phase and provide practical strategies that can be used in the classroom for this purpose.

Figure 1.6

Connecting Through Park Walks (Pollinator Unit)

UNDERSTAND: DEVELOPING "BIG PICTURE" THINKING

Understand

In the Understand phase of inquiry, we support students to take a mountaintop view and see the "big picture." As we invite students to zoom out, they locate patterns and relationships in their learning. Here students synthesize their findings and reflect on the evidence they have to make a claim. What are some ways that we can help students take a macro perspective? First, we engage students in *systems thinking*, where they identify the parts, relationships, and behaviors that emerge from a system. This helps them see what's really happening in an issue and supports the development of solutions in the Act phase. Likewise, we invite students to make connections between concepts and articulate their own conceptual understandings. We do this by asking students to reflect on and respond to conceptual questions, using the facts of a case study as evidence for ideas (p. 83). This ensures that learning about an issue, which is locked in time, place, and situation, becomes applicable to other contexts now and in the future. All the while, we develop students' **intercultural understanding** and media and information literacy skills, including the ability to critically interpret sources. Intercultural understanding integrates both knowledge of one's own and other cultures, as well as attitudes like compassion, respect, and open-mindedness that are fundamental to living peacefully and in harmony with others and nature (United Nations Educational, Scientific, and Cultural Organization, 2010). Interdisciplinary thinking underpins these experiences: Students draw conclusions using learning from across the disciplines. Chapter 3 discusses interdisciplinary learning, as a component of an integrated curriculum. Chapters 6 and 7 detail how we can support the development of systems thinking and conceptual thinking in students, including tools and strategies we might use for these purposes.

Figure 1.7

Understanding the Beehive System Through Model Making (Pollinator Unit)

ACT: PARTICIPATING AS GLOBAL CITIZENS

In the Act phase of inquiry, we support students as they prepare to take action. To do so, we start from the self, asking our learners to reflect on their identities and their behaviors as individuals, encouraging them to act as critical consumers in relation to the issue explored. This includes our consumption

Act

of information and the underlying messages, worldviews, or biases that may be communicated through it. We foster global citizenship by establishing **democratic classrooms** where students can participate meaningfully in decision-making processes. This includes innovating to develop appropriate, needs-based solutions that could improve local or global conditions in a sustainable way. Importantly, action extends to promote equity, inclusion, and justice in the classroom, community, and beyond.

In this phase, we provide the space and time for students to take purposeful action and reflect on their impact as citizens of the world. Actions might be small in scale, but we need to remember that these moments are teaching opportunities that model being active in society. Recognizing that young people *can* make a genuine, measurable difference is the biggest hurdle for our students to jump. For this reason, an important component is the self-reflection that accompanies powerful learning about issues. How have our perspectives changed? Despite the fact that solving complex problems requires resilience, imagination, and bravery, once students believe in themselves, the sky's the limit. This is exemplified in the Changemaker Spotlight on innovator Boyan Slat. Equipped with a passion and deep concern for plastic pollution, he was motivated to search for answers to this massive issue when he was only in high school. Chapter 2 explores ways we can design democratic classrooms, which promote values such as inclusivity, respect, participation, and voice. Chapter 8 shares ways for students to develop as changemakers, engage critically with information, and create solutions as global citizens. Chapter 9 closes this book with action steps and strategies for becoming a Worldwise Educator to bring each of the phases to life in the classroom.

Figure 1.8

Acting as Stewards by Creating a Butterfly Garden and Nursery (Pollinator Unit)

BOYAN SLAT

"Once there was a Stone Age, a Bronze Age,

and now we are in the middle of the Plastic Age."

At age 16, Dutch teenager Boyan Slat became acutely concerned about plastic pollution while scuba diving in Greece. Though the issue is massive in scale (with the oceans containing more plastic than fish), he became frustrated to learn there were no large-scale efforts to combat it. Returning to high school, Boyan dedicated his science project to this focus to uncover its root causes and why it was considered nearly impossible to solve.

After graduating high school, Boyan presented his innovative idea to rid the world's seas of plastic waste in a 2012 TEDx talk titled "How the Oceans Can Clean Themselves." Having studied ocean currents, he theorized that plastics would accumulate in specific areas and afford significantly quicker cleanup. Boyan's first prototype was discredited by many who promoted education and prevention over cleanup. Instead of giving up, Boyan used others' concerns as motivation to achieve his goal. And he has.

In 2013, then 23-year-old Boyan founded The Ocean Cleanup, a nonprofit organization that is "developing advanced technologies to rid the world's oceans of plastic." It operates to achieve two overarching goals: (1) to clean up existing pollution and (2) "close the tap" or stop plastic pollution from entering the oceans from its main

(Continued)

(Continued)

source: rivers. To that end, The Ocean Cleanup invented the first scalable solution coined The Interceptor, a 100% solar-powered device that removes plastics autonomously. Now in version 4.0 after gleaning lessons from case studies of prior models, the project is on its way to meeting its goal of reducing floating ocean plastic by 90% in 2040.

Conceived by a high school student who became concerned about a complex global challenge without clear solutions, today The Ocean Cleanup team is comprised of more than 90 engineers, scientists, and technologists working together to clean the world's oceans. Boyan Slat's story showcases how persevering with creativity and bravery can allow individuals to meaningfully address global challenges.

Learn more at: https://theoceancleanup.com/

Together the *Connect, Understand, Act* learning process prepares students to take an active role in our globalized world. It does so in an integrated way so that students experience *connectedness*. It is important to note that the limitations of written text mean that we've presented our model in a unidirectional, linear way. Inquiry, however, is recursive; as such, we would expect to see students moving back and forth between these phases throughout an inquiry (Marschall & French, 2018). For example, we may move from Connect to Understand, but then go back to Connect to explore another question. Instead of thinking about *moving through* the cycle, it is more useful to consider the *purpose* of single or multiple learning engagements: Is the learning intention to help students engage the heart, head, and hand? Is it to scaffold big picture thinking? Or is it to give students opportunities to participate as global citizens? To see this in action, we recommend taking a closer look at the pollinator unit in Appendix A. A number of other sample unit plans can be found on our companion website.

Tenets of a Pedagogy for People, Planet, and Prosperity

As instructional designers, we are continuously making decisions in the classroom. Should we introduce an activity with the whole class or in small groups? What resources, materials, or prompts will we use to scaffold student thinking? As students explore relevant issues within the Connect, Understand, Act cycle, powerful learning emerges. We describe this learning as *purposeful, experiential, contextual, interconnected,* and *transferable*. These words encircling the Worldwise Learning Cycle name what the learning should *feel like* to students. What *instructional moves* then might we use to support these outcomes?

To foster learning about real-world issues, we've articulated tenets of a Pedagogy for People, Planet, and Prosperity (Figure 1.9). These core principles name the overarching practices we employ in Worldwise Learning. Although they are linked to specific descriptors for how we want learning to feel for our students, they are interconnected and could fit in multiple categories.

Figure 1.9

Tenets of a Pedagogy for People, Planet, and Prosperity

Because we want learning to be . . .	Then in our teaching, we . . .
Purposeful	Champion social-emotional learning as integral to academic learning.
	Use real-world issues as organizers for learning.
	Engage students in shared decision making.
Experiential	Provide immersive, whole-body learning experiences, including in nature.
	Make use of the power of story to communicate, build empathy, and connect with others.
	Design inquiry-based experiences for the application of learning, such as projects.
Contextual	Promote perspective-taking, dialogue, and an awareness of self and others.
	Develop intercultural understanding, including a recognition of bias and stereotypes.
	Use a case study approach.
Interconnected	Make authentic links between, across, and beyond disciplines.
	Develop the ability to *think in systems*.
	Promote global citizenship to extend to all living beings.
Transferable	Scaffold conceptual thinking that transfers.
	Advocate for critical consumerism, extending to media and other sources of information.
	Promote solution-focused thinking, purposeful action, and reflection.

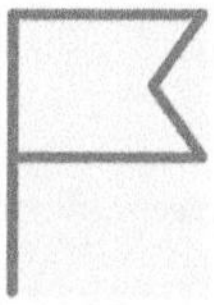

Integrating these tenets into our teaching makes learning purposeful, experiential, contextual, interconnected, and transferable for our students. At the beginning of each subsequent chapter, you will find the tenets relevant to the chapter focus, so you can see how these look in action. While each of these tenets is *macro* in scope, they are contextualized across the chapters and linked to specific teaching strategies.

If our expectation is that effective learning empowers students to act, we can no longer present learning in disjointed chunks that compartmentalize the heart, head, and hand. We can no longer use a passive model of education, where students have little to no decision-making power and ownership over their learning. Chapter 2 looks at how Worldwise Learning intentionally designs democratic classrooms where students have opportunities to discuss ideas, actively participate, and develop solutions. Before moving on to the next chapter, take a moment to pause and reflect using the following questions.

PAUSE AND REFLECT

- How might you be able to organize some of your students' learning using local, global, or intercultural issues?

- What connections can you make to the Worldwise Learning Cycle? How does this relate to the curriculum and instruction within your context?

- Think about the tenets of a Pedagogy of People, Planet, and Prosperity. Which resonate with you and why? How can you envision these in your instruction?

CHAPTER TWO
CREATING INCLUSIVE, DEMOCRATIC CLASSROOMS

PARTICIPATION

VOICE

DECISION-MAKING

CO-PLANNING:
CREATING THE ROAD MAP
WITH STUDENTS

ACTIVE LISTENING
AS A TEACHER–RESEARCHER

INTEGRATING THE SELF, THE SOCIAL, AND THE COGNITIVE

SOCIAL

COGNITIVE

SELF

RIGHTS,
RESPONSIBILITIES,
PEACE, AND CONFLICT

VOTE

MAKING A JUST COMMUNITY
THROUGH PARTICIPATION

UNITED NATIONS
Convention on the Rights of the Child

CREATING INCLUSIVE, DEMOCRATIC CLASSROOMS

"Children learn more from what you are than what you teach."

—W. E. B. Du Bois, Sociologist, Writer, and Civil Rights Activist

This chapter explores the following Tenets of a Pedagogy for People, Planet, and Prosperity:

- Champion social-emotional learning as integral to academic learning.

- Engage students in shared decision making.

- Promote perspective-taking, dialogue, and an awareness of self and others.

- Promote global citizenship to extend to all living beings.

- Promote solution-focused thinking, purposeful action, and reflection.

Educators teach far more than content. Through our behaviors and pedagogical decisions, we promote or reject democratic values, such as respect, voice, and participation. We enable or discourage students to identify as active citizens who engage in issues in their communities. In other words, *who* we are and *how* we teach is just as important as what we teach. If our intention is to develop inclusive classrooms, how can we ensure that students are seen, heard, and valued? Likewise, if our expectation is that students will *do something* with their learning in the wider world, how do our classroom structures support this aim? We cannot expect that a passive mode of education will create agentic learners or nurture active citizens.

In 2016, only 61.4% of the citizen voting-age population reported voting in the United States election (United States Census, 2017). And although there was record turnout for the 2020 election, sources project this represents about 66.5% of the voting-age population (Schaul, Rabinowitz, & Mellnik, 2020). That's two out of every three adults. Compare this to other countries: Turkey (89% of voting-age population), Sweden (82.1%), Australia (80.8%), Belgium (77.9%), and South Korea (77.9%) (DeSilver, 2020). If we want students to take an active role in society, they need *practice*. They need to listen to others, discuss ideas, exchange diverse opinions, read information critically, and share in decision making. By showing students we value their thoughts and creating supportive structures for participation, we shape a learning environment that develops responsible, respectful individuals. In this chapter, we explore the democratic classroom as a way to integrate **social-emotional learning (SEL)**, honor student identities and experiences, and build student agency in Worldwise Learning.

RECOGNIZING A 1918 LYNCHING IN NORTH CAROLINA

Shannon Hardy is a middle grades educator and experienced project-based learning (PBL) facilitator at Exploris School, an innovative K–8 public charter school located in downtown Raleigh, North Carolina. To foster authentic student participation, she uses the Design for Change (DFC) methodology, bringing together PBL with social change. Through the DFC process, her students dissect issues prior to taking action in their local communities.

In 2016, Hardy's students became deeply concerned about systemic racism in the news media. They chose this issue for their eighth-grade project focused on the driving question: "How can we end racism?" During the initial DFC stage, students explored the perspectives of affected groups prior to analyzing the root causes of the issue. Students interviewed civil rights pioneer Joe Holt, Jr., an African American teacher's son whose family paved the way for the integration in Raleigh schools in 1956. Further research led them to uncover other historical injustices and acts of violence, including a nearby unrecognized 1918 lynching. Students became upset that their history books did not address these stories. When discovering that school buildings throughout the city were named after white

Figure 2.1

Students With Civil Rights Pioneer Joe Holt, Jr.

supremacists, the students chose to act by requesting that Wake County Commissioners and the Wake County School Board name a future school after Holt's mother. While their petition was unsuccessful, students learned how to use their voices for social good.

At the end of the year, students recruited a new cohort of eighth graders to carry on their work. They also initiated the Citizen's Promise pledge to recognize any persons who have been victims of injustice, including to "no longer remain silent or passive in the face of white supremacy, racial hatred, or any social injustice." Students collected more than 600 citizen signatures, along with a soil sample as a metaphor for the site of their county's 1918 lynching. They took these commitments and the soil jar to the National Memorial for Peace and Justice in Montgomery, Alabama, to include in the exhibit.

Since 2016, eighth-grade Exploris School students have carried the torch of their predecessors in the struggle to end racism. "The work is never done," Hardy explains. "Every year, students learn what actions were effective by the previous students and how they can contribute. In the end, it was never a project. It was empowering students to own their learning and to make the world better."

Scan this QR code to learn more about Exploris School students' work for racial justice, or visit https://sites.google .com/exploris.org/ 1918georgetay lorlynching/

The Democratic Classroom

American philosopher John Dewey (1916) argued that democracy is "more than a form of government; it is primarily a mode of associated living" (p. 96). This view of democracy—as a way of living and being through our relationships—extends to the classroom where children develop self- and social awareness, the ability to regulate their emotions and impulses, and share power with others, including adults. Here the classroom acts as a microcosm of society as we wish it to be. In the democratic classroom, an **integrated approach** is used to unify the student learning experience into a coherent whole. The self, the social, and the cognitive dimensions of students intertwine to achieve this aim. This approach recognizes that we cannot separate the emotional self from the analytical self. We cannot abstract learning from the environment in which it occurs. We cannot separate our past experiences from new learning.

What does this look like? As students acquire knowledge, skills, and conceptual understandings, democratic classrooms promote values, such as inclusion, equality, respect, voice, and participation. Unpinned by the principle of shared control, teachers and students co-construct the learning process. Yet this does not mean that teachers are laissez-faire or permissive. Democratic classrooms hold high expectations for all learners. To this end, teachers act as role models, showing respect for children's ideas, valuing individual contributions, and providing opportunities for authentic participation. As a result, students come to understand their rights and responsibilities as members of the classroom community and as members of society at large.

Democratic classrooms allow learners to recognize themselves as equal citizens, despite the fact that they are "only children." Lawrence Kohlberg (1980), founder of the Just Community School model in the United States in the 1970s, describes the importance of embedding opportunities for authentic participation saying, "The only way school can help graduating students become persons who can make society a just community is to let them try experimentally to make the school themselves" (p. 35). Democratic classrooms provide the space required to experiment. They act as a counterpoint to the competition and individualism students so often see in the world.

Grounded in trusting relationships, mutual respect, a sense of belonging, and student agency, the democratic classroom integrates SEL through everyday routines and experiences. For example, we may dedicate spaces and design protocols for students to talk through conflict. We may use collaborative learning opportunities that rely on perspective-taking. Such experiences purposefully build students' social-emotional competencies, such as self-awareness, social awareness, and relationship skills (Collaborative for Academic, Social, and Emotional Learning, 2020). As students reason about the beliefs, thoughts and emotions of others, they also develop the so-called Theory of Mind that precedes the formation of empathy (Singh & Duraiappah, 2020, pp. 41–42). Integrating SEL in this way promotes equity and inclusion, affirming the diverse backgrounds and experiences of our learners. Importantly, a culturally sustaining, democratic approach to SEL promotes positive self-image and identity development. It is not an instrument of compliance or control, which disproportionally disadvantages students of color (Simmons, 2021). Characteristics of democratic classrooms are summarized in Figure 2.2.

EMPOWERING STUDENTS AS CITIZENS

The democratic classroom is underpinned by two sets of complementary concepts: *rights and responsibilities* and *peace and conflict*. As students learn about their rights, such as those in the United Nations Convention on the Rights of the Child, they recognize their responsibility to engage in behaviors that protect the rights of others. Likewise, as a diverse learning community, students establish structures that create and sustain peaceful interactions with each other. By peaceful, we do not mean free of conflict. **Conflict** will always remain a part of navigating diverse perspectives. In fact, recognizing that conflict is not a bad thing to be avoided but a source to develop

Figure 2.2

Characteristics of Democratic Classrooms

Definition: A democratic classroom is a safe, inclusive learning environment, where students actively practice democratic values, understand their rights, and take responsibility for their behavior as both individuals and members of a community.

Characteristics:

- High-trust relationships between teachers and students
- Intentional modeling of democratic values and processes
- Shared power between teachers and students
- High degree of student voice and agency
- Respect for children's ideas and contributions
- Intentional sharing of diverse perspectives
- Confrontation of difficult issues from the past and present in purposeful ways
- Use of dialogue and group decision making
- Development of the whole self, including students' critical consciousness

our understanding is crucial for our students. We can help students learn to manage and resolve conflict in positive ways. Strategies we might use, such as Socratic Seminar (p. 119), teach learners how to take turns, listen to ideas, summarize thoughts, or add on to others' ideas. In the remaining chapters of this book, we have intentionally included strategies that develop students' ability to engage in dialogue with their peers. Many rely on sharing control with students, such as the co-planning strategies found in this chapter and those that ask students to design their own solutions in Chapter 8.

*By making controversial topics into objects of investigation, we can build the **critical consciousness** of our learners and support their empowerment.*

To some teachers, educating about these concepts, in particular the area of human rights, might feel controversial. Yet if we never guide our learners through controversial topics, how well prepared will they be to make sense of the contentious issues they encounter outside of school? How will they know how to channel strong emotional reactions they may have? How will they be able to maneuver through political or religious sensitivities? By making controversial topics into objects of investigation, we can build the **critical consciousness** of our learners and support their empowerment. By critical consciousness, we refer to students' awareness of the social and political systems that shape society and how it functions. To be active citizens, students must become aware of systems of oppression and structural inequalities that enable socially and ecologically unjust ends, with the aim of disrupting them. Hugh Starkey, Professor of Citizenship and Human Rights Education, affirms this commitment to our students stating, "Human rights are only rights when people know about them and can therefore exercise them" (as cited in Schmidt, Manson, & Windschitl, 2000, p. 8). Figure 2.3 elaborates on how we embed learning about the concepts of *rights and responsibilities* and *peace and conflict* in the democratic classroom.

Figure 2.3

Connecting Democratic Concepts to Democratic Classroom Practices

Concepts	Definition	In the Democratic Classroom, we . . .
Rights and Responsibilities	**Rights:** Legal, social, or ethical principles that frame what people are owed or allowed to do. **Responsibilities:** Duties, associated with actions and attitudes within one's power or control.	Support a safe, inclusive learning environment characterized by trusting relationships. Empower learners to exercise their rights both inside and outside of school. Encourage student behaviors that relate to civic action (e.g., enacting one's duties).
Peace and Conflict	**Peace:** Composed of both negative peace (the absence of war and conflict) and positive peace (attitudes, institutions and structures that create and sustain peaceful societies). **Conflict:** A difference between the needs and interests of two parties, which can be either positive or negative.	Develop understanding that "peace starts with me," advocating for mindfulness and kindness at the personal level, in addition to community and global levels. Encourage learners to see peace as a dynamic process rather than a static endpoint. Position conflict as part of understanding perspectives, engaging in dialogue, and making decisions with others. Build student interpersonal skills, including the ability to communicate, collaborate, and manage conflict.

Our learners come to us with a wealth of experience. They are not blank slates, nor is a mandated curriculum equally accessible for all students. Students' backgrounds, identities, and perspectives inform their beliefs and in turn shape their understanding of the curriculum (Myers & Zaman, 2009). Building on and developing the **identity** of each student as part of the learning process makes education an emancipatory act that helps our learners find meaning in the world. This echoes the words of educator and critical theorist Paolo Friere (2000) who said, "Liberating education consists in acts of cognition, not transferals of information" (p. 79). We can teach students to memorize content, but that knowledge takes no life of its own until the learner recognizes how it relates to their lived experiences. They need to make it *their own*.

Part of a democratic classroom approach means valuing students' experiences and viewing them as assets to support learning. This includes their racial, cultural, and linguistic identities, as well as their lived experiences from home, prior schooling or the community. By **assets**, we mean viewing each child's thoughts, culture, and traits as strengths, which can contribute to the richness and diversity of classroom learning. As we integrate our students' experiences into the curriculum, we can highlight diverse perspectives and provide a platform for every child to have a voice. We can show our learners what it means to co-exist in a highly diverse society through their interactions in the classroom. They can *live it*. Because new learning is constructed on prior learning, the more we help learners engage their prior knowledge, the more likely they will also be able to acquire knowledge and skills, understand deeply, and apply their learning.

While integrating students' lived experiences into the curriculum can support learning, we must also be aware that some life events may have been traumatic, such as discrimination, divorce, violence, homelessness, or disasters. In fact, data collected by the Centers for Disease Control and Prevention (n.d.) from 2009–2018 determined that nearly two thirds of surveyed adults reported at least one adverse childhood experience between birth and 18, with more than a quarter reporting three or more adverse childhood experiences. While we may not fully understand the extent of the trauma they've experienced, we do need to be cognizant that past adverse experiences will affect the way our learners engage with the curriculum. This is particularly true with out-of-school experiences related to COVID-19 and its consequences on families and communities.

Building on and developing the identity of each student as part of the learning process makes education an emancipatory act that helps our learners find meaning in the world.

Student-Centered Planning in the Democratic Classroom

While there are many ways to value and integrate students' identities and experiences, we recommend beginning with the planning process. Inviting our students to be part of the planning process enhances the likelihood that a unit will be relevant and meaningful *to them*. Given that they are the "end users" of the curriculum, it is vital that their ideas are captured to inform our planning. Such a form of liberatory design looks to "create shared truths,

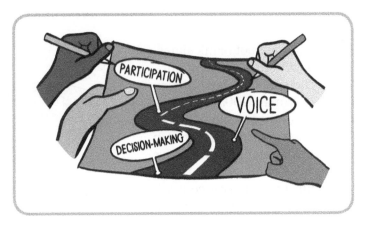

stories, and ultimately learning" (Stanford dSchool, 2020).

Often, teachers ask students to take part in pre-assessment activities before or at the start of a unit to assess specific knowledge, skills, or conceptual understandings. Pre-assessment data can inform planning by creating a map of curricular outcomes to focus our instruction. Inviting students to participate in planning goes one step further, involving aspects of our learners that are much more challenging to assess: their strengths, passions, concerns, and experiences. When we involve students, we model decision making and consensus building. We tell them, "I, as a teacher, have just as much to learn from you, as you from me." We change the power dynamics in our classroom and communicate that the learning journey applies to everyone in the room, regardless of age or status. Creating the road map for learning *with our students* also counts as a meaningful learning experience in and of itself, teaching them about the democratic concepts of *voice* and *participation* through the decision-making process.

So what does this look like? When we engage our students in co-planning, we ask two key questions:

1. What are our students' strengths, passions, concerns, and experiences?

2. What significant issues connect to students' lives, invite deep learning, and compel students to act?

While the first question seeks to unearth information about students' prior knowledge and experiences, the second question considers contemporary issues, community connections, and curricular outcomes. What is happening in the world today that we can connect to? What resources or case studies might we draw from in our community? How do particular issues relate to the school, state, or national standards we are asked to address with our learners? We can identify meaningful learning contexts by looking for the intersection of these two questions (see Figure 2.4). By bringing together students' strengths, passions, and concerns with significant issues, we can ensure that learning widens their perspectives. Parents also provide valuable insights that complement students' thinking in co-planning activities. We encourage educators to invite parents to the table as part of the planning process, where possible.

Not every co-planning activity will occur at the beginning of a new unit. We may engage learners in opportunities to share their strengths, passions, and concerns at the beginning of the year, which are refreshed and drawn on at regular intervals throughout the year. Likewise, we may invite students to give feedback in the middle of a unit to shape a project. Common classroom routines, such as Morning Meeting, can be used for this purpose. Depending on the age and developmental stage of our learners, we may provide more or less structure to these co-planning activities. It is important to note that students can also provide feedback on many other aspects of the classroom. For

Figure 2.4

Identifying Meaningful Learning Contexts

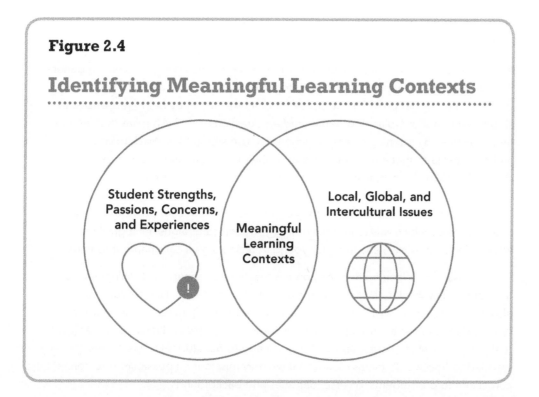

example, on the way they are assessed, how they work with their peers, or the design of the classroom environment. An example of powerful co-planning is exemplified in the Spotlight on High Tech High.

••• SPOTLIGHT ON CO-PLANNING WITH STUDENTS

HIGH TECH HIGH

High Tech High is a network of 16 public charter schools serving K–12 students in San Diego, California. Guided by four design principles, *Equity*, *Personalization*, *Authentic Work*, and *Collaborative Design*, High Tech High is highly committed to student-centered approaches, such as co-planning. High Tech High uses projects as a focal point for teaching and learning experiences and collaborates with students in two distinct ways to gather their feedback and set a direction.

One way is that teachers generate ideas for future projects, guided by current events and situations that they believe will spark student enthusiasm and interest. These project ideas are then discussed with students using the Project Tuning Protocol (see below for link to protocol). As students and teachers engage in dialogue, they build trust, empathy, and a deeper understanding of each other. As school leader Melissa Daniels says of this process, "When you sit down at a table with students to do a Project Tuning, and you've got students and teachers together, there's this equity that's communicated and practiced. We're all here, talking about this project idea, and your idea as a seventh grader is just as valuable."

(Continued)

(Continued)

Another way that teachers co-plan with students is by developing an idea of a general theme or topic and launching an inquiry together with students before a project is defined. The teacher provides the space for co-construction by being responsive to students and not overplanning. *What student questions exist? What are their interests and concerns?* By listening deeply, teachers can use student feedback to develop authentic projects that empower students in their local communities. For example, during the 2016 election, first graders were aghast to discover the percentage of voting age Americans who actually vote in elections. "What do you mean grown-ups don't vote, when they have the right to vote?" they exclaimed. This concern drove their inquiry and related project, which was to create voter registration campaigns. First graders went to local college campuses, encouraging young adults to sign a commitment to vote.

The success of co-planning depends on the teacher's openness and willingness to use student feedback to shift learning experiences. As Melissa Daniels suggests, it's about thinking creatively to ensure we reach all learners, "[i]t's really important to stand back and think, what are the opportunities for learning here and how can we adjust to really speak to what's happening in the world and to our students' lives?" Being overly wedded to *how we do things* means that we may miss out on possibilities to connect the curriculum to our students' diverse identities and backgrounds.

Scan this QR code to access the Project Tuning Protocol featured in this spotlight, or visit **teachworldwise.com/ resources**.

Figure 2.5

Co-Planning at High Tech High

For more on High Tech High and their approach to project planning, see https://gse .hightechhigh.org/design/

The Worldwise Learning Planning Process

How does co-planning fit into the wider Worldwise Learning planning process? We advocate for the planning steps and tools found in Figure 2.6. Note that choosing an organizing issue is only one of the ways that students can participate in planning. They can also support the development of unit questions or design learning experiences such as projects. Where there are school-based constraints, ensure student participation is authentic and produces meaningful changes to the design of a unit. If a unit context is fixed, focus instead on inviting students to co-construct questions or learning engagements.

Scan this QR code to access a video walkthrough modeling the unit planning process, or visit **teachworldwise.com/resources**.

Figure 2.6

Worldwise Learning Planning Process

1. **Choose a Standards-Aligned Organizing Issue (Meaningful Learning Context):** Involving students to the greatest extent possible, choose a relevant local, global, or intercultural issue as an organizer for the series of lessons or unit. Ensure that this issue aligns with curricular standards from your context. When including students in the identification of issues, use a strategy for co-planning to scaffold the collection of all voices. As students engage with issue identification, they can also jot initial questions, which can inform Step 5. Issue identification may occur weeks before the launch of a unit.

2. **Create the Unit Web:** Once an issue has been chosen, consider the disciplines or strands that would be part of the intended learning. Create a Unit Web (Erickson & Lanning, 2014) to map knowledge, skills, and concepts related to areas of the unit. The web will facilitate the construction of unit conceptual understandings in Step 3. While adding detail to your web, keep curricular standards (knowledge and skill learning) in mind that you may choose in Step 4. A QR code connecting to a short video about how to construct a Unit Web can be found on page 20.

3. **Write Conceptual Understandings:** Looking at the unit web, articulate conceptual understandings that represent the transferable ideas students should walk away with at the end of the study. By writing these conceptual understandings as learning outcomes, we can align knowledge and skill learning in Step 4 and construct questions to guide student learning in Step 5 of this process. More about how to create conceptual understandings can be found in Chapter 7 (pp. 199–200).

4. **Determine Curricular Standards:** From the unit web process, disciplinary and interdisciplinary knowledge and skills will emerge as integral to the unit study. Drawing from the curricular standards adopted within your context, choose specific knowledge and skill outcomes for students to develop in the unit.

5. **Construct Guiding Questions:** In this stage, write guiding questions that will facilitate inquiry through the Connect, Understand, Act cycle. Factual questions build issue-awareness, focus knowledge and skill acquisition, and name case studies that will be uncovered in a unit. These are drawn from the knowledge and skill learning named in curricular outcomes. Conceptual questions enable students to see the "big picture," uncover relationships between concepts, and form their own conceptual understandings. These questions are written using the conceptual understandings articulated in Step 4. Provocative questions, also called debatable questions, invite students to take a stance on an issue and use their learning to justify their thinking. These can be specific to a context (factual) or transferable across contexts (conceptual). Examples of these three question types can be found under the Case Study Approach strategy in Chapter 3 (pp. 83–86) and the Conceptual Questions strategy in Chapter 7 (pp. 214–216). Where possible, invite students to take part in generating the factual questions of a unit based on their strengths, passions, concerns, and experiences.

(Continued)

Figure 2.6 (Continued)

6. **Design Assessments:** Design the summative assessment and assessment criteria. This assessment reveals students' understanding of an important conceptual understanding (or two) and reflects knowledge and skill learning named in curricular standards. Formative assessments can be named at this point or returned to as learning experiences are crafted.

7. **Design Learning Experiences:** Last, use the curricular standards, conceptual understandings, and questions to design and sequence learning experiences. By writing each of the questions on a sticky note, these can be grouped and ordered over a number of weeks. In this step, consider how the questions move from building self-awareness and connection toward understanding and action. Consider the dispositions and SEL that underpins the design of learning experiences. Record dispositions or SEL outcomes alongside learning experiences to ensure mini-lessons or lesson-level questions relate to them for student reflection. Involve students to the greatest extent possible. For example, they can propose projects, specific case studies, or connections to the local community to explore.

Strategies for Democratic Classrooms

At the heart of the democratic classroom is being a considerate, active listener of children's perspectives and ideas. We take both the role of a researcher and the role of a co-participant, as we learn about and from our students. For this reason, we can say that the following strategies are underpinned by a "pedagogy of listening" and guided by a number of principles of listening that guide our interactions with learners (modified from Clark, 2005).

Experiences should be:

Scan this QR code to watch a short video modeling how to use questions to sequence a unit, or visit **teachworldwise.com/ resources**.

- **Participatory:** We view children as experts and agents in their own lives.
- **Reflexive:** We share the purpose of activities with children and youth and include them in the interpretation of data, where appropriate.
- **Student-Focused:** We explore students' lived experiences as a way to both provide authentic reflection opportunities and to gather insights about learners.
- **Multimodal:** We recognize that children and youth communicate ideas and opinions through different modes (e.g., speaking, writing, drawing, photography, etc.).

The following strategies are broken into two broad categories:

1. **Strategies to Explore Rights, Responsibilities, Peace, and Conflict:** These strategies help students understand aspects of rights, responsibilities, peace, and conflict in relation to the learning environment and learning process. They can support learners in understanding how these concepts relate to the school, local community, or wider environment, depending on students' age and developmental stage.

2. **Strategies for Collaborative Decision Making and Co-Planning:** These strategies can be used to gather information about students' strengths, passions, concerns, and experiences, in particular as part of a co-planning process. That said, many can be modified for other collaborative decision-making processes. For example, Empathy Maps (p. 65) could be used to explore classroom set-up at the beginning of the school year.

STRATEGIES FOR DEMOCRATIC CLASSROOMS

Strategy	Description	Page Number
STRATEGIES TO EXPLORE RIGHTS, RESPONSIBILITIES, PEACE, AND CONFLICT		
Co-Constructed Class Charter	Students co-construct a class charter using the concepts of *rights* and *responsibilities*.	46
Rights, Needs, and Wants	Students differentiate between the concepts of *rights*, *needs*, and *wants*, connecting to concrete examples from their lives.	48
A Peaceful Place	Students design a peaceful place in the classroom to support reflection and mindfulness.	51
Circles of Peace	Students draw connections between personal, community, and world peace using a graphic organizer.	53
STRATEGIES FOR COLLABORATIVE DECISION MAKING AND CO-PLANNING		
Passion Maps	Students map out their passions for use in personalized learning experiences throughout the school year.	56
Issues Inventory	Students share their strengths, passions, concerns, and experiences, which are recorded and drawn from over the school year.	59
Deconstructing Standards	Students unpack learning outcomes and determine how best to address them over a school year.	61
Sort, Group, Name	Students ask, analyze, and group questions related to a unit issue to form areas of inquiry.	63
Empathy Maps	Students consider what they think, feel, say, and do in relation to an issue.	65

STRATEGY FOR DEMOCRATIC CLASSROOMS
Co-Constructed Class Charter

Best for: Grades K–8

Purpose: Involving students in the construction of classroom agreements engages them in setting expectations while having ownership over the process. The Co-Constructed Class Charter goes beyond traditional classroom agreements by being constructed using articles from the UN Convention on the Rights of the Child. Through the strategy, students come to understand which rights we need to uphold for powerful learning. An important piece of learning from this strategy is that rights are not conditional on responsibilities. That is, rights cannot be taken away as punishment. However, the opportunity to infringe other people's rights can be withdrawn. The class charter should not be viewed as a behavior management tool. Rather it is a set of democratically negotiated expectations using the UN Convention on the Rights of the Child as a values framework. This strategy has been modified from UNICEF Canada (n.d.).

How It Works:

1. **Introduce the Charter and Rights:** Share the goal to create a charter about our rights and responsibilities in the classroom to support learning. By creating a charter collaboratively, all voices are included in establishing expectations for how we interact. Let students know that the UN Convention on the Rights of the Child will be used to guide the process. Briefly review the aims of the Convention with students.

2. **Discuss and Select Rights:** In groups of three to five, invite students to select the articles from the Convention that specifically relate to students' lives in school. Ask students to choose the top five rights that they believe need to be upheld in the classroom. We recommend the child-friendly icons from UNICEF, which are also available in a number of languages. Students can cut out the icons that represent their most important rights for the classroom, as is shown in Figure 2.7.

3. **Review and Establish Class Rights:** Review the rights each group chose as part of their small group discussion. Look for patterns: Which rights were commonly chosen across groups? As a class, discuss how these articles relate to their lives at school and support their learning in the classroom. As a class, select the five or six most popular and relevant articles for the class charter.

4. **Identify Behaviors and Responsibilities:** As a class, identify the behaviors and responsibilities associated with the five to six most popular rights. Invite students to work together in small groups to develop the wording of the charter and share with the whole class. Where appropriate give students sentence frames such as:

   • Upholding this right means we need to . . .

   • Upholding this right in the classroom looks/sounds/feels like . . .

Scan this QR code to access a folder with all these UNICEF materials, or visit unicef.ca/en/resources-teachers

Figure 2.7

Groups Choose Rights to Uphold for Learning

Figure 2.8

Example Class Charter

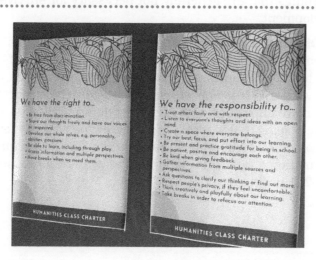

5. **Display and Reflect:** As a class, vote on the design and placement of the charter. Students and adults can sign the charter if desired. Review the charter with students throughout the year.

Extension: Classroom Culture Survey: At points throughout the year, create the opportunity for students to voice how well they felt valued and included. Did all members of the classroom community (e.g., students and teachers) uphold the charter? Where might we make improvements?

STRATEGY FOR DEMOCRATIC CLASSROOMS
Rights, Needs, and Wants

Best for: Grades K–8

Purpose: Democratic classrooms ensure students feel their rights are respected. As educators, we have a responsibility to facilitate explicit learning opportunities where students can make sense of the abstractness of *human rights* with concrete, age-appropriate examples. In this strategy, students come to understand similarities and differences between rights, needs, and wants. They make connections between rights and expectations for behavior in the classroom. This strategy has been modified from UNICEF Canada (n.d.).

How It Works:

1. **Introduce and Define Words:** Share the intention of the activity with learners, which is to understand the similarities and differences between rights, needs, and wants. Share the following definitions with students:

   - **Rights:** Freedoms we have to meet our needs for survival, growth, and development. These are granted to all people regardless of context.

   - **Needs:** Things that are necessary for survival, growth, and development. (These needs are protected as rights in the Convention on the Rights of the Child.)

   - **Wants:** Things that are generally not necessary for survival, growth, and development.

2. **Sort and Discuss Cards:** Provide pairs or trios of students a set of Rights, Needs, and Wants cards to sort along a spectrum of "Least Important" to "Most Important" (Figure 2.9). For example, a new phone would be a want and less important, whereas nutritious food would be a need and more important. Encourage students to discuss each of the cards before placing it along the spectrum, giving reasons for why a card might be more or less important than another. The Spectrum Sort, a concept formation strategy, is elaborated on with other examples on pages 210–211 in Chapter 7.

Scan this QR code to access a set of sort and discuss cards to use with your students, or visit **teachworldwise .com/resources**.

Figure 2.9

Spectrum Sort for Rights, Needs, and Wants

Least Important ←————————————————→ Most Important

---

3. **Pair Share:** Invite two pairs to look at each other's sorts and make comparisons. What is similar or different? Are there any common cards on the Most Important side of the spectrum? Why did students place these cards here?

4. **Analyze Most Important Cards:** As a class, ask students to share their Most Important cards and why they were placed on the end of the spectrum. How did they decide which cards were the most important? Scaffold student responses by giving them the sentence frame "_____ was a Most Important card because . . ." Encourage students to connect their Most Important cards to the concepts of *rights*, *needs*, and *wants*. What do they notice? Why would some needs be protected as rights?

5. **Connect to the Classroom:** Support students in making connections to the classroom and to the behavior of all students and teachers. Given the cards they felt were the most important, how do these impact on learning? What can be done to ensure children and teachers in the class have all their rights met? What are the responsibilities of the teacher? What are the responsibilities of students?

Scan this QR code to access a placemat of Maslow's hierarchy of needs, or visit **teachworldwise.com/ resources**.

Modification: Sort using Maslow's Hierarchy of Needs (Grade 4 and Up)

For older students (Grade 4 and up), we can choose to introduce Maslow's Hierarchy of Needs (Figure 2.10) and ask students how specific human rights connect to each level of the pyramid. For instance, which rights match with

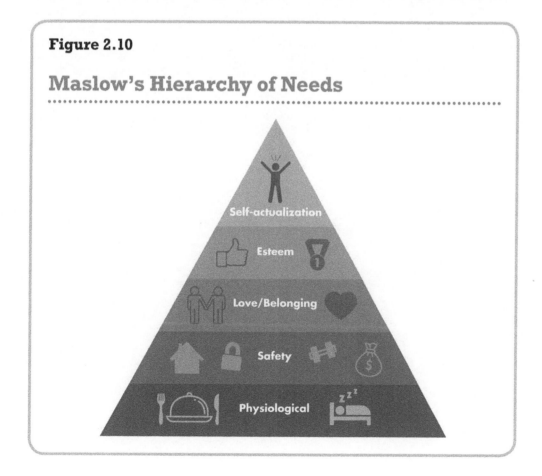

Figure 2.10

Maslow's Hierarchy of Needs

- Self-actualization
- Esteem
- Love/Belonging
- Safety
- Physiological

fundamental human needs, such as food, water, or shelter? Which rights have more to do with love and belonging? Sorting using the Hierarchy of Needs helps students see how human rights go beyond the physiological needs required for survival.

Extension: Absolute and Non-Absolute Rights (Grade 5 and Up)

Freedom of opinion and expression are basic conditions of democratic participation that our students must be competent and confident to exercise (Gollob, Krapf, Ólafsdóttir, & Weidinger, 2010, p. 29). Yet these are *non-absolute rights*. Absolute rights cannot be interfered with or limited in any way, for example the rights not to be tortured or enslaved. Few human rights are absolute. Most rights can be limited in certain circumstances, and in many situations rights need to be balanced. For example, imagine a group of students using derogatory language on a playground. Their rights to an opinion and to self-expression must be balanced with the rights of others to be treated equally and to be free from discrimination. Extend the sorting activity by asking students to sort rights named on cards into absolute and non-absolute piles. Can they give scenarios where one non-absolute right might be in conflict with another?

STRATEGY FOR DEMOCRATIC CLASSROOMS
A Peaceful Place

Best for: Grades K–5

Purpose: A key understanding we foster in the democratic classroom is that peace begins within each individual. This means every member of the classroom community contributes to the classroom as a peaceful place. In this strategy, we create a physical *peaceful place*, a quiet refuge in the classroom where students can choose to identify feelings and emotions, find their inner calm, or resolve conflicts with their peers. This strategy helps reaffirm the habits we seek to embed and makes the concept of *peace* more concrete for young learners.

How It Works:

1. **Explore Peace:** After engaging in a read aloud, such as *The Peace Book* by Todd Parr, *Peace is an Offering* by Annette LeBox, or *The Peace Stick* by Nidhi Misra, ask students the question: "What might a *peaceful* place look like, sound like, feel like?" Unpack responses in a Y-chart (Figure 2.11). These can be used to establish norms for use of the space.

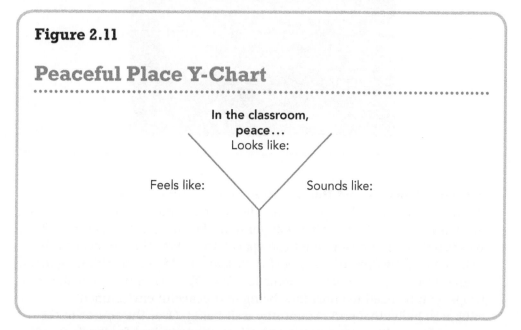

Figure 2.11

Peaceful Place Y-Chart

In the classroom,
peace...
Looks like:

Feels like:

Sounds like:

2. **Discuss and Choose Space:** Given the ideas explored in the Y-chart, invite students to brainstorm a space to become the classroom peaceful place. In classrooms with little space, this could be as simple as an extra table at the back of the room, where students might be able to reflect. After students have recommended a number of areas and discussed their pros and cons, hold a vote to decide on a space.

3. **Design and Decorate:** Give students ownership over the space by designing and decorating it. An example Peaceful Place can be seen in Figure 2.12. Here Grade 1 students used a large box, which they covered

with paper and decorated with artwork evoking peaceful experiences. Students also wrote the word *peace* on their decorations in their home languages, reflecting their linguistic diversity. Inside the space, students added favorite books, paper, and drawing materials to encourage quiet reflection.

Figure 2.12

A Peaceful Place

4. **Practice Routines and Reflect:** After constructing a space and discussing how it will be used, provide explicit opportunities for learners to try it out. How did they feel going into and coming out of the space? What could be improved about the space? How does this connect to their well-being? How does this support their learning? Systems thinking tools shared in Chapter 6, such as Behavior-Over-Time Graphs or Feedback Loops, can be used to chart how being in a peaceful environment enhances individual and community well-being. Over the course of the year, make modifications to the space based on student feedback.

STRATEGY FOR DEMOCRATIC CLASSROOMS
Circles of Peace

Best for: Grades K–8

Purpose: The Circles of Peace model (modified from Crawford & Shelit, 2012) helps students understand the interrelatedness of individual and group behaviors on community and world peace. A key idea here is that peace is dynamic rather than static: We must continually work toward it. At the personal level, it can only be achieved through self-care, self-awareness, and reflection. As students engage in positive, respectful interactions with each other, personal peace transforms to become community peace. Discussions using the Circles of Peace can help students identify how they contribute to the **classroom climate** and to the community more broadly.

Scan the QR to access a poster version of the Circles of Peace, or visit **teachworldwise .com/resources**.

Figure 2.13

Circles of Peace

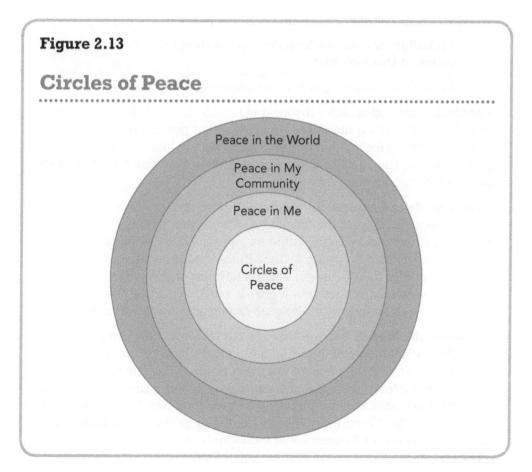

Peace in the World

Peace in My Community

Peace in Me

Circles of Peace

How It Works:

Because the Circles of Peace is a model that visualizes relationships between personal, community, and global peace, we can use it in a variety of ways depending on our aims and the age and developmental stage of our students.

Here are a few ideas:

Scaffold Discussions: During class meetings, on special days like the International Day of Peace (September 21st), or in relevant units, facilitate discussions using the Circles of Peace model. Morning Meeting, or other forms of discussion, provide excellent opportunities to model communication skills such as active listening, building on other's ideas, taking turns, and using respectful language. Use questions to focus the discussion such as:

- What behaviors might promote peace in you?

- What might it feel like, sound like, or look like if you're not at peace?

- What might you do if you notice you're not at peace?

- What behaviors might promote peace between individuals?

- What strategies might we use to manage a conflict with a friend?

- Could we measure how peaceful a community is? How might we do this?

- How can individuals contribute to global peace?

- Is it possible for communities to create systems that promote peace? What might this look like?

- Is the work of achieving peace ever finished? Why or why not?

Construct Analogies: After discussing the Circles of Peace, ask students to individually write a metaphor or simile about peace, such as "Peace is like . . . ," "Peace feels like . . . ," or "Peace sounds like . . ." These can be placed around the circle map to remind students as they reflect on their actions throughout the year.

Visualize Relationships: For young children, sensory experiences can support storytelling and the formation of concepts. In this case, the Circles of Peace can be represented as a peace pool. By filling a shallow pool with water and dropping a stone in the middle, students can see the ripple effects their personal actions have on others and the world. An example peace pool is shown in Figure 2.14. After having this experience, students can draw images of themselves engaging in peaceful behaviors.

Annotate the Model: Explain that the circles show how people's individual actions, in collaboration with others, help create a more peaceful world. Over the school year, record ideas directly on the model to show examples of personal, community, or global peace. For example, respectful behavior shared during a class meeting could be recorded in the "Peace in My Community" circle. During or at the end of units on particular issues, add examples of individuals and organizations that promote peace at the community or global level.

Set Intentions and Celebrate Behaviors: Using the graphic organizer, ask students to set intentions for a day or a week that relate to personal peace. For example, "If I feel angry, I will take one deep breath before interacting with others." Ask students to recognize times when they find it

Figure 2.14

Using a Peace Pool to Show Relationships

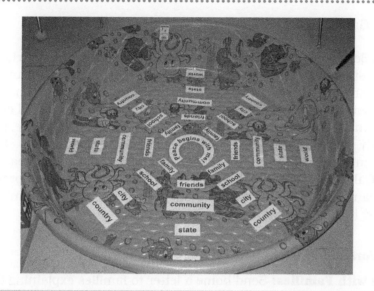

challenging to feel peaceful. This may be after a playground conflict, when engaging in learning that feels challenging, and so on. Say to students that we will set intentions to try to change our behavior, so we experience more personal peace. We can give them sentence frames for this, such as:

- If I feel . . . , I will . . .

- When . . . , I . . .

Invite students to write down their intentions and share with a classmate. Research shows that if we share our intentions with others, we're more likely to feel committed to them. At the end of a day or a week, ask students to debrief with their classmate. How did they do in keeping their intention? What was tricky or challenging for them? What successes did they have? Share as a class and celebrate both self-awareness as well as changes to behavior. Behavior change occurs over time, so making this a regular routine will benefit students.

STRATEGY FOR DEMOCRATIC CLASSROOMS
Passion Maps

Best for: Grades K–8

Purpose: Serving as the launch of passion projects, a passion map is a strategy that helps students identify and organize their interests, talents, and passions visually using a web. The passion map helps students envision pathways for aligning their identity with goals for academic learning and global citizenship. To inform the development of passion maps, students reflect, share, and brainstorm with their parents. Then they present their maps to their classmates. The following protocol comes from Katelyn Patterson, a Grade 2 teacher in Los Angeles, California. Although framed around the idea of passion projects, this strategy can also be used to gather student passions to inform unit planning over a year (e.g., choice of issues or specific case studies).

How It Works:

1. **Share with Families:** Send home a letter to families explaining the semester-long passion project before engaging students in passion mapping.

2. **Introduce the Map:** Introduce the passion map to students and explain how it will inform their passion project focus. Provide any models or work samples of a passion map (if available).

3. **Brainstorm Passions:** Guide the students in brainstorming their interests, talents, and passions using webbing (hand drawn or using technology). Discuss how others can help inform our passion maps as they notice interests or traits we may not have realized. A sample passion map can be found in Figure 2.15.

4. **Engage in Interviews With Families:** In class, prepare students to conduct an interview with their parents by writing clear, specific questions. Questions should be framed to help students find out about their parents' perceptions of their passions and strengths. At home, students conduct the interview, recording responses on the template and returning it to school. Informed by the interview, students add additional interests and talents to their passion maps.

5. **Present Maps:** Invite each student to present their passion maps to peers. Classmates ask probing questions and offer additional observations to each student related to their interests, talents, and passions. They can use sentence frames to give feedback such as:

   - I wonder . . .

   - I notice about you . . .

   Ask students to add additional ideas to their passion maps, as is appropriate.

Figure 2.15

A Student Passion Map

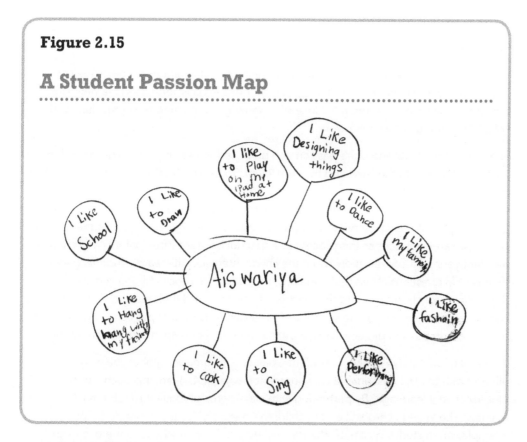

6. **Select Topics:** Prompt students to review their final passion maps and reflect on what is most important to them. From this, students select the focus for their passion projects and identify goals for learning, including how they may take action.

7. **Construct Individualized Learning Plans:** Co-plan Individualized Learning Plans with students, a living document informed by each student's passion maps and learning needs. Confer with each student to identify what they would like to accomplish academically in alignment with their passion maps. Relate this to curricular goals, such as literacy development or research skills. Students complete the plan individually then share with an accountability partner, classmates, and parents.

●●● SPOTLIGHT ON PASSION MAPS WITH KATELYN PATTERSON

Katelyn Patterson is a California-based primary grades educator whose teaching philosophy aligns with passion-based learning. Katelyn describes her role as a passion-based educator as "finding something that sets a spark in a child and helping them facilitate that spark until they can carry that flame on their own." She views her role

(Continued)

(Continued)

as a guide who helps students identify what their interests are and supports their self-discovery and learning. Holistically, Katelyn believes passion-based learning is a framework that reinforces the relevance of schooling, connecting the curriculum to the child, the community, and the world.

The process of identifying one's passion and purpose for learning may take a month or longer, evolving with the child and the curriculum. To begin, Katelyn engages her students in creating a passion map whereby they each present their identities and interests while peers act as observers, commenting what they notice and wonder. As part of this launch project, students interview their parents about what they glean about their child's passions. Katelyn describes this process as impactful because often parents and children have not yet had a conversation about the child's interests. Afterward, students generate their central questions about their passions, narrowing their focus for the semester with the guidance of classmates and the teacher. Students record their research in notebooks. Katelyn protects an hour of the school day to students' individual passion projects along with classwide passion projects chosen by the children that help inform the curriculum.

As a facilitator, Katelyn connects students' passions to broader global challenges aligned with the UN Sustainable Development Goals (SDGs), an approach she calls "intersectional learning." By partnering with classrooms globally through the UN initiative The World's Largest Lesson, children's perspectives are expanded. For example, when studying climate change, Katelyn took her students to the ocean and researched the effects of pollution on marine animals, sharing their research with children in Cambodia, Canada, Indonesia, and other regions of the United States. Following exposure to the SDGs, children began to address them in their passion projects. For example, one student was interested in architecture. He spent the day with his father studying construction sites in downtown Los Angeles, remarking that he saw no female employees. The student suddenly became concerned about gender equality in the construction industry and whether women felt like this career was accessible to them.

Students' passion projects culminate in a presentation to the community and a Sustainability Statement, a commitment to advancing one or more SDGs (see Figure 2.16). In past years, second graders have committed to lifestyle changes due to their learning, such as one student's family adopting a plant-based diet. While Katelyn remarks there are many academic benefits to implementing passion-based learning, such as improved communication skills and time management, her primary goal is to foster students' global citizenship. Follow Katelyn Patterson on Twitter at @_katepatterson_.

Scan this QR code for a related strategy that can be used at the launch of passion projects, Identity Maps. You will see an example of practice from middle school educator Julia Fliss, as well as an accompanying strategy protocol. This content is also available at **teachworldwise.com/resources**.

Figure 2.16

Grade 2 Student's Culmination Presentation

STRATEGY FOR DEMOCRATIC CLASSROOMS
Issues Inventory

Best for: Grades 4–8

Purpose: This strategy invites students to identify a challenge or problem in the community to frame a student-led project or inquiry. By creating an inventory of news articles, students develop media literacy skills and awareness of current events and social, cultural, and environmental issues. It also provides an opportunity for students to share what they care about and how they might collaborate to take action. The following protocol comes from Shannon Hardy, a middle school educator in Raleigh, North Carolina, as part of a Design for Change U.S. #DoGoodFromHome Earth Day challenge.

How It Works:

1. **Introduce the Protocol:** Introduce the curricular focus, timeline, process, and desired outcomes of using the protocol. For example, we may choose to use this protocol at the beginning of the year to collect student passions and concerns related to community issues. Likewise we can use it to launch a project, coupling it with a driving question such as: "What can we do to make a difference in a week?" In this respect, the protocol can work to frame interdisciplinary projects that may occur as part of a disciplinary unit (see more about projects as part of the Interdisciplinary Learning Continuum on page 75).

2. **Issues Selection:** Identify student-friendly news sites that adapt reading levels and content based on the students' ages, for example, Newsela, The Day, or Time for Kids. Students then conduct an initial news media search and create an inventory of issues they care about onto a digital board, such as a Padlet (Figure 2.17). Next, students organize the articles into categories (e.g., hunger, energy production).

3. **Form Teams and Research:** Students with similar concerns form teams. Groups conduct additional research into their chosen issues, including an analysis of individuals who may have vested interests in them. They can answer questions like: Who is affected? How do they feel? What are the probable root causes of the issue? Students check in regularly with group members to compare sources of information added to the inventory. Each group uses a note-catching document for research and collaboration, where the teacher can insert comments and questions. Students use strategies, such as perspective-taking strategies (Chapter 4) or systems thinking strategies (Chapter 6) to understand issues being investigated. This prepares them for developing solutions and actions (Chapter 8).

Figure 2.17

Example Padlet Board of Student-Selected Local Issues

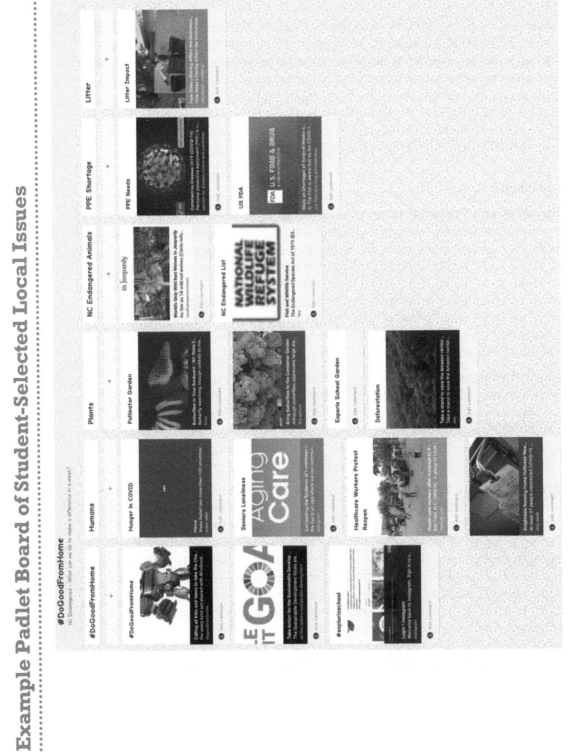

STRATEGY FOR DEMOCRATIC CLASSROOMS
Deconstructing Standards

Best for: Grades 4–8

Purpose: Co-planning with students affords a unique opportunity to amplify their voices, learn what interests them, and create student ownership at the beginning of the year. The following protocol is from middle school language arts teacher Julia Fliss in Evergreen, Colorado. She engages students in deconstructing the Colorado Content Standards, the Learning for Justice Social Justice Standards, and the SDGs. Together, Julia and her students co-create the curriculum, linking the standards with student passions to drive student-led inquiries.

How It Works:

1. **Introduce Standards:** Provide digital or print copies of the year's academic standards, including those from organizations relevant to the teacher's discipline. If appropriate, include the school's mission statement as a guiding document. For Grade 4 or 5 students, consider reducing the number of standards or paraphrasing them.

2. **Make Connections:** Invite students to highlight key words, phrases, and symbols from the standards that connect to their identities and interests. As a class, students curate notes that help create common language and goals for curriculum design (Figure 2.18).

3. **Co-Plan Curriculum:** Using curated ideas linked to the standards, co-plan inquiry units on issues that matter to students. For example, students may care about water-related issues. In the language arts class, learning experiences may include reading about water issues, communicating about the environmental impact of water footprints, conducting research through personal interviews and media, and creating art to represent key citizenship ideas and concepts.

4. **Personalize Learning:** Find spaces in the curriculum for individualized learning experiences. This may entail each learner developing a Personalized Action Plan through which to research a self-selected issue and determine how to use one's voice to teach others.

Figure 2.18

Deconstructing Standards With Students

Colorado Standards: On a sticky note, write your name + 3 words/ideas/targets from the CO 6th Grade Standards that you connect with the most. See my example.

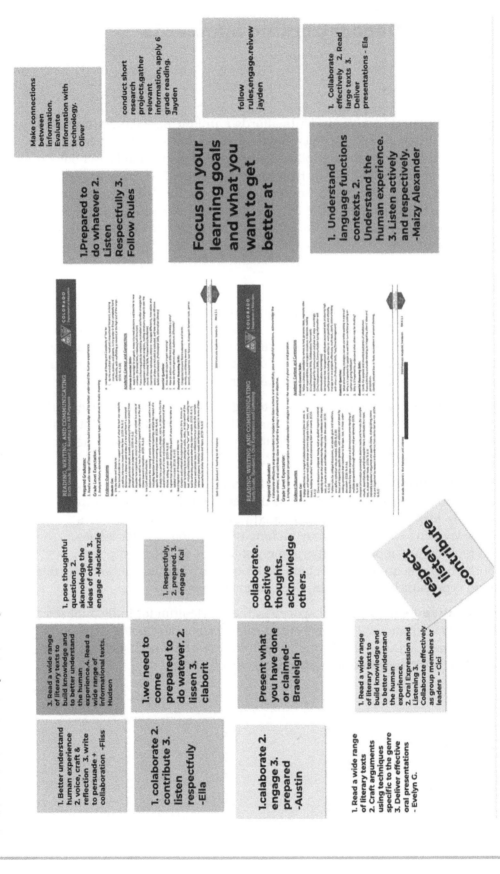

STRATEGY FOR DEMOCRATIC CLASSROOMS
Sort, Group, Name

Best for: Grades K–8

Purpose: This strategy asks students to generate, sort, and categorize their questions as a way to identify broad areas for exploration in a unit. It provides an opportunity to discuss what makes quality inquiry questions, such as using open instead of closed questions. Likewise, because student questions can sometimes be very divergent, it provides overarching lines of inquiry that can be more easily integrated into a unit.

How It Works:

1. **Generate Questions:** Invite students to write questions they have about a particular issue or aspect of an issue, ensuring they have sufficient content knowledge to ask meaningful questions. Students may benefit from being introduced to an issue before engaging in this step, for example, by reading a short article or watching a video that summarizes main aspects of it. To ensure class trends can easily be identified, an option is to limit the number of sticky notes each student has (e.g., "Write your top three questions"). This will facilitate sorting in the next step.

2. **Sort and Group Questions:** After students have written questions, ask them to work in small groups or as a whole class to identify themes. Tell students to read and sort their group's questions by the type of information sought, for example, "These questions are all about reasons why discrimination exists." During their sort, ask students to put questions into like groups based on their similarity. These should be clustered in columns or rows, so individual questions can be seen.

3. **Name Groups:** Last, instruct students to give each group a name that reflects the main information it seeks. Groups should be named with single nouns or short phrases (e.g., Reasons, Consequences, etc.).

4. **Share Categories:** Have each group read out the categories they identified from their questions. What similarities are evident across the class? How could each group's thinking be synthesized into a class chart? At this point, make sure you collate each group's categories into one class chart. This will ensure student feedback is easier to process while modifying planning.

5. **Modify Planning:** Make connections between the student-constructed categories and the unit overview and timeline. How might students' categories be addressed over the course of the unit? Figure 2.19 (see next page) shows how students used Sort, Group, Name to describe aspects of climate change they wanted to address in a unit. These became the overarching lines of inquiry that guided unit learning.

Extension: Diamond Ranking

Depending on the number of categories developed as part of this process, students can engage in a diamond ranking activity to prioritize areas based on their

interests or how ideas might be sequenced (e.g., what might need to be learned first?). As shown in Figure 2.20, the diamond has one card at the top, with two cards sitting one level down, followed by three, then two, and finally one. All cards on the same level are of equal ranking. This image shows how students brainstormed and ranked possible projects related to the unit issue of human resource extraction and use. Student groups then created 1-minute elevator pitches to show why these projects would represent powerful learning in the unit.

STRATEGY FOR DEMOCRATIC CLASSROOMS
Empathy Maps

Best for: Grades K–8

Purpose: Empathy maps are a design thinking strategy traditionally used to visualize attitudes and behaviors. They record information in a number of categories, creating a shared understanding of needs to support decision making. Empathy maps can be used with students to inform the planning process, while also activating prior knowledge. They may be used before or at the beginning of an exploration into an issue, before a project, or in the middle of a unit to guide next steps. Although empathy maps are typically not used sequentially, this modification asks students to do an individual reflection first, before discussing the issue with peers. Empathy maps can also be used as part of perspective-taking and perspective-getting experiences in the Connect phase of the Worldwise Learning Cycle (see Chapter 4).

Scan this QR code to download the Empathy Map template for co-planning, or visit **teachworldwise.com/resources**.

How It Works:

1. **Introduce the Map and Purpose:** Empathy maps are divided into four sections: Think, Feel, Say, Do. Each of these sections have corresponding questions to prompt reflection specific to unit planning (Figure 2.21). In the center is a box for the issue being presented to students. Being

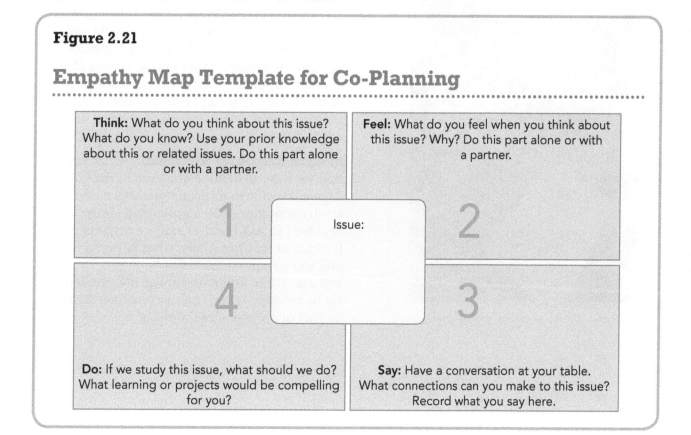

Figure 2.21

Empathy Map Template for Co-Planning

Think: What do you think about this issue? What do you know? Use your prior knowledge about this or related issues. Do this part alone or with a partner.

1

Feel: What do you feel when you think about this issue? Why? Do this part alone or with a partner.

2

Issue:

Do: If we study this issue, what should we do? What learning or projects would be compelling for you?

4

Say: Have a conversation at your table. What connections can you make to this issue? Record what you say here.

3

mindful of the *reflexive* principle of listening, share the purpose of the empathy mapping with students. Let them know the goal is to gather their insights to inform classroom experiences in the unit. If students have limited background knowledge about the issue, use a short article or video to introduce it before continuing.

2. **Encourage Individual Reflection:** For the *Think* and *Feel* sections of the map, encourage children to engage in individual or partner reflection before talking in small groups. Here we ask students to activate their prior knowledge, making connections to what they know and think about an issue. For younger children, the empathy map can be completed as a whole class, or students can record their responses in small groups as part of a screencast.

3. **Invite Small Group Conversations:** Next, invite small groups of children (3–4) to have conversations about the topic as part of the *Say* section of the map. What connections can they make to what they think, know, and feel? As students speak, direct quotes should be charted on the map. A recorder at the table can support this process. Sentence starters can help learners articulate their ideas and can be put up on a board or at tables to facilitate discussion:

   - When I think about _____, I . . .
   - Something similar to this issue is . . .
   - This issue makes me feel . . . because . . .
   - A connection I made was . . .
   - Something I wonder is . . .

4. **Recommend Actions:** Based on their individual and small group reflections, what do students believe learning about this issue should look like? In the *Do* section of the map, students write down learning experiences, project ideas, or other suggestions for learning about the issue at hand. This step can be done individually, as partners, or in small groups, depending on the age and context.

5. **Analyze Responses (Optional):** Remembering that we want to include students to the greatest degree possible in drawing conclusions from the feedback produced by co-planning strategies, next we can ask them to analyze responses. Looking at multiple maps, what patterns and trends can we find? Students can use highlighters to annotate similar information that exists between maps and discuss their findings as part of a whole-class meeting.

Figure 2.22

Students Share Their Empathy Maps

Worldwise Learning is far more than learning about issues in the world. It is about developing students as local and global citizens who advocate for themselves and others. Democratic classrooms provide purposeful opportunities for participation and decision making, nurturing the values and dispositions required to become agents of change. They model our expectation that children actively construct their learning, instead of passively receive it. Through instructional decisions, such as the strategies shared in this chapter, we can harness the power of students' identities as assets that enhance learning. In the next chapter, we explore interdisciplinary learning as it relates to real-world issues and how this approach can support the development of global competence. Before diving into the next chapter, take a moment to pause and reflect on your learning.

PAUSE AND REFLECT

- What attributes of a democratic classroom currently exist in your classroom? How might you engage your learners in more opportunities for participation and decision making?

- To what extent are students able to share and build on their identities as part of your classroom community? How might this be enhanced?

- Where might there be opportunities for co-planning with students in your classroom? What might this look like?

CHAPTER THREE
COMPLEX ISSUES KNOW NO DISCIPLINES

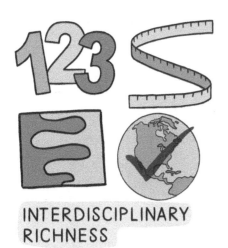

INTERDISCIPLINARY RICHNESS

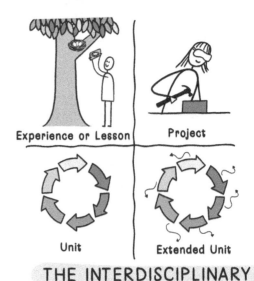

Experience or Lesson — Project — Unit — Extended Unit

THE INTERDISCIPLINARY LEARNING CONTINUUM

DISCIPLINES AS VEHICLES TO UNDERSTAND ISSUES

"UP AND OUT" TRANSFER

DISCIPLINARY, MULTIDISCIPLINARY, AND INTERDISCIPLINARY APPROACHES

COMPLEX ISSUES KNOW NO DISCIPLINES

"The community, in short, is the world in miniature. If we encourage children to observe directly the complex relations between people and the land, between nature and society, they will grasp the realities of their homes, their school, the town, village or city, and will be able to understand the wider world."

—Tsunesaburo Makiguchi, Educator and Founder of Soka Gakkai

This chapter explores the following Tenets of a Pedagogy for People, Planet, and Prosperity:

- Use real-world issues as organizers for learning.

- Make authentic links between, across, and beyond disciplines.

- Provide immersive, whole-body learning experiences, including in nature.

- Scaffold conceptual thinking that transfers.

- Use a case study approach.

Understanding Issues Using Interdisciplinary Learning

When the disciplines intertwine, they can create coherent narratives for our students about complex issues. Immersive issues-focused learning breaks down disciplinary walls. It enables students to grapple with the interconnected nature of the world to better understand it. This contrasts to a traditional approach, where instruction focuses on the mastery of information partitioned into subject areas and taught discretely. As Sweeney shares (2017), "Such a fragmented approach reinforces the notion that knowledge is made up of many unrelated parts, leaving students well-trained to cope with obstacle-type or technical-based problems but less prepared to explore and understand complex systems issues" (p. 142). Simply put, significant issues cannot be solved out of a *single discipline* of knowledge. If we want students to be able to tackle challenges in their lives, they need to connect their learning to authentic contexts with creativity and flexibility.

An integrated approach views the disciplines as resources from which we can draw purposefully to make sense of the world. In this book, we refer to this process as **interdisciplinary learning**, although we recognize that other

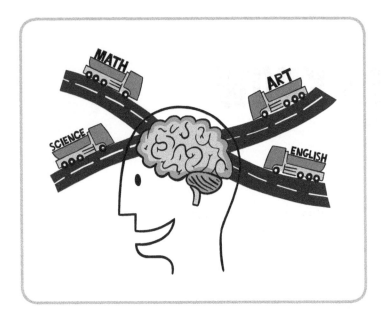

terms like transdisciplinary learning can be used to describe the real-world application of knowledge we are aiming to achieve. Interdisciplinary learning enables students to make sense of complex phenomena. For this reason, we can say it centers "on life itself rather than on the mastery of fragmented information within the boundaries of subject areas" (Beane, 1997, p. 18). This change of perspective emphasizes the importance of taking learning out into the wider world, where students demonstrate their global competence. Here the subject areas are vehicles to support learners in deeply understanding and interacting with issues (Murdoch & Hornsby, 1997).

Interdisciplinary learning also helps make our classrooms more equitable, inclusive environments. As Sarangapani (2003) argues, modern schooling is "based on abstraction, decontextualization, and literacy" (p. 208). By providing opportunities for experiential, interdisciplinary learning, we increase access to the curriculum and engage with knowledge that ordinarily falls between the cracks of subject areas boundaries. This broadens our students' thinking and reiterates the importance of practical uses of learning. By asking whose knowledge might have been marginalized in the single-subject approach, we can attempt to integrate multiple *ways of knowing* that connect to the diverse backgrounds and experiences of our learners.

●●● SPOTLIGHT ON INTERDISCIPLINARY LEARNING

Grade 7 students from UWC South East Asia in Singapore have been engaging in a unit focused on plastic waste and pollution to understand that *People's use of resources can lead to intended and unintended consequences for people and the environment.* Focusing on the effects of plastic waste going into waterways, they considered the role of individual human activity, and collectively how consumer choices, waste management systems, and river systems lead to the accumulation of ocean plastics. In particular, they investigated how plastic breaks down in the ocean over time to create microplastics. Microplastics are small pieces of plastic less than 5mm in length. To give a comparison, a United States dime is about 18mm in diameter, about three times as long as the largest piece of microplastic. Once these plastics get in the waterways, they are mistaken for food or ingested unintentionally by organisms. The consumption of plastic waste affects the entire food chain, because larger organisms eat smaller animals who have undigested plastic in their stomachs.

To apply their learning to a local outdoor context, students collaborated in a beach clean-up. They collected, sorted, and measured the waste collected as research. This brought

Figure 3.1

Collecting and Sorting Microplastics at the Beach

together learning from science, social studies, and mathematics. It integrated social-emotional learning as students worked together and persevered through challenges. Students were astonished by the number of microplastics on the beach and grasped the difficulties of trying to get plastic waste out of the ocean. Abena, a Grade 7 student, reflected on this experience saying, "There were small pieces of trash everywhere you looked closely and you could stay in one spot digging the plastic nurdles out of the sand forever. I realized the extent to which waste has impacted our environment, as there wasn't a single stretch of beach that didn't require a clean-up. I felt a bit accomplished when I saw all the trash that was collected in the end, but I did wish we had more time, as I was unsatisfied with the amount of trash that remained on the beach."

The Role of Disciplinary Knowledge

Disciplinary knowledge plays an important role in developing the background knowledge needed to form concepts and understand issues. Each discipline offers us a lens through which we can view and interpret the world. Likewise each discipline is made up of critical content our students need to learn to be effective citizens. Worldwise Learners must be literate and numerate to navigate global challenges, and this goes beyond traditional notions of literacy to include areas such as media literacy, information literacy, data literacy, and digital literacy. Developing essential literacies also supports student agency, enabling students to act autonomously, and self-direct their learning within an environment.

Where particular disciplines cannot be meaningfully integrated, students require instruction to develop the requisite knowledge, skills, and understandings. Therefore, disciplinary units often run concurrently to interdisciplinary ones in our classrooms. For example, a unit on multiplication may occur at the same time as a unit on water. However, the question still remains of how students will use their learning. Do we expect them to take disjointed learning, put the puzzle pieces together, and somehow apply it to relevant contexts all by themselves? Have we modeled how the pieces fit together, and when we actually use this learning in real life? Unless we explicitly plan for its application, **disciplinary learning** can remain a passive classroom exercise. As Hideki Watanabe from Japan's Soka University rightly suggests, our students "become creators of the future by facing the changes in society not passively but *proactively*" (H. Watanabe, personal communication, November 2, 2020). We have an obligation to help our students connect disciplinary learning to the world around them so they can become creators of the future.

A Fruitful Exploration of Interdisciplinary Learning

So what constitutes disciplinary, multidisciplinary, and interdisciplinary learning? Nissani (1995) uses the metaphor of fruit to describe and compare them. If disciplinary learning is represented by singular fruits, like an apple, an orange, or a guava, multidisciplinary learning is a *fruit salad*. In the fruit salad, we can see pieces of each individual fruit. We know when we're eating a piece of pineapple or a piece of grapefruit. Each fruit may be chopped up and mixed together, yet we can distinguish them from each other. In the same way, multidisciplinary learning still begins and ends with subject-based knowledge. It does not attempt to synthesize disciplinary perspectives into a unique whole, nor to meaningfully connect learning to complex issues.

Scan this QR code to access an overview contrasting multidisciplinary and interdisciplinary learning with two unit contexts, or visit **teachworldwise.com/resources**.

When we move to interdisciplinary learning, however, these fruits are blended to become a *smoothie*. As we have experienced, when drinking a smoothie we cannot discern the blueberry from the kiwi. In fact, the amalgamation of fruits leads to a unique taste that is beyond each singular fruit. Think about strawberry banana, for instance. The distinctive flavor of each fruit is replaced by a new taste that emerges from the combination of multiple fruits. This is also the case with interdisciplinary learning: Using issues as meaningful organizers for learning, the disciplines meld so that they are no longer individually recognizable. Each of these three approaches is represented in Figure 3.2 along with a definition.

Figure 3.2

Disciplinary, Multidisciplinary, and Interdisciplinary Approaches

Disciplinary	Multidisciplinary	Interdisciplinary
Individual Fruits	Fruit Salad	Smoothie
An approach that divides content into separate and distinct disciplines, such as science, mathematics, and social studies. This term covers the full range of subjects, both those more traditional, such as language arts, and newer areas of study, such as media literacy.	An integrated approach that focuses on the different disciplines and the diverse perspectives they bring to illustrate a topic, theme, or issue. A multidisciplinary approach uses the viewpoint of more than one discipline to study the same topic. These distinct viewpoints are not necessarily synthesized by students.	An integrated approach that generates an understanding of themes and ideas that cut across disciplines and an understanding of the connections between disciplines and the world. An interdisciplinary approach seeks to bring together disciplinary perspectives into a unique whole.

Sources: Definitions modified from United Nations Educational, Scientific, and Cultural Organization International Bureau for Education. (2020). *Glossary of curriculum-related terms.* http://www.ibe.unesco.org/en/news/ibe-unesco-global-consultation-revised-curriculum-glossary and Icons via The Noun Project.

It is important to note that none of these approaches are inherently associated with quality. It is just as possible to create poor interdisciplinary learning engagements as it is to create strong disciplinary ones. Likewise we don't "do interdisciplinary learning" with the sole aim of integration. As with any aspect of our planning, we need to work backward from our aims and choose the most relevant approach for our purpose. If our goal is to directly relate learning to authentic contexts, then an interdisciplinary approach, which unifies disciplinary knowledge, will better allow us to connect classroom learning to the world outside our doors. You will find criteria for assessing the interdisciplinary richness of a unit later in this chapter.

"Up and Out" Transfer

Worldwise Learning facilitates transfer by asking students to go "up and out," that is *up* to the level of transferable, conceptual understanding and then *out* to the wider world. "Up and out" transfer brings together students' use of two kinds of thinking: conceptual thinking and interdisciplinary thinking. This idea is visualized in Figure 3.3.

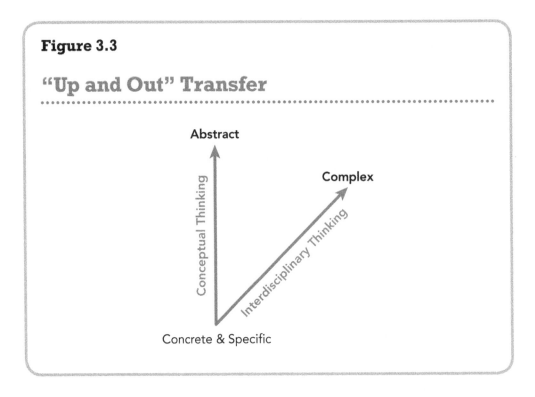

Figure 3.3

"Up and Out" Transfer

Abstract

Complex

Conceptual Thinking

Interdisciplinary Thinking

Concrete & Specific

UP TO THE ABSTRACT

As explored in Chapter 1, we want our curriculum and instruction to move beyond a two-dimensional model that is *inch-deep, mile-wide*. To do so, we organize the teaching of knowledge and skills around transferable conceptual understandings. We provide our students with opportunities to construct their own understandings, using knowledge and skill learning as evidence to support their ideas. When we say Worldwise Learning facilitates transfer *up*, we refer to students' ability to take their thinking to more abstract levels. Instead of referring to a *specific* issue, students begin to develop transferable ideas that cut *across* issues. For example, let's say students undertake a case study into how Malala Yousafzai courageously uses advocacy and protest to stand up for her rights and the rights of others. By asking conceptual questions such as "How might people stand up for human rights?" students articulate ideas at the conceptual level, such as *People can stand up for <u>human rights</u> by voicing their <u>ideas</u> publically using <u>protest</u> or <u>advocacy</u>*. Note that concepts are underlined. This understanding could then be applied to other rights activists, such as John Lewis or Coretta Scott King. Strategies to support students' conceptual thinking are explored in Chapter 7.

OUT TO THE COMPLEX

Interdisciplinary thinking is key to global competence, taking students' learning *out* of the classroom to complex, real-world contexts. Why? Because it lays the foundation for "deep learning," which involves the capacity for transfer to novel situations (Boix Mansilla, 2016). Interdisciplinary thinking supports our students in mobilizing their learning across subject lines as they make sense of and develop solutions to issues. When we say Worldwise Learning facilitates transfer *out*, we refer to students' ability to apply interdisciplinary thinking to situations in the wider world. By applying knowledge, skills, understandings, and dispositions for a *purpose*, learners see the relevance of their learning and its ability to be used flexibly. For example, after learning about the importance of pollinators, kindergarten students design their own butterfly garden in part of the school yard. This real-world context requires students to think across the disciplines as they answer questions such as:

- What part of the yard might be best given where children walk or play? (Social Studies)

- What host plants do local butterfly caterpillars eat? What flowering plants do local adult butterflies like? (Science)

- What is our budget? How many plants can we order, given our budget? How might we space them out in our plot? (Mathematics)

- How might we communicate to the school community about the purpose and upkeep of this butterfly garden? (English Language Arts)

Here we can see how applying learning to a rich context requires the creative use of knowledge, skills, and understandings from across the disciplines. Transfer becomes natural when learning occurs under the actual conditions of life: contemporary issues, embedded social-emotional learning, and an ever constant nudge to take that learning outside the classroom through application and action. Instead of learning being stored away in memory for an exam or some unknown, hypothetical future situation, we open the possibility for students to inquire critically into issues and take appropriate actions to improve their communities *now*. Developing active learners has never been more imperative. As Feng (2012) argues, the capacity for interdisciplinary thinking must be developed "so that a learning society can emerge in which individually and collectively we can face up to complex and uncertain challenges that lie ahead with more open, flexible, holistic and creative minds" (p. 33).

The Interdisciplinary Learning Continuum

When we talk about providing interdisciplinary learning experiences to students, we sometimes think about an extreme version, with students only learning through interdisciplinary approaches without the scaffolding and support of disciplinary learning. However, disciplinary learning provides important frameworks that help students both understand deeply and apply thinking rigorously to complex situations. We don't need to choose between disciplinary and interdisciplinary approaches. They can cohabit our learning environments in harmony. We can couple them intentionally to provide students access to different kinds of thinking.

We can think of interdisciplinary learning as existing on a continuum related to the frequency and degree of access students have to interdisciplinary thinking (Figure 3.4). Depending on our purpose, we can move along this continuum

We don't need to choose between disciplinary and interdisciplinary approaches. . . . We can couple them intentionally to provide students access to different kinds of thinking.

Scan this QR code for a printable version of this continuum, or visit **teachworldwise.com/ resources**.

Figure 3.4

The Interdisciplinary Learning Continuum

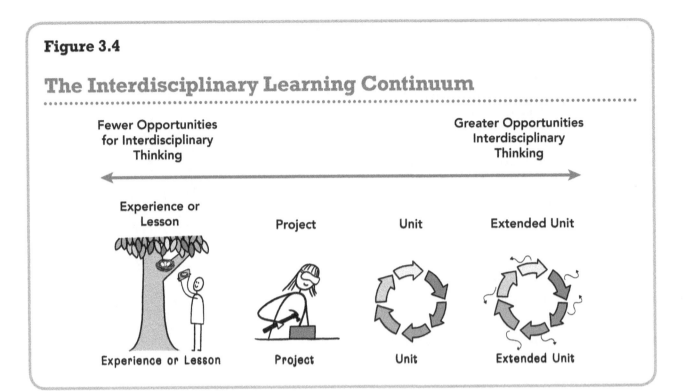

Fewer Opportunities for Interdisciplinary Thinking

Greater Opportunities Interdisciplinary Thinking

Experience or Lesson

Project

Unit

Extended Unit

Experience or Lesson

Project

Unit

Extended Unit

and provide different types of learning experiences for our students. Some experiences may be short in duration, such as an individual experience or a project. This means that students can still have opportunities to develop interdisciplinary thinking within disciplinary units. For example, we may choose to ask students to apply their learning from a disciplinary middle school science unit on pathogens to a real-life scenario: antibiotic resistance. This allows students to think outside the disciplinary box, look for connections across ideas, and consider their applicability to the world. Recognizing that schools can place restrictions on teachers regarding how they structure and deliver the curriculum, this continuum also provides an answer to the question: How might an interdisciplinary approach work in my classroom despite my constraints?

SINGLE EXPERIENCES AND LESSONS

At one end of the continuum are one-off experiences or lessons, which may provide students with immersive experiences in nature, opportunities to transfer understanding to real-world contexts, or the chance to take purposeful action related to local and global challenges. For example, Grade 3 students who have learned about migration in social studies are invited to engage local community members in a survey to chart, map, and write stories about their journeys, meaningfully weaving in mathematics and English language arts. Please scan the QR code for a sample lesson plan related to the Connect phase. Visit our companion website for additional lesson plans.

Scan the QR code for a sample lesson plan related to the Connect phase, or visit **teachworldwise.com/ resources**.

PROJECTS

PBL Works (n.d.) describes a project as "an extended period of time to investigate and respond to an authentic, engaging, and complex question, problem, or challenge" (para. 7). Projects include multiple experiences or lessons. These

Figure 3.5

Grade 4 Biodome Project

Scan this QR code to access Annika's full slidedeck with explanations of natural cycles, or visit **teachworldwise .com/resources.**

can be nested within broader units, where disciplinary learning may be occurring. An example project comes from Grade 4 students, who have learned about the planet's natural cycles (e.g., rock cycle, water cycle, and carbon cycle). As an end-of-unit project, teacher Kris Leverton invited his learners to create a biodome to identify and communicate how natural cycles work together to sustain life. Because students needed to both create their dome and explain how it worked using a slide presentation, the project integrated science, social studies, English language arts, and digital literacy. Take a look at the completed biodome from Grade 4 student Annika in Figure 3.5. Projects can be short (a couple of days) or long (multiple weeks) depending on their focus and aim.

UNITS

Units framed around local, global, or intercultural issues provide even greater access and more frequent opportunities to think in interdisciplinary ways. Units are typically 4 to 8 weeks in length, depending on the number of hours students spend engaged in unit learning per week. For instance, Grade 2 learners take part in a 6-week unit on the food production system. Learning focuses on plant life cycles, the effects of farming on the soil and organisms, the production of processed and unprocessed foods, and how foods travel as part of the production process. The unit fuses together learning from science, social studies, English language arts, and visual arts, as students learn about and represent their findings about food production.

EXTENDED UNIT

An *extended unit* refers to a unit that is longer in duration, for example, one that runs over a semester or year. The design of some extended units, sometimes referred to as *courses* in middle schools, means that interdisciplinary learning is integral to the way the content is organized. For instance, at UWC

South East Asia in Singapore, middle schoolers engage in a semester-long course on Social and Environmental Entrepreneurship Development (SEED), which brings together learning about sustainability, systems thinking, and change-making through the idea of entrepreneurship.

Strategies for Interdisciplinary Learning

The following strategies deviate slightly from those in other chapters. Building from the co-planning strategies found in Chapter 2, these strategies can be used in the planning process (p. 43) to develop interdisciplinary units. Although Slow Looking (pp. 79–80) can be used with both students and educators to facilitate close observation, the three other strategies included in this chapter are distinctly meant to support educators to engage in dialogue and thinking at various stages of the planning process.

STRATEGIES FOR INTERDISCIPLINARY PLANNING

Strategy	Step of Planning Process	Description	Page Number
Slow Looking	Across the Planning Process	Teachers engage in Slow Looking to locate possibilities, perceive complexities, and design learning for students.	79
Criteria for Interdisciplinary Richness	Step 2: Create the Unit Web	Teachers use criteria to assess the interdisciplinary richness of their unit design.	81
Case Study Approaches	Step 5: Construct Guiding Questions Step 7: Design Learning Experiences	Teachers identify case studies aligned to unit learning and use these to design questions to drive an inquiry.	83
Interdisciplinary Contexts	Step 7: Design Learning Experiences	Teachers design learning experiences by drawing from local interdisciplinary contexts.	87

STRATEGY FOR INTERDISCIPLINARY PLANNING
Slow Looking

Steps of the Planning Process: Slow Looking can be used across multiple steps of the planning process, such as Step 1 (Choosing a Standards-Aligned Organizing Issue), Step 5 (Construct Guiding Questions), or Step 7 (Designing Learning Experiences).

Purpose: When we slow down and look around us, we begin to realize that interdisciplinary links surround us. For example, that tree in the playground can be an opportunity to explore insect habitats (science), leaf symmetry (visual arts), or trunk circumference (mathematics). Yet this requires that we find the time to engage in Slow Looking. Shari Tishman (2018), author and researcher at Harvard University's Project Zero, describes **Slow Looking** saying,

> Whatever sensory form that it takes, slow looking is a way of gaining knowledge about the world. It helps us discern complexities that can't be grasped quickly, and it involves a distinctive set of skills and dispositions that have a different center of gravity than those involved in other modes of learning. (p. 2)

For us to see the wealth of learning that exists in our community, we need to *slow down*. Slow Looking, often underemphasized in school experiences, counterbalances our natural tendency toward fast looking (Tishman, 2018, pp. 5–6). Using Slow Looking allows us to be present, observe closely, and identify links we can bring into learning experiences.

How It Works:

Slow Looking can be used with both students and educators to nudge them to go beyond first glances. Protocols, such as Project Zero's Visible Thinking Routines, can enable individuals to appreciate the complexity of the everyday. Some of these are discussed in Chapter 4, which focuses on the importance of perspective-taking and perspective-getting. A table, showing practices we can use for Slow Looking can be found in Figure 3.6. Examples relate to the classroom, but are just as applicable for supporting our planning of rich, interdisciplinary learning. These strategies are drawn and modified from Tishman (2018).

Using these overarching practices, here are a few ways educators can engage in Slow Looking during the planning process:

1. **Search for Concepts:** Knowing the context and concepts to be explored in a unit, we can undertake a school or community walk with these in mind. Employing the Using Categories practice, we open our perspective about where learning about these concepts may exist around us. For example, "Where is *pattern* visible in the school? How can I use these spaces for authentic learning about *pattern* with my students?"

Scan this QR code to access Project Zero's dedicated Educator Tool for Slow Looking, or visit pz.harvard .edu/sites/default/files/ Slow%20Looking%20 -%207.11.2018.pdf

Figure 3.6

Practices for Slow Looking

Practice	What This Looks Like
Using Categories: Students use specific categories, such as shape, material, and so on, to guide a looking experience.	Students use the categories of size, material, and type to collect and sort lunch waste as part of a unit on waste management.
Creating Inventories: Students list and record every item of a specific kind or those found in a particular location as part of a looking experience.	Students undertake an inventory of local green spaces in the community as part of a unit on urban planning.
Set a Schedule: Students plan repeated visits or viewings over time to better understand phenomenon and how they change based on conditions.	Students schedule repeated visits to the same garden over time as part of a unit on pollinators. Visits intentionally occur at different times of the day and in different weather conditions.
Adjusting the Scale and Scope: Students change the scale and scope in a viewing using their bodies or tools like a camera to see objects with fresh eyes.	Students zoom in and zoom out of underwater panoramic images of the Great Barrier Reef to study ecosystem biodiversity and the magnitude of coral reef bleaching.
Employing Juxtaposition: Students place examples of a phenomenon in a collection to discern subtle similarities and differences.	Students curate photographs from the same U.S. Civil Rights Movement event, such as the 1960 Sit-Ins, comparing and contrasting the photographers' techniques.

2. **Make Observations Around a Guiding Question:** Using the Creating Inventories practice, we may structure a 20-minute observation accompanied by journaling. With a guiding question such as, "What connections can I make to this interdisciplinary unit? Where are the various disciplines present?" we can create a list of connections as we walk around the school or local community.

3. **Choose a "Sit Spot":** Using the Set a Schedule practice, we may choose to have a "sit spot" on school grounds or in the local community that we return to over a number of days. How does the space change depending on the day, time, and weather? What opportunities exist to make this location a place for learning? How might multiple visits change student perspectives on the space?

4. **Perspective Exploration:** Applying the Employing Juxtapositions practice, we can analyze resources for perspectives, which are dominant or silenced. For example, we may put out all mentor texts for a unit on a table. Taking a slow walk around the table, we can ask ourselves, "Which perspectives and worldviews are evident when looking across these texts? Whose voices may be missing that we may need to include?" This can allow us to identify texts, which provide a range of perspectives to students.

STRATEGY FOR INTERDISCIPLINARY PLANNING
Criteria for Interdisciplinary Richness

Step of the Planning Process: Step 2 (Create the Unit Web)

Purpose: Regardless whether interdisciplinary learning occurs as a lesson, short experience, project, or unit, we want learning engagements to be high quality for our learners. This means ensuring that experiences bring together the disciplines in a way that reflects authentic contexts and transferable conceptual learning. So how might we plan for interdisciplinary richness in a unit? We can consider a number of criteria (modified from Nissani, 1995) and reflective questions, always keeping in mind that our intention is never integration for integration's sake. Our goal is to purposefully draw from the disciplines as resources to help students make sense of issues and facilitate transfer to novel contexts. Figure 3.7 shows criteria for interdisciplinary richness that

Scan this QR code to access a reflective unit planning tool featuring the set of criteria in Figure 3.7, or visit **teachworldwise.com/ resources**.

Figure 3.7

Criteria for Interdisciplinary Richness

Criteria	Meaning	During the planning process, we ask ourselves . . .
Number	The number of different disciplines drawn into a unit.	Which disciplines might we purposefully bring together in this lesson, project or unit given its focus?
Distance	The proximity of disciplines to each other (e.g., history and geography are closer to each other than history and visual art).	How similar or different are disciplines in this lesson, project, or unit to each other? How does this support the intended learning?
Integration	The extent to which disciplines are mixed and blended together (e.g., kept as individual fruits, made into a fruit salad or blended into a smoothie).	How *finely blended* might the disciplines in this lesson, project, or unit be to support meaningful learning?
Authenticity	The degree to which the integration of disciplines reflects real-life contexts and consequently facilitates students' ability to transfer their learning.	How well does the integration of these disciplines mirror the authentic issue we are exploring?

can support us in our unit planning. Chapter 9 presents additional strategies for designing interdisciplinary learning experiences centered on global challenges.

Here is an example protocol for how we might use this criteria to evaluate the interdisciplinary nature of a unit:

1. **Choose a Standards-Aligned Unit Context:** Involving students to the greatest extent possible, choose a relevant local, global, or intercultural issue as an organizer for the series of lessons, project, or unit (see co-planning strategies in Chapter 2). Ensure that this issue aligns with curricular standards from your context.

2. **Pause and Reflect:** Before beginning the unit webbing process, pause and reflect. Using the criteria for interdisciplinary richness, hold a conversation with colleagues structured around the questions:

   1. Which disciplines might we purposefully bring together in this unit given its focus?
   2. How similar or different are disciplines in this unit to each other? How does this support the intended learning?
   3. How *finely blended* might the disciplines in this unit be to support meaningful learning?
   4. How well does the integration of these disciplines mirror the authentic issue we are exploring?

From our thinking about these questions, identify modifications you might make to increase the interdisciplinary richness of the unit. For example, we may realize when engaging in this reflection that our chosen disciplines are very similar to each other (e.g., science and social studies). We may ask ourselves how we may authentically integrate other areas of learning, for example mathematics or music, to deepen learning.

Scan this QR code to watch a video showing how to create a unit web, or visit **teachworldwise.com/ resources**.

Create the Unit Web: Place the local, global, or intercultural issue in a circle in the middle of your web. This can be done on a piece of chart paper, a whiteboard, or digitally. Begin to consider the disciplines or strands that would be part of the unit. Knowledge, skills, and concepts are mapped against each of these disciplines or strands. As concepts are generated under each discipline or strand, underline them. As outcomes of the unit web, we articulate conceptual understandings to guide instruction as well as assess the breadth and depth of disciplinary knowledge and skills being drawn into the unit.

STRATEGY FOR INTERDISCIPLINARY PLANNING
Case Study Approaches

Steps of the Planning Process: Step 5 (Construct Guiding Questions) and Step 7 (Design Learning Experiences)

Purpose: In Worldwise Learning, we take a case study approach to support students in investigating relevant examples of issues. Marschall and French (2018) describe a case study as "a particular instance or example that may be investigated to illustrate a concept or generalization, for example, an event, person, time period, problem, or hypothetical situation" (p. 142). Case studies provide opportunities to inquire into authentic contexts. At the same time, they reflect unit conceptual understandings and provide a meaningful framework for teaching disciplinary knowledge and skills. Case studies can foster interdisciplinary thinking by providing a relevant context for connecting knowledge and skills from across the disciplines. Sample online databases housing diverse case study resources, such as literature, film, and news media, are located on our companion website.

Once we have written unit conceptual understandings (Step 3), we can begin to think of specific contexts for students to study that align to them. This supports the development of guiding questions (Step 5). Importantly, these case studies relate to students' prior knowledge and experiences, ensuring that our diverse learners can form connections to them. As such, we recommend exploring learning opportunities found in the local community; from here, linkages may be made to other contexts. For example, in an interdisciplinary unit on energy, a teacher in Singapore wants her students to understand that *Passive building design can reduce a city's use of energy for cooling.* This unit brings together learning from social studies (Urban Planning), science (Materials and Heat Transfer), and mathematics (Angles and Surface Area). Using the question, "How might architecture protect a city against heat?" the teacher introduces two case studies:

1. **Singapore,** where a number of buildings have garden terraces and climbing vines on the exterior walls to reduce the need for air conditioning (a near context reflecting the location of the school)

2. **Hyderabad, India,** where rooftops are painted white to reflect sunlight and help keep building interiors cool (a far context relating to the national and cultural background of many students)

By investigating and juxtaposing these two contexts, students are able to identify concepts and create their own big ideas.

To choose case studies and design unit guiding questions we can take the following steps:

1. **Review the Unit Issue and Conceptual Understandings:** From Steps 1 to 4 of the planning process, remind yourself of the unit issue, conceptual understandings, and curricular standards (knowledge and skills) to be explored. Case study ideas generated in the next step should align to these.

2. **Brainstorm Case Studies:** Identify a number of case studies that could be studied given the issue, conceptual understandings, and curricular standards in a unit. Start with case studies closest to student experiences and spiral out to far contexts. Figure 3.8 shows how we can align case studies to an issue and conceptual understanding. Note how the case studies introduce complexity over time. The conceptual understandings have been developed with reference to the corresponding grade's standards in the Next Generation Science Standards (2013).

Figure 3.8

Connecting Case Studies to Issues and Conceptual Understandings

Grade	Issue	Conceptual Understanding: *If we want students to understand that . . .*	Case Studies: *Then as case studies we may use . . .*
Kindergarten	Animal Needs	Animals can survive in an environment by meeting their needs.	Domesticated animal needs (e.g., dog or cat) Local, wild animal needs (e.g., bees, frogs, doves, wolves, etc.)
Grade 2	Biodiversity	Scientists measure biodiversity within and across habitats by identifying the variety of native plants and animals in a place.	Local land habitat (e.g., park, forest, etc.) Local water habitat (e.g., pond, river) Habitat from a far context (e.g., rainforest, mangrove, etc.)
Grade 4	Natural Hazards	Urban planning can reduce the negative consequences of natural hazards on communities.	Building standards to reduce earthquake damage in California (USA) Vertical tsunami evacuation structures (Indonesia) An automated volcano warning system to forecast volcanic eruptions (Italy)
Grade 7	Climate Change	Life-sustaining elements and compounds cycle between the atmosphere, hydrosphere, biosphere, and lithosphere through a number of processes.	Photosynthesis and cellular respiration Decomposition of natural matter (e.g., composting food waste) Burning of fossil fuels

3. **Consider Students' Prior Knowledge and Experiences:** At this stage, reflect on which case studies will both connect to students' prior knowledge and experiences, yet offer new insights. As reflected in Figure 3.8, we may choose multiple case studies, start with those which are more familiar or local, and extend to far contexts. Students can co-design the case study options for a unit in this step by giving feedback or prioritizing those case studies they are most interested in exploring.

4. **Refine Case Study Choices:** After considering how students may connect to possible case studies, decide on the few that will drive student learning. Although we may provide opportunities for students to choose their own case studies for independent or small group investigation, here we are considering case studies that all students will be exposed to in a unit. Sequence how case studies may be introduced over a unit, moving from familiar to distant contexts.

5. **Construct Guiding Questions:** Once we identify specific case studies, we can construct guiding questions to facilitate learning experiences. There are three types of guiding questions: factual, conceptual, and provocative questions.

   - **Factual questions:** These questions address unit knowledge and skills and highlight the case studies that students will draw from to articulate conceptual understandings. Because they lead back to the issue being explored, these questions are locked in time, place, or situation and, therefore, do *not* transfer. These questions also address knowledge and skills named in curricular standards. Examples for our Energy unit may include:

     ○ How are fossil fuels used to keep buildings cool? What are the consequences of this on the planet?

     ○ What strategies do buildings in Singapore use to keep them cool without the use of fossil fuels? How do these work?

     ○ What strategies do buildings in Hyderabad use to keep them cool without the use of fossil fuels? How do these work?

   - **Conceptual questions:** Written in third person and present tense, conceptual questions *do* transfer. They are written broadly to allow for a range of student responses, but also guide teaching and learning toward unit conceptual understandings. These questions support students in articulating their own big ideas. Each conceptual understanding is unpacked using roughly two to three conceptual questions. In the Energy unit, we may ask the following conceptual questions about cities, heat, and energy use:

     ○ Why do cities often retain heat?

     ○ How might different materials increase or decrease heat transfer?

     ○ How might architecture protect a city against heat?

     ○ How can people design buildings to reduce energy use?

   - **Provocative questions:** Also known as debatable questions, these questions invite students to take a stance on an issue and use their learning to justify their thinking. They can either be factual or conceptual in nature. A unit usually has one to two provocative questions, which can be revisited over time (Erickson, Lanning, & French, 2017, p. 55). A sample provocative question for the Energy unit could be:

- ○ Whose responsibility is it to manage the heat produced by urban planning and building design?

More examples of guiding questions from across the K–8 continuum can be found in the Conceptual Questions strategy in Chapter 7 (pp. 214–216).

6. **Design Learning Experiences:** Once we have identified case studies, we can design learning experiences for students. Given the age, developmental ability, and research skills of our students, we decide how much support they will need to be successful in learning about these contexts. We also consider contexts that will enhance the interdisciplinary nature of these case studies (see pp. 87–90). For an in-depth look at how different case study approaches align to different types of inquiry learning, see pp. 143–148 of *Concept-Based Inquiry in Action* (Marschall & French, 2018).

STRATEGY FOR INTERDISCIPLINARY PLANNING
Interdisciplinary Contexts

Step of the Planning Process: Step 7 (Design Learning Experiences)

Purpose: In Worldwise Learning, we both bring the world into our classrooms and go out to explore it. Broadly speaking, there are three *buckets* we can draw from to enhance the interdisciplinary nature of a case study: people, places, and projects. Embedding people, places, and projects can support the development of dispositions, as students grapple with authentic challenge. We define people, places, and projects as:

- **People:** Learning directly from individuals or groups about their experiences, thoughts, or work. For example, Grade 1 students might interview the school custodian as part of a unit on Communities.

Figure 3.9

Undertaking a Design Challenge at Berlin Brandenburg International School as Part of a Cities Unit

- **Places:** Locations where learning occurs, which can be changed to reflect a case study. For example, a Grade 5 unit on Geometry may take the learning outdoors to explore perpendicular and parallel lines in the neighborhood. Depending on the age of students, places may also be virtual.

- **Projects:** Learning prompted by an authentic, engaging, and complex question, problem, or challenge. For example, Grade 3 classes undertake a design challenge to locate user-centered improvements that could be made to the community as part of a unit about Cities. As discussed in Chapter 2, the aims and scope of a project can be negotiated with our learners.

How It Works:

1. **Determine Case Studies and Guiding Questions:** As part of the planning process, choose case studies aligned to the issue, conceptual understandings, and curricular outcomes of a unit (see previous strategy). Articulate factual, conceptual, and provocative questions that will sequence and facilitate learning experiences about these case studies.

2. **Consider People, Places, and Projects:** Having identified case studies, consider the ways that people, places, and projects may be used to develop authentic learning experiences that connect to the wider world. For example, in a middle school unit on Resource Extraction and Use, students investigated the types of waste produced at the end of break time by tipping a trash can and sorting waste by material. Here the school community (Place) was used as an interdisciplinary context to explore a localized case study. This engagement connected to social studies, mathematics, and English language arts, as students sorted, graphed, and represented findings about community waste. Figure 3.10 shows additional examples of how People, Places, and Projects can be utilized to enhance the interdisciplinary nature of a unit. A Spotlight on outdoor learning at the Green School New Zealand also follows, illustrating a powerful example of the use of place in a unit. One strategy to identify people, places, and projects, Community Mapping, can be found on page 284.

3. **Reach Out and Make Connections:** Consider practical aspects of integrating people, places, or projects into your unit. Who might you need to connect with to design these experiences for students? What permissions might you need to leave school grounds? Leverage the collective knowledge and experiences of your community: teachers, parents, or those in the local community. Remember that digital resources can support this process. Individuals who cannot meet physically can create short screencasts or be interviewed virtually.

4. **Plan and Schedule Experiences:** Integrating people, places, and projects into our units takes planning and scheduling. Knowing your intended unit start date, when might this experience need to take place? Will it launch a unit, or is it part of a student investigation? Plan ahead, because many individuals require at least a few weeks' notice. Pencil in dates so that these experiences do not get forgotten about in the whirlwind of the school year.

Figure 3.10

People, Places, and Projects as Interdisciplinary Contexts

	Examples	What This Looks Like in a Case Study
People	Interviews Surveys Parent Involvement	Middle school students survey their peers about experiences with cyberbullying in digital spaces, identifying trends for analysis in a unit on Personal and Community Well-being.
Places	Field Trips Neighborhood Walks Nature Experiences	Grade 1 students take a neighborhood walk to look for signs and symbols and how they communicate information as part of a unit on Safety.
Projects	Investigations Design Challenges Service Projects	Grade 4 students undertake a design challenge to improve the school environment for differently abled students as part of a unit on Human Rights.

●●● SPOTLIGHT ON PLACE

OUTDOOR LEARNING AT THE GREEN SCHOOL NEW ZEALAND

Situated on the Oakura River, middle school students at the Green School New Zealand used this local context as a way to launch powerful interdisciplinary learning about natural systems. Inquiring into the issues of river pollution and soil erosion, learners investigated the role of the *riparian zone* along the riverbank. This area borders rivers, bridging the land and the freshwater ecosystem. To recognize the importance of the riparian zone, students first visited sites to compare natural riparian ecosystems with riverbanks on farms, where plants had been cleared. This allowed them to understand the natural functions of riparian plants to make banks stable, reduce pollution, and prevent soil erosion.

At the start of the project, students engaged in a BioBlitz to measure the biodiversity of their local river area. To do so, they used Seek by iNaturalist, an iPad app that allows users to engage and interact with the natural world by scanning the plants or animals

(Continued)

(Continued)

found in a habitat. Students at the Green School also collected water samples to analyze water quality, which would allow them to compare readings before and after their project. Focused on the idea of rivers as common resources, students considered thought-provoking questions, such as "Who is responsible for what's in a river, given that it travels through land?"

Grounded in learning from disciplines such as science, social studies, and mathematics, students then concentrated on replanting the local riverbed. Students learned to recognize and identify native plants, placing them at the correct height on the bank when they took action as stewards. This immersive and highly contextualized project fostered their connection to nature, as they came to understand the complexity that lies within this tiny strip of land. Of this experience, founding principal Stuart MacAlpine states, "You can't care *in theory* about nature, you have to actually understand the huge depth of sophistication of ecosystems. Then the awe and wonder comes, and you feel a genuine sense of stewardship." Through this experience, students gained deep understanding and developed their identities as changemakers.

Scan this QR code to access National Geographic's Guide to the BioBlitz strategy, or visit media .nationalgeographic .org/assets/file/ NationalGeographic BioBlitzGuide.pdf

Figure 3.11

Riparian Planting at Green School New Zealand

Chapters 1, 2, and 3 have outlined conditions for transformative education. With the backdrop of our globalized world, we argue that learners today require and deserve a new form of schooling that allows them to connect with, understand, and take action on issues important to them:

- Transformative education requires *active learning*. By including opportunities for conceptual and dispositional learning, we counter a passive approach to learning centered on decontextualized knowledge and skill learning.

- Transformative education requires *students' awareness of our local and global interconnectedness*. Using a Pedagogy for People, Planet, and Prosperity, we develop students' ability to see and understand the complexity of our planet and our place in it.

- Transformative education requires that *students feel seen, heard, and valued*. Using a democratic classroom approach, we enable our learners to internalize values such as inclusion, ownership, voice, and participation, while also giving them active practice in respectful interactions with others.

- Transformative education requires that *learning is relevant and purposeful*. Interdisciplinary learning intentionally draws from across the disciplines to allow our students to directly connect to issues in their communities. Facilitating near and far transfer, it promotes flexible and creative use of student learning.

We now look to the Connect phase of the Worldwise Learning Cycle. The Connect phase develops issue-awareness, perspective-taking, and empathy as students begin investigating a local, global, or intercultural issue. Before moving on to the next chapter, take a few moments to reflect on your learning from this chapter and how it relates to your unique context.

PAUSE AND REFLECT

- How often do students experience their learning as fruit, as a fruit salad, or as a smoothie in your classroom? Why is this?

- Given your school context, how might you leverage lessons, projects, units, and extended units to promote interdisciplinary thinking?

- Engage in a 20-minute Slow Looking experience. Choose a place common to you, but outside of your home or classroom. Use these questions to scaffold your experience: What disciplines exist here? What concepts exist here?

- How might people, places, or projects be used as interdisciplinary contexts within your case studies?

PART II

CONNECT: ENGAGING THE HEART, HEAD, AND HAND

Aims of the Phase

- Develop issue-awareness about significant local, global, or intercultural issues.

- Foster self-awareness and perspective-taking about an issue.

- Promote empathy and connectedness to others and nature.

CHAPTER FOUR

PERSPECTIVE-TAKING AND PERSPECTIVE-GETTING

PERSPECTIVE-TAKING TO
ZOOM IN AND OUT ON ISSUES

LOOKING INWARD:
MENTAL MODELS FRAME
AND DISTORT VISION

EMOTION DRIVES ATTENTION;
ATTENTION DRIVES LEARNING

LOOKING OUTWARD: PERSPECTIVE-GETTING

LOOKING OUTWARD: PERSPECTIVE-TAKING

PERSPECTIVE-TAKING AND PERSPECTIVE-GETTING

"Learning to look through multiple perspectives, young people may be helped to build bridges among themselves; attending to a range of human stories, they may be provoked to heal and to transform."

—Maxine Greene, Educational Philosopher, Teacher, and Social Activist

This chapter explores the following Tenets of a Pedagogy for People, Planet, and Prosperity:

- Champion social emotional learning as integral to academic learning.

- Promote perspective-taking, dialogue, and an awareness of self and others.

- Develop intercultural understanding, including a recognition of bias and stereotypes.

- Develop the ability to *think in systems*.

This chapter begins the Connect phase of the Worldwise Learning Cycle, which develops students' issue-awareness, perspective-taking, and empathy as they learn about a meaningful issue. Recall from Chapter 2 that Worldwise Learning uses an integrated approach that educates the whole child. This entails students *looking inward*: perceiving the thoughts, emotions, and identities that collectively form self-awareness. Likewise, it means *looking outward*: recognizing others' perspectives and uncovering what has influenced them. For example, in the following Spotlight on Human Rights and the Food System, young children formed connections to their own lives and emotions through multiple case studies. From this foundation, they formed deep understandings about the root causes of food injustice across time and place, as well as the motivation to act as informed consumers.

As explained in the Introduction, we advocate for a curriculum that teaches to the heart, the head, and the hand of each student. In this chapter, we focus on **perspective-taking** and **perspective-getting** as capacities required to care, think, and act as global citizens. By perspective-taking, we refer to "the capacity to identify and take on often conflicting points of view" (Organisation for Economic Co-operation and Development, 2018a, p. 14). By perspective-getting, we name the intentional process of seeking out others' perspectives to better understand a personal history, event, situation, or issue. Together these competencies reflect the interconnected nature of learning domains as students

- recognize and understand multiple perspectives in an increasingly diverse and global society,
- communicate respectfully across differences, and
- value and respect diverse beliefs and ways of knowing.

••• SPOTLIGHT ON PERSPECTIVE-TAKING

HUMAN RIGHTS AND THE FOOD SYSTEM

Students from Grades 1 to 3 at Island Montessori School in Wilmington, North Carolina, were engrossed in a unit focused on the overarching question, "How are human rights connected to the food system?" Before playing a short contemporary video of migrant workers in California, the teacher asked the children to "step inside" the perspective of those portrayed in the clip. *What emotions do their faces show? What did they think it would be like living as a migrant worker?* Using the Project Zero See, Think, Wonder routine the children turned and talked to their peers. A first grader shared, "I see sadness. I think it must be a terrible way of life. I wonder why they have to work so hard." A third grader then remarked, "They don't get a lot of money for working

Figure 4.1

The Migrant Mother

"Destitute pea pickers in California. Mother of seven children. Age thirty-two. Nipomo, California"; Library of Congress Prints and Photographs Division

Digital ID: (digital file from original neg.) fsa 8b29516

18 hours. I think they should be paid more." Following this initial shared experience, students collaborated in small groups to analyze photographs taken by Dorothea Lange, a Depression-era photographer known for her 1936 portrayal of the "Migrant Mother" (Figure 4.1). Children were asked to infer whether the subjects' basic human needs were met and why they think so.

After exploring this historical context, teacher Sally Petermann returned students' focus to our modern-day food system where an estimated 925 million people experience chronic food insecurity using examples such as cacao farming in the Ivory Coast and agricultural labor in North Carolina. She explained:

> Children often do not know where their food comes from, who farms it, or their working conditions. By analyzing diverse historical contexts, I want students to understand how the unfair treatment of agricultural workers has continued across time and place. Most importantly, I want children to realize their power as consumers to not support such practices when they purchase foods and other foods.

At the completion of the unit, students made local-to-global connections by researching the origin of foods at their local supermarket chain. They learned about the mistreatment of migrant workers in Florida, prompting them to write letters to the store manager requesting that foods be sourced from fair trade farms. Some children concluded that supporting local farmers makes it easier for consumers to track whether their money supports the humane treatment of workers.

Perspectives as Lenses for Understanding Complex Issues

Perspective derives from the Latin verb *perspicere*, meaning "to look through." As a noun, perspective often connotes viewing objects or situations through diverse lenses relative to time and space. Applying this metaphor to the study of global challenges, perspectives can be used as lenses to enable students to *zoom in* and *zoom out*. This allows students to identify patterns, processes, and interactions between people and places (National Geographic Society, 2017).

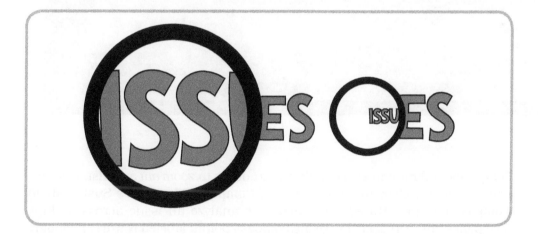

Let's look at an example of *zooming in* to understand a persistent and complex global challenge: migration and refugeeism. On their interactive World Population History site, Population Connection (2016) depicts the 2,000-year journey of human civilization from 1 CE to present-day (and projected into 2050). The viewer can explore how population growth and movement can be analyzed using diverse perspectives: historical, environmental, social, and

To access the World Population History site, visit https://worldpopulationhistory.org/

political (see Figure 4.2). As the historical timeline advances, the dots on the map show human movement and growth. By pausing and zooming in, students can learn more about the events and interactions that correlate with those patterns. For example, the signing of the 1830 Indian Removal Act resulted in the U.S. federal government stealing indigenous peoples' ancestral lands in exchange for land west of the Mississippi River. The Cherokee Nation, however, refused this relocation policy. They were forcibly removed in 1838 to a reservation 1,000 miles away in an event that became known as the Trail of Tears, leading to the deaths of 4,000 Cherokees from disease, starvation, and exposure. By zooming in on individual migration events such as the Trail of Tears, students can better understand the factors that underlie migration as a whole.

Figure 4.2

World Population Map

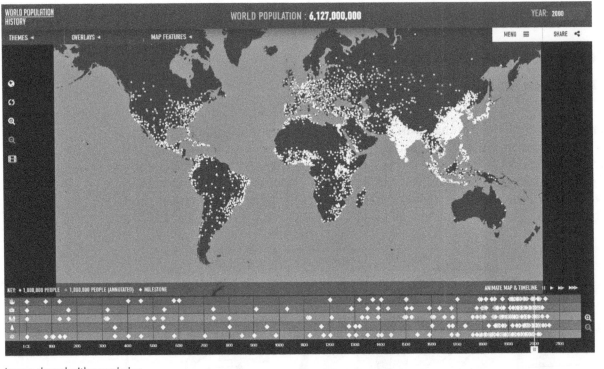

Image shared with permission.

Perspective-taking can also enable our students to *zoom out* and visualize connections across elements. For instance, Compass Education's Sustainability Compass tool (p. 216) allows students to analyze an issue across multiple disciplines and perspectives. Using compass points labeled Nature, Economy, Society, and Well-Being, one can identify cause and effect relationships and the leverage points that may produce changes in a system. For example, students are introduced to the issue of single-use plastics through the film *Bag It: Is Your Life Too Plastic?* (Hill & Beraza, 2010). This film highlights the environmental and human health implications of single-use plastics, as well as the contributing roles of government, culture, and economics.

Figure 4.3

Bag It: Is Your Life Too Plastic?

Image shared with permission.

Using the Sustainability Compass, students make connections between single-use plastics and the compass points:

- **Nature:** land, air, and water pollution; overflowing landfills; methane production; toxic leachate; greenhouse gas emissions; climate change; oil drilling; nonrenewable resource loss; habitat loss for animals; animal endangerment and extinction.

- **Economy:** profits by companies producing single-use disposable products like coffee cups and take-out containers; cost of environmental pollution and waste.

- **Society:** plastic-bag fees and bans; store policies; plastic industry lobbying; "throw-away lifestyle"; loss of connection to nature.

- **Well-Being:** convenience; human health impacts of chemical additives like bisphenol A and phthalates (endocrine disruption and disease-causing).

By looking at this issue holistically in a 360-degree way, it becomes evident that using diverse perspectives as lenses helps our students deepen their understanding of complex, interconnected issues.

In contrast, viewing global challenges through a single lens often results in stories that are incomplete or that perpetuate stereotypes. For this reason, we advocate that students take a multi-perspectival approach to knowing our world (Tishman, as cited in Boudreau, 2020). Because the capacity to understand perspectives is critical in an increasingly complex, diverse world (Boix Mansilla, 2015), it must be nurtured through classroom practices. As explored in Chapter 2, creating democratic learning environments entails the intentional sharing and honoring of diverse perspectives. In this chapter, we highlight how numerous discussion-based and experiential approaches can support children's development of perspective-taking. Before we do, we must emphasize that there are circumstances when perspective-taking is not appropriate.

When Perspective-Taking Is Not Appropriate

If not structured carefully, perspective-taking in the curriculum may have no educational value and could even cause harm to our learners. For example, in their research on experiential learning techniques like role-playing historical events, Dack, van Hover, and Hicks (2016) found that the majority of exercises lacked an explicit instructional purpose and reinforced misconceptions about the content. Worse yet, simulations can trivialize tragic events. In her chapter, "Simulating Survival," Schweber (2003) poignantly explains the dangers of re-enacting historical atrocities like the Holocaust:

> By virtue of their format alone, simulations fundamentally pervert Holocaust history. The form of a simulation warps its historical referent. By treating tragic subject matter as a "game," by making it "fun" for students to learn, by leavening the heavy history of this era, one compromises or diminishes the seriousness of the events themselves. Put differently, according to these assumptions, the Holocaust is inherently tragic, tragedy demands reverence or at least a seriousness of venue through which to study it. (pp. 140–141)

Further harm may be caused by perspective-taking methods that disregard participants' emotional reactions. For example, "living history" role-plays involving students assigned as plantation owners and slaves have been reported in the media (Associated Press, 2019). Such experiences can cause **racial trauma**, "a type of physical or emotional injury uniquely impacting Black and Brown children in school spaces" (Jones, 2020, para. 4). Educators must be cognizant of the emotional violence role-playing experiences can cause.

Teacher reflection and critical evaluation should accompany the design of any perspective-taking experience. In Figure 4.4, we outline characteristics of harmful perspective-taking experiences and what we might do instead. Importantly, when involving complex and emotionally charged subject matter, it is critical to plan for follow-up experiences to help students contextualize and process their learning and emotions.

Looking Inward: Understanding the Self

Before we can look outward, we need to learn to look inward and build our self-awareness. The limbic region of the brain is known as the *emotional brain.*

Figure 4.4

Characteristics of Harmful Perspective-Taking

Harmful Perspective-Taking . . .	Instead . . .
Asks students to act in the role of an oppressor (e.g., slave owner; Nazi during the Holocaust).	When the event pertains to oppression, inequality, and/or human rights violations, structure perspective-taking to emphasize the agency of oppressed persons (e.g., the bravery and success of Harriet Tubman) or focus on the actions of the bystanders.
Perpetuates a dangerous, violent, or dominant ideology, such as White supremacy or colorblindness.	
Trivializes or romanticizes tragic events or conflicts (e.g., war, colonization).	Ensure historical perspective-taking is accurate and involves no explicit oppression, although hardships or unequal social structures may be at play.
Groups students using characteristics that represent real-life oppression (e.g., race, gender).	Ask students to opt-in, instead of opt-out of an experience, which may produce strong emotions.
Includes cultural appropriation or reinforces stereotypes about a cultural group (e.g., creating totem pole crafts or wearing Indigenous apparel for a singular event).	Empower students from diverse backgrounds to share *real* stories and experiences related to issues (e.g., discrimination) with clear ground rules and protocols.
Manipulates children's emotional response to teach empathy.	Ask students to debrief using reflective tools such as journaling in case they are uncomfortable talking aloud about their experiences.

Its architecture balances emotion with reason and guides our behavior. Social psychologist Jonathan Haidt (2006) offers a helpful analogy to explain the emotional and cognitive systems of the brain regions: the Rider and the Elephant. The Rider represents the rational, analytical mind whereas the Elephant is the emotional mind whose often unconscious behaviors are driven by feeling and instinct. This duality in the brain offers an explanation for why humans are sometimes resistant to change or can't make decisions. Chip and Dan Heath, brothers, authors, and experts on motivation and social entrepreneurship, urge us to sync the two. They explain:

> Perched atop the Elephant, the Rider holds the reins and seems to be the leader. But the Rider's control is precarious because the Rider is so small relative to the Elephant. Anytime the six-ton Elephant and the Rider disagree about which direction to go, the Rider is going to lose. He's completely overmatched. (Heath & Heath, 2010, p. 7)

Simply stated, when experiencing strong emotions, our students struggle to self-regulate (Goleman & Senge, 2014). **Self-awareness**, an understanding

of how emotions, thoughts, and beliefs affect behaviors, is critical to one's overall well-being and ability to live a fulfilled life (Singh & Duraiappah, 2020). Students' emotional state can also affect their ability to understand others' perspectives, resulting in what is known as the *empathy gap*. For these reasons, we must be mindful to guide the Rider *and* inspire the Elephant in our learners. We can do this by creating a safe environment where students are encouraged to form emotional connections. Coupled with healthy discussions, educators can nurture students' capacity for empathy and compassion for oneself and others through **mindful awareness**, or "paying attention, on purpose, to present experience as it emerges moment by moment without being swept up by judgments" (Siegel, 2012, pp. 43–44). Mindfulness practices like Deep Listening on page 108 are one approach to encourage students to *take a pause* and connect with their inner world and surroundings.

We must help students surface and examine their mental models so they can shift them.

In addition to creating a safe climate, educators can support students' self-awareness by developing their **perspective consciousness**, the recognition that one's perspective and worldview are not universally shared, yet shape and influence our beliefs and behaviors (Hanvey, 1982). Importantly, our perspectives are guided by **mental models**. These are deeply held beliefs, assumptions, and stories we hold about ourselves, others, and the world. Peter Senge and colleagues (1994) liken mental models to a "pane of glass framing and subtly distorting our vision, [determining] what we see" (p. 235). In other words, mental models act as cognitive and emotional frameworks that impact how we interpret our experiences. Having fixed mental models contributes to the complex sustainability issues we face today: climate change, habitat destruction, war, social injustice, and more (Laininen, 2019). For example, the mental model that our planet has inexhaustible resources leads to unsustainable behaviors, such as using new plastic bags in every supermarket shop. We must help students surface and examine their mental models so they can *shift* them. Using open discourse and reflection, we can enable students to "see below the surface" of specific situations and issues. Tools shared later in this chapter, such as the Iceberg Model (p. 110) and the Ladder of Inference (p. 113), can help our students bring their thinking down to the level of mental models.

As we use strategies to look inward, we may discover some of our students' perspectives are unhelpful or even harmful, such as prejudiced or deficit beliefs about individuals or a group of people. It is our responsibility to help students recognize and challenge their mental models, while making sure that their Elephants do not take charge. Chapter 5 explores how stories can be used to broaden students' worldviews.

Looking Outward: Understanding Others

Once learners develop self-awareness, they are better able to understand others' diverse perspectives. Social awareness or *looking outward* is also foundational for developing **empathy**. Philosopher and psychiatrist Dr. Alfred Adler once said, "Empathy is seeing with the eyes of another, listening with the ears of another, and feeling with the heart of another" (as cited in Demetriou, 2018, p. 2). This ability to understand others' thoughts, beliefs, and feelings—known as Theory of Mind—develops in children naturally from a young age.

Scan this QR code to access discussion strategies from Facing History and Ourselves that can be used to facilitate perspective-taking, or visit facinghistory.org/resource-library/teaching-strategies

This capacity counters our natural tendency for egocentric thinking that is often biased and fails to consider the limitations of our own unique point of view (Paul & Elder, 2006). How do we help students look outward? As mentioned, a key strategy we use to support student perspective-taking is dialogue. Coupled with active listening, dialogue with others highlights that there is no singular way to interpret an event or issue. Teachers may use a number of discussion strategies to support students as they express their perspectives, as well as listen respectfully to the perspectives of peers. We may use small-group discussion, for example, with café conversations or Socratic Seminars (see p. 119). We may invite students to engage in written conversations using graffiti boards or gallery walks. We may use discussion protocols that ask students to role-play from the perspective of another human or non-human species such as Panel Discussions (see p. 121).

Like other learned skills, students develop the capacity for perspective-taking through experience.

Importantly, we must determine our students' readiness for exploring complex, and perhaps controversial, issues through classroom discussions. Like other learned skills, students develop the capacity for perspective-taking *through experience*. The more students practice weighing diverse perspectives, the better equipped they will be when confronting sensitive topics. For this reason, a teacher may engage students in role-playing an assigned point of view before they share their own. Similarly, opening a unit using a Four Corner Debate with a less emotionally provocative prompt like "Buying stuff makes people happier" may elicit more viewpoints than a controversial one.

Project Zero's Thinking Routines are flexible inquiry-based protocols that can also support perspective-taking in the classroom. Routines like Circle of Viewpoints, Step Inside, and Think, Feel, Care invite students to take the perspective of a specific person, living creature, or character in a story. An

Scan this QR code to view the complete Project Zero's Thinking Routine Toolbox, or visit pz.harvard.edu/thinking-routines

example of Think, Feel, Care is found in the following Spotlight. Other thinking routines invite students to share their own perspective. For example, Lenses for Dialogue engages students in exploring how they see the world through unique lenses, such as one's race or gender, as they view a piece of artwork. Students then share and seek to understand their peers' perspectives using prompts like, "Tell me more about why you see/think/feel . . ."

PROJECT ZERO'S THINK, FEEL, CARE THINKING ROUTINE

Scan this QR code to check out the Think, Feel, Care routine, or visit agencybydesign .org/sites/default/files/ AbD%20Think%20 Feel%20Care%20.pdf

Grade 3 students in Lorraine Jacobs-Hyde's class at Berlin Brandenburg International School engaged in a unit about Cities. After exploring Berlin and comparing it with other cities, students identified features that were required to create an effective city. They focused on why the features would be included in a city design. In teams, students were given a variety of materials and invited to build their own city from the perspective of a user, for example, a child, an individual in a wheelchair, and so on. Using the Think, Feel, Care routine, students were asked to put themselves into others' shoes and to consider how their decisions impacted these individuals positively and negatively. This was followed by a gallery walk, where teams needed to provide feedback to each other about the design and inclusiveness of each city. Considering how each of the cities supported accessibility, they made suggestions for improvement. Based on the feedback received, teams iterated on their original design to make improvements to their city and justified their thinking.

Figure 4.5

Reflection Using Think, Feel, and Care

Perspective-Getting:
Seeking Out Diverse Perspectives

The ability to perceive others' thoughts, desires, and emotions is deemed critical to a cooperative society, yet we humans struggle to do this accurately. We often make incorrect inferences about others' feelings or intentions, which can lead to stereotypes, distrust, or conflict. While it may seem obvious, the most effective way to understand another person's perspective is to *ask them* (Epley, 2014). In this chapter, we highlight a few ways students can actively seek others' perspectives through perspective-getting.

Like a journalist, there are many ways students may authentically gather others' perspectives: through interviews, photography, sound or video recordings, and more. Oral history interviews are a common practice whereby students interview family or community members to glean their unique perspective relative to a topic or event. The process can be adapted for different age groups, such as kindergarteners asking their parents about their family history to upper elementary students interviewing local civic leaders about their roles in the community. Regardless of purpose, Jenks (2010) reminds us that "oral history should be conducted in the spirit of critical inquiry and social responsibility, and with recognition of the interactive and subjective nature of the enterprise" (p. 31).

Other practices for perspective-getting include Cathy Berger Kaye's MISO Research (short for media, interviews, surveys, and observations) (p. 123) and Photovoice, a form of youth participatory action research (p. 126). Both methods engage students in responsible research about a community issue or need through investigation, planning, action, and reflection. In doing so, students develop civic consciousness and deepen their self-awareness as they interact with diverse people and communities.

Strategies for Perspective-Taking and Perspective-Getting

As we share in Chapter 2, the democratic classroom is a safe, connected space where students can discuss issues happening in the world. Students feel comfortable expressing beliefs, sharing stories, and asking questions. Likewise, they honor others' ideas, feelings, and perspectives. What are the qualities of safe spaces that promote challenging discussions and perspective-taking? UK-based global education community ThoughtBox recommends the following agreements that support equitable, inclusive classroom dialogue (see Figure 4.6).

Figure 4.6

Five Agreements for Safe Spaces

Quality	In the Classroom . . .
Free of judgment	Students welcome and view different opinions as valid.
	Students meet controversy with respect and civility.
	Teachers appropriately structure experiences, so all students can share viewpoints without interruption or criticism.
Active listening	Students listen carefully to what others are saying, even when they disagree with what is being said.
	Teachers scaffold active listening skills (e.g., giving sentence frames, asking students to paraphrase, etc.).
Conscious challenges	Students challenge or criticize the idea, not the person.
	Teachers encourage students to use evidence and provide reasons for their arguments.
	Teachers promote the importance of productive cognitive struggle.
All voices welcome	Students have opportunities to collect their thoughts before being asked to speak.
	Teachers vary the type of discussion (e.g., group, pairs, talking sticks) to allow all voices to be heard.
Respect	Students understand the difference between challenge and aggression.
	Students recognize how opinions are shaped by our contexts and our beliefs.
	Teachers model respectful interactions.

The following strategies help students uncover perspectives in themselves and others. Beginning with the self, students learn how thoughts, feelings, and beliefs are interconnected and shape our mental models. Following this development, students are better equipped to understand the perspectives and behaviors of others. We include both perspective-taking and perspective-getting strategies that guide students in exploring the points of view of diverse people or parts in a system. Note that strategies in Chapter 2, Chapter 5, and Chapter 8 (e.g., Focused Observation on p. 261) can also be used to support perspective-getting. It is important to be aware that children with different abilities in learning and development, such as autism and Down syndrome, may have different perspective-taking capabilities and require modifications to the strategies.

STRATEGIES FOR PERSPECTIVE-TAKING

Strategy	Description	Page Number
Deep Listening	Students become mindful by sitting quietly and listening carefully to the multiple layers of sounds around them.	108
Iceberg Model	Students use the Iceberg Model to learn about the multiple levels of perspectives influencing behaviors in a system.	110
Ladder of Inference	Students analyze how perceptions and beliefs influence perspectives and actions by going up and down the rungs of a ladder.	113
The Sustainability Compass	Students uncover information about an interconnected issue through the four compass-point lenses: Nature, Economy, Society, and Well-being.	116
Socratic Seminar	Students engage in a structured, guided discussion to listen to and share perspectives centered on a shared text.	119
Panel Discussion	Students empathize with the thoughts, feelings, and experiences of diverse human and non-human species relative to a specific issue through role-play.	121

STRATEGIES FOR PERSPECTIVE-GETTING

Strategy	Description	Page Number
MISO Research	Students collect multiple sources of information to glean diverse perspectives on a community issue or need.	123
Photovoice	Students capture and raise awareness about community conditions through photography.	126

STRATEGY FOR PERSPECTIVE-TAKING
Deep Listening

Best for: Grades K–8

Purpose: Deep listening fosters mindful awareness as students learn to focus without judgment on their thoughts and emotions. Whereas hearing is a mechanical sense that automatically processes information at a rate 10 times that of sight, listening is a skill that requires active focus and practice (Horowitz, 2012). Mindful listening promotes self- and social awareness, nurturing one's capacity to be fully present and form authentic connections with others (Rakel, 2018).

How It Works:

1. **Introduce Deep Listening:** Explore the difference between the sense of hearing and deep listening, such as reading this description by Thích Nhất Hạnh, "Deep listening helps us to recognize the existence of wrong perceptions in the other person and wrong perceptions in us. The other person has wrong perceptions about himself and about us. And we have wrong perceptions about ourselves and the other person. And that is the foundation for violence and conflict and war." Discuss: How can deep listening promote inner and outer peace? How can we practice it?

2. **Choose a Spot to Practice Deep Listening:** Identify a location for students to listen intentionally to a variety of natural and human-made sounds. Explain that students will sit still in a comfortable position to attune their hearing to diverse sounds they notice. Students may choose to close their eyes.

3. **Practice Deep Listening:** Help students monitor their reticular activating system that filters important sensory inputs, including sounds, thus blocking out unimportant information. Students take a few deep breaths and practice listening to sounds that are far away; afterward, bring the focus closer to their immediate surroundings, including the body. To bring awareness to the sounds, invite students to notice them as they are (without judgment or explanation).

4. **Reflect:** After a few minutes of deep listening, invite students to share what they heard and how listening with heightened awareness can connect us closer with ourselves, other people, and nature.

Figure 4.7

Students Practicing Deep Listening

Students at Loka School in North-India practicing Deep Listening. After sitting quietly and listening carefully they shared their observations and identified 32 different sounds. The sound of a bee passing their face. A tractor ploughing the fields. A grunting buffalo. A heartbeat.

STRATEGY FOR PERSPECTIVE-TAKING
Iceberg Model

Best for: Grades K–8

Purpose: The Iceberg Model is a visual framework that uses the metaphor of an iceberg, where only 10% of an event or issue appears visibly above the water line. The remaining 90% is hidden from view. Understanding this 90% requires "deep, below-the-surface understanding," including analyzing multiple levels of perspectives influencing the behaviors in the system. At the bottom of the iceberg are mental models, which shape individual and group behaviors. Notably, truly transformative change occurs at the level of mental models and ripples upward toward the surface. The Iceberg is a versatile framework comprised of other systems thinking tools like Connected Circles, Causal Maps, and Behavior-Over-Time Graphs as explored in Chapter 6. The protocol below serves to introduce the framework holistically.

How It Works:

1. **Introduce the Model:** Display the Iceberg visual and explore the concept of surface-level understanding about an event or issue. How are we limited by what is seen? Introduce the underlying structures of the

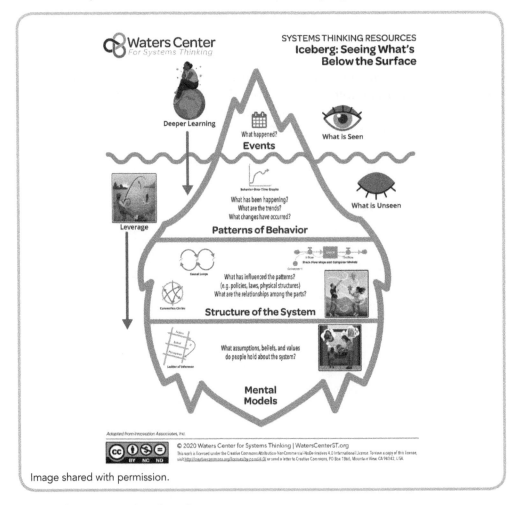

Image shared with permission.

iceberg or event: patterns of behavior, structure of the system, and mental models. Discuss how analysis at each level helps us better understand what is happening and where leverage points exist to create systems change. This process of going beneath the surface is sometimes called *lowering the water line*.

2. **Introduce the Event:** Choose an observable event to analyze, such as a series of recent oil spills in California's Central Valley. Write the event at the tip of the iceberg. Explain that this top level of thinking is how we typically perceive the world. Discuss the dangers of *surface-level fixes* that only address the symptoms at the surface level.

3. **Go Beneath the Surface:** Identify observable patterns of behaviors connected to the event by asking questions like, "What has been happening? What are the trends?" We often find that similar events have been happening over time. In the chosen example, oil spills have been linked to the controversial practice of hydraulic fracturing or *fracking* that has been occurring in the region since the 1980s.

4. **Identify the Underlying Structures:** Continue to go deeper by identifying the structural level of the event or issue. Ask students, "What causes the patterns we observe?" Structures may include physical things like roads or organizations like governments, policies, and habitual behaviors.

5. **Uncover Mental Models:** At the bottom of the iceberg are mental models, the assumptions, deeply held beliefs, and values people hold that are often unconscious. Discuss how mental models influence how we see an event like oil spills.

6. **Reflect**: After exploring the Iceberg Model, reflect on the experience. How does the iceberg help broaden one's perspectives? Why is it helpful to analyze multiple levels of perspectives when analyzing a situation or issue?

Iceberg in Action

Grade 3 learners in Daniel Withington's class used the Iceberg Model to unpack behavioral issues in the classroom that impede their learning. Specifically, the class considered patterns and structures that created a noisy classroom. They noticed how certain types of games, like imaginative play and hide 'n' seek, seemed to cause challenging transitions back to learning. Daniel asked his learners to think about how to alter their event by changing mental models. They brainstormed ways to use mindfulness and other techniques to calm and refocus the class.

(Continued)

(Continued)

Figure 4.8

Using the Iceberg to Understand Behavior

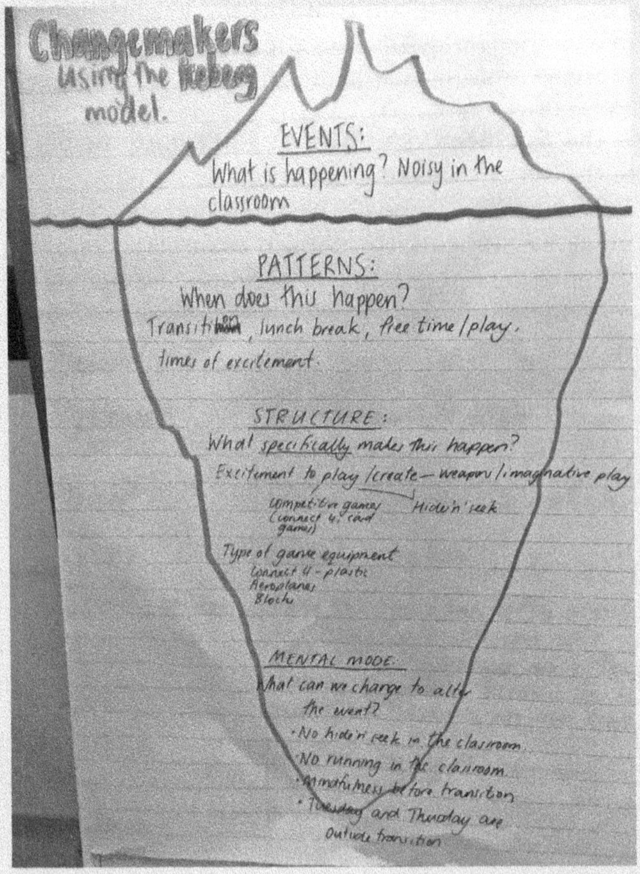

Changemakers using the iceberg model.

EVENTS:
What is happening? Noisy in the classroom

PATTERNS:
When does this happen?
Transitions, lunch break, free time/play, times of excitement.

STRUCTURE:
What specifically makes this happen?
Excitement to play/create — weapons/imaginative play
Competitive games (Connect 4, card games)   Hide 'n' seek
Type of game equipment
Connect 4 - plastic
Aeroplanes
Blocks

MENTAL MODE:
What can we change to alter the event?
• No hide 'n' seek in the classroom
• No running in the classroom
• Mindfulness before transition
• Tuesday and Thursday are outside transition

STRATEGY FOR PERSPECTIVE-TAKING
Ladder of Inference

Best for: Grades K–8

Purpose: First proposed by organizational psychologist Chris Argyris in 1970, the Ladder of Inference is a series of mental processes one uses (often subconsciously) to make sense of observations. Ultimately, how we process and assign meaning to information is influenced by our beliefs, assumptions, and prior experiences (our mental models). To understand the reasons for behavior, it is helpful to go *up and down* the rungs on the Ladder of Inference. This model can also support students in resolving conflict. As Vice President of the Waters Center for Systems Thinking, Mary Quinnan explains,

> The Ladder of Inference allows students to dive deeper into how they respond to conflict based on their perspectives. Using the Ladder, students can examine what information they process in a situation, how they attach meaning to this information, the belief or beliefs they develop as a result, and finally how they then act on those beliefs. Talking through the Ladder provides a reflective opportunity to develop an understanding for differing perspectives and needs.

The following protocol was inspired by the Waters Center for Systems Thinking.

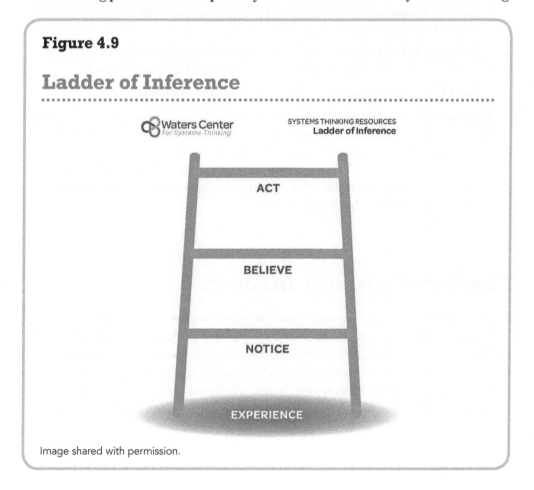

Figure 4.9

Ladder of Inference

Image shared with permission.

How It Works:

1. **Choose an Individual Situation to Analyze:** Select a compelling example with sufficient details to analyze using the Ladder of Inference. These may include:

   - Personal experience
   - Primary source text (such as an interview or documentary film clip as illustrated in Figure 4.10)
   - Fictional story (such as a picture book)

2. **First Reading (or Viewing):** Before analyzing the chosen example, read or watch the story, asking questions as needed to ensure comprehension. Ask students to share what they understand and connections they made.

3. **Second Reading (or Viewing):** During the second reading or viewing, engage students in applying the Ladder of Inference. Select a Ladder of Inference template with the appropriate level of complexity, posting it on chart paper or giving students a handout of it to record their responses. For younger students, it may be helpful to pause during the second reading or viewing to ask the following guiding questions starting on the bottom rung:

   - **Observe:** What is happening around the individuals? What do they see, hear, touch, taste, or smell?
   - **Notice:** What do they notice? What information from the experience did they selectively pay attention to?
   - **Assign meaning:** What cultural and personal meaning or conclusions to do they assign to the experience?
   - **Develop beliefs:** What beliefs did they form based on their conclusions? How do these beliefs reinforce what they noticed?
   - **Act:** What action did they take based on their beliefs?

4. **Discuss:** Engage the whole class in discussing what lessons they gleaned from using the Ladder of Inference. Did they need to change their own perspectives to understand the other perspectives better? What did they learn by doing so? How can we be more mindful when we are in a situation and prevent ourselves from jumping to conclusions about others' beliefs and behaviors?

Ladder of Inference in Action

To illustrate the power of storytelling for changing perspectives and driving a change in behaviors, Grade 7 students watched a short video of a girl named Manisha living in a Kolkata slum. Manisha was invited to take part in a Photovoice experience to document community hygiene practices and increase awareness of the issue with family and friends (see Photovoice strategy on p. 126). A leading cause of malnutrition and death in children ages 5 and younger, diarrhoeal disease is a widespread global issue. It is also preventable through adequate sanitation, hygiene, and clean drinking water (World Health Organization, 2017).

The video begins with the question, "Could a photo change the way we approach hygiene?" After watching the video, students reflected on how changing what she noticed in her community consequently changed her beliefs about the importance of hygiene as well as her behaviors. At the end of the project, she advocates for hygiene improvements with the adults in her community. Students used the Ladder of Inference to infer Manisha's observations, thinking, and reasoning. An example is shown in Figure 4.10.

Figure 4.10

Ladder of Inference: Manisha's Photovoice Experience

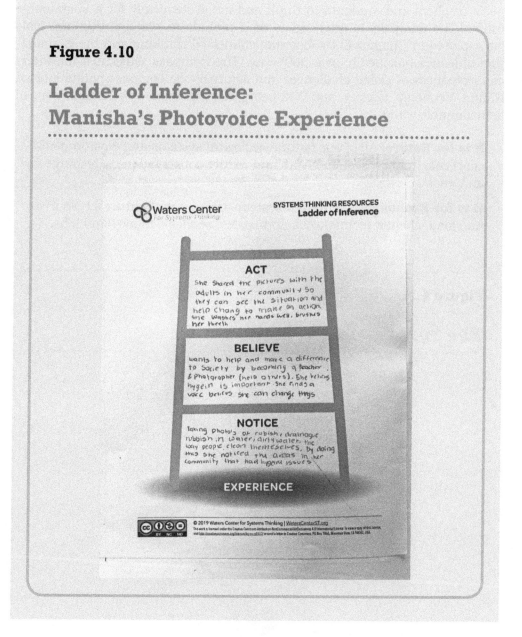

STRATEGY FOR PERSPECTIVE-TAKING
The Sustainability Compass

Best for: Grades K–8

Purpose: Developed by Alan AtKisson, the Sustainability Compass (or Compass for short) is a tool of Compass Education, an organization that supports teachers and students to think and act systemically for a sustainable future. The Compass is intended to be a prelude to systems thinking tools (as explored in Chapter 6) by fostering connected thinking and the examination of issues holistically in a 360° way. The Compass illustrates the interconnectedness of global challenges and solutions via compass points labeled Nature, Economy, Society, and Well-being that represent system conditions of a sustainable world:

- **N is for Nature:** All of our natural ecological systems and environmental concerns, from ecosystem health and nature conservation, to resource use and waste.

- **E is for Economy:** The human systems that convert nature's resources into food, shelter, technologies, industries, services, money and jobs.

Figure 4.11

The Sustainability Compass

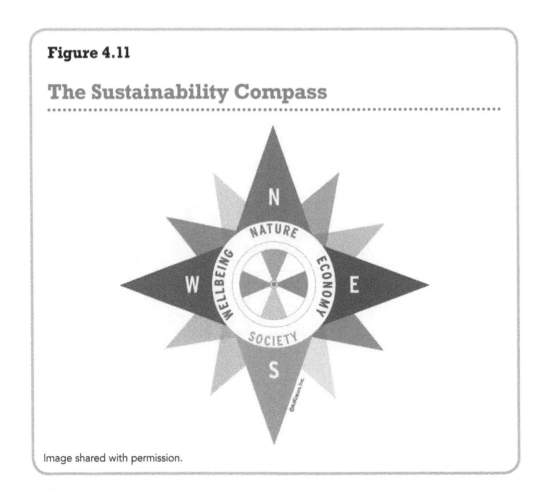

Image shared with permission.

- **S is for Society:** The institutions, organizations, cultures, norms, and social conditions that make up our collective life as human beings.

- **W is for Well-being:** Our individual health, happiness, and quality of life. (Compass Education, 2017, p. 3)

By analyzing an issue through these lenses, students can better understand the connections between individual behaviors, collective actions, and the world around us. The Compass is a versatile tool to examine any topic or issue, engaging students in questioning, analysis, and problem solving.

How It Works:

1. **Introduce the Compass:** Display the Compass tool and explore the interconnectedness of the four points (Nature, Economy, Society, and Well-being) using an example, such as fast fashion. For example, fast fashion impacts nature through the production, distribution, consumption, and disposal of clothing, impacting soil, water, and air, as well as the climate over time. Fast fashion contributes to the economy in positive and negative ways, such as producing jobs but also exacerbating income inequalities when employees are not paid fairly. Fast fashion influences societal norms and behaviors, such as contributing to a consumerist culture. Environmental and labor laws also regulate what is produced and sold in the marketplace. Last, our individual and collective well-being is impacted by fast fashion, because society places pressure on consumers regarding how to dress. We may feel happy when purchasing a new outfit, but these feelings can fade quickly.

2. **Select an Issue:** Once students grasp how to use the Compass tool, introduce an interconnected, meaningful issue to unpack using multiple perspectives. For example, Figure 4.12 highlights Grade 3 students analyzing the positive and negative effects of the COVID-19 pandemic. By using diverse lenses, students uncover the complexities inherent in the issue, building a foundation for understanding multiple systems.

3. **Unpack the Issue:** Invite students to work in small groups, using the compass points as lenses to identify positive and negative effects related to each quadrant. Students may write on a physical template or use sticky notes on chart paper. Encourage students to record as many perspectives as possible in each quadrant.

4. **Make Connections:** Prompt students to reflect on the interconnections between Nature, Economy, Society, and Well-being. For example, they may draw arrows to illustrate how the system conditions intersect.

5. **Formulate Questions:** In addition to uncovering interconnections, the Compass provokes students to ask deep questions as they discern what they do not yet know about the issue. Student responses and questions can also be used to develop guiding questions to frame an inquiry on the issue.

Sustainability Compass in Action

Using COVID-19 as a stimulus, Grade 3 teacher Dan Withington from UWC South East Asia invited his students to analyze the impact of the coronavirus pandemic using the Sustainability Compass. Using each compass point as a lens and working collaboratively, students unpacked the effects of this virus. The impartial nature of this thinking tool challenged student perspectives with a wide variety of positive and negative repercussions of COVID-19, evoking some thought-provoking debate.

Figure 4.12

Using the Sustainability Compass to Unpack the Coronavirus

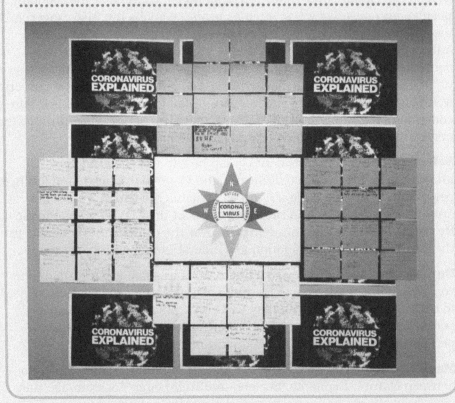

STRATEGY FOR PERSPECTIVE-TAKING
Socratic Seminar

Best for: Grades 3–8

Purpose: A structured, discussion-based method named for the Greek philosopher, Socratic Seminar engages students in listening to and sharing perspectives centered on a shared text. Guided by open-ended questions, Socratic Seminar is a student-facilitated, inquiry-based approach that nurtures critical thinking, respectful discourse, and a democratic classroom culture. Its ultimate aim is to support meaning-making and consensus through close textual analysis and group discussion (as opposed to argument or debate). The following protocol was adapted from Facing History and Ourselves.

How It Works:

1. **Choose a Compelling Text:** Before initiating this strategy, select a text that affords inquiry and diverse interpretations. A text can be any written or spoken discourse, such as fiction or nonfiction text, poem, news article, or other form of expression like visual art. If appropriate, two contrasting texts may be selected for comparison and close analysis. The selected text for discussion should be short, equivalent to one paragraph to one page of written text.

2. **Prepare the Students:** Introduce the chosen text. In preparation for the seminar, model how to annotate a text while reading or viewing closely using sticky notes, a highlighter, and so on. Explain that the purpose of Socratic Seminar is to deeply understand the meaning of a text rather than to argue or debate. Students will rely on their notes to prepare for the discussion.

3. **Prepare the Seminar Questions:** Model the creation of open-ended questions that provoke inquiry and discourse. With practice, students can craft their own and serve as discussion leaders. Use the QR code in the margin to access sample Socratic Seminar Stems for writing different types of open-ended questions, such as analyzing point of view or author's purpose.

Scan this QR code to access sample Socratic Seminar question stems, or visit facinghistory .org/resource-library/ teaching-strategies/ socratic-seminar

4. **Set the Stage:** Prepare the physical space, such as arranging chairs in a circle, to allow for eye contact and discussion. Co-create norms with students for sharing perspectives and for listening respectfully (e.g., speak to the group, not only to the teacher or discussion leader, no personal opinions or attacks, no interruptions). Choose a discussion leader who will guide participants to deeper understanding of the text using questioning and clarifying statements, model respect for diverse interpretations, and follow the seminar process. Some students may also be assigned other roles, such as observer or recorder.

5. **Engage in the Socratic Seminar:** The discussion leader begins with an open-ended question followed by other questions to provoke inquiry, critical analysis, and dialogue. As needed, participate in the seminar to

refocus students' attention or to model alternative interpretations and perspectives. With practice, students may assume responsibility for planning and conducting future seminars.

6. **Reflect:** Engage students in assessing the effectiveness of the seminar through discussion or reflective writing. Sample prompts include the following: Was the seminar focused on the text rather than on opinion? Did the discourse result in a deeper, shared understanding of the main ideas? How might we improve our capacity for inquiring into texts and perspective-taking through collaborative discussion?

Socratic Seminar in Action

In their Values, Beliefs, and World Religions unit, a Grade 7 class explored Hate Speech using the Connected Learning Alliance's Socratic Smackdown game. In this gamified version of Socratic Seminar, students read a text, explore key questions, and engage in a scored conversation using a range of discussion strategies. In this strategy, Grade 7 students learned how hate speech can infringe on the freedom of religion, yet be protected by freedom of speech. In giving time to prepare for the discussion, learners were able to formulate their thinking, share ideas informally in small groups, and hear diverse perspectives. This allowed them to make deeper connections and consider evidence (e.g., direct quotes) that relates to their ideas.

Connecting freedom of speech and freedom of religion in a reflection after the discussion, Grade 7 student Tanay said, "If governments offer too much freedom of speech, rampant hate speech could occur and there is a possibility that it would lead to violence. On the other hand, if there is too little freedom of speech to protect freedom of religion, governments can effectively censor their citizens. A delicate balance is needed to protect the freedom of speech while still taking care to prevent hate speech against religions."

Scan this QR code to access the Socratic Smackdown strategy, or visit clalliance .org/wp-content/ uploads/2020/02/ SocraticSmackdown .pdf

STRATEGY FOR PERSPECTIVE-TAKING
Panel Discussion

Best for: Grades 2–8

Purpose: A panel discussion engages students in empathizing with the thoughts, feelings, and experiences of diverse human and non-human species relative to a specific issue. By role-playing and engaging in dialogue with classmates, students broaden their perspectives, deepen their connections with others and the natural world, and learn about global challenges. The following protocol is from Rachel Musson of ThoughtBox. An accompanying Spotlight on Discussion-Based Learning follows.

How It Works:

1. **Plan:** Choose an issue, in which students may explore diverse (human and non-human) perspectives, such as climate change. Identify groups affected by the issue (e.g., organisms, industry, government, media, community members). Prepare information cards about each affected group along with guiding prompts, such as "If you were a (polar bear), how would you feel about (climate change)? What would you say about the state of the world right now?" Ensure that one individual is the interviewer who will ask a series of questions and guide the discussion.

2. **Introduce the Issue:** Introduce the issue by posing a question like "How does climate change affect animals?" Engage in a brief class discussion to assess students' prior knowledge followed by reading or viewing a short text to present relevant background information. Explain that students will take the perspective of a specific group affected by the issue under study.

3. **Prepare for the Panel:** Place students into groups of five to six. Using their information cards, allow 5 minutes for students to become familiar with their roles, underlining key ideas and recording statements they might make during the discussion. Note that the interviewer should prepare questions to ask the other panel members. Students may also conduct their own background research to supplement the information provided to their group.

4. **Discuss:** In their panel groups, students hold a 20-minute discussion on the issue. First, panelists introduce themselves in 1 minute or less, explaining who they are and what their life is like. Afterward, the interviewer guides the discussion using their prepared questions. Remind students to listen carefully to what each panelist has to say, jotting down notes.

5. **Reflect:** Afterward, engage the whole class in reflecting on the experience of taking another's perspective and empathizing with their experiences, thoughts, and feelings. What commonalities did the groups share? What were the challenges of assuming another's perspective? How might we learn more?

"We have a responsibility to bring this sort of learning into the classroom and have a space where young people can talk about what's happening in the world around them."

—Rachel Musson, Founder and Director of ThoughtBox

ThoughtBox is a UK-based membership community of global educators offering inquiry-based curriculum and professional development focused on helping young people develop healthy relationships and make sense of our changing world. Underpinned by a holistic framework designed to nurture social, emotional, and environmental well-being, or *triple well-being*, ThoughtBox primary and secondary curricula comprise discussion-based learning journeys exploring key global issues like equity and climate change.

Founded in 2019 by former secondary teacher Rachel Musson, ThoughtBox creates a space of empowerment for both teachers and students. She elaborates: "We have an opportunity now to make systemic shifts in the way that we're responding to crises and the habits that we know are causing them. Activism isn't for everyone. We can't all go to the streets, but we can all do something that is a significant step in a direction of change, including starting a conversation with someone about important issues."

To nurture connection in the classroom, ThoughtBox learning journeys highlight how to create safe spaces using guided discussions. Integral to their approach is nurturing students' self-awareness and social-emotional well-being. For instance, students may feel eco-anxiety or be overwhelmed by the climate crisis. Instead of denying their feelings, educators can build students' confidence in speaking about how emotions are affecting them and how to navigate ways forward. By establishing agreements for safe spaces (see Figure 4.6), such as the practices of active listening and modeling respect for diverse perspectives, educators can build a classroom environment centered on empowerment. Importantly, educators are learners in these spaces, too. "Through discussion-based learning, exploring questions on important matters, teachers and students get to be *human* together," Musson explains. "Instead of standing, teachers are able to sit down with their students and say: Let's learn together."

While ThoughtBox lessons include a variety of discussion models to adapt to students' diverse needs, they include the following general steps to nurture "out-of-the-box" thinking: (1) *Open the box* (introduce the topic), (2) *Go inside the box* (explore what we know), (3) *Unpack the box* (open up discussions), (4) *Close other boxes* (correct falsehoods), and (5) *Go outside the box* (encourage continuation). Reflective of its inquiry-based approach, Rachel explains that discussions "encourage children to leave lessons with more questions than they started."

Reaching more than one million students in 55 countries, ThoughtBox inspires a new future of learning by working alongside educators, policy makers, and innovators. To learn more, please visit https://www.thoughtboxeducation.com/

STRATEGY FOR PERSPECTIVE-GETTING
MISO Research

Best for: Grades K–8

Purpose: Developed by Cathy Berger Kaye (2010), MISO Research engages students in investigating issues in an authentic way. Students act as researchers to learn how an issue manifests, such as in their community, and seek out diverse perspectives. The following protocol was inspired by the International School of Paris.

How It Works:

1. **Create a Research Plan:** Students identify a research purpose, such as a community need or initiative, and create a plan for gathering diverse perspectives about it. The following questions can be adapted for diverse ages to guide students' research plan:

   - **Purpose:** What do I want to find out? What are my research questions?

   - **Form:** How will I find out? What information will I collect?

   - **Gather:** From whom will I gather information? Who will my participants be?

   - **Analysis:** How will I analyze the data?

   - **Share:** How will I share what I learned? For which audience?

2. **Locate Media Sources:** Media sources include newspapers, podcasts, radio, and more. Many student-friendly searchable media databases exist, such as National Geographic Kids, Newsela, ReadWorks, Smithsonian TweenTribune, and Time for Kids.

3. **Conduct Interviews:** Interviews help students learn the perspectives of the issue or phenomenon under study from a small number of people. During this phase, students use listening for understanding (e.g., do not interrupt or insert personal opinions). Prior to conducting interviews, students practice writing effective open-ended questions. StoryCorps offers question generators that may be helpful as students plan their interviews.

4. **Write and Send Survey:** Surveys help students collect data efficiently from a larger number of participants compared to interviews. There are many types of survey questions (such as multiple choice and rating scale) and ways to collect survey data (such as Google Forms, Mentimeter, or by hard-copy forms), each adaptable for a specific group of students.

5. **Observe:** Through observation, students use their senses to gather information firsthand. This includes identifying the *location* (Where will you go?); *activities* (What will you do there?); and *data collection methods* (How will you record what you observe?).

6. **Analyze:** After data have been collected, students analyze the information. This may include creating graphs, transcribing interview data and highlighting themes, categorizing information, and so forth. It

Scan this QR code to access the StoryCorps question generators, or visit storycorps .org/participate/ great-questions

is important that students remain objective and seek to understand the answers to their research questions without inserting their perspectives or biases.

7. **Share Findings:** Following their research, students present their findings to an authentic audience. Storytelling strategies presented in Chapter 5, such as ArcGIS StoryMaps or other data visualization methods, may be effective for this purpose.

Modification: Use MISO to Determine Best Research Methods

Instead of asking students to use all four types of research as part of a study, invite students to reflect on which of the four methods might be best given a research question. Using a MISO quadrant, such as the one in Figure 4.13, go through each research question and determine which method might be most appropriate to answer it. For example, in a Grade 1 unit about Community Goods and Services, these questions (in no particular order) were connected to the following research methods:

- **Media:** What do different communities look like?

- **Interview:** What are the jobs in our community? What skills and tools do you need to do these jobs?

- **Survey:** What do people like best about their community?

- **Observation:** Who lives and works in our community? What do they do?

Scan this QR code for a sample slide deck we have constructed for introducing MISO to students, or visit **teachworldwise.com/ resources**.

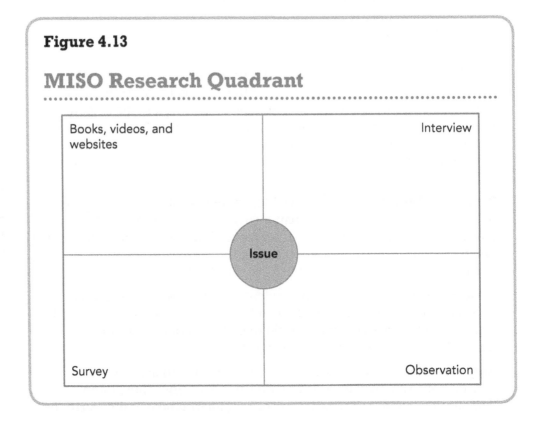

Figure 4.13

MISO Research Quadrant

Books, videos, and websites	Interview
	Issue
Survey	Observation

MISO in Action

Students at Loka School in North-India interview family and community members to learn about others' experiences and memories of their local area. In this example, a young girl interviews a woman in the village about how it has changed throughout the years.

Figure 4.14

Community Stories

STRATEGY FOR PERSPECTIVE-GETTING
Photovoice

Best for: Grades 2–8

Purpose: Photovoice is a type of Youth-led Participatory Action Research (YPAR), whereby young people capture and raise awareness about community conditions through photography and videography. Grounded in Paulo Freire's (1970) notion of "critical consciousness," this approach gives voice to those with limited power to document and reflect on the sociopolitical forces shaping community issues to create change. With young students, Photovoice provides insight into their lives and an opportunity to share their perspectives. The following protocol was inspired by the University of California, Berkeley YPAR Hub (http://yparhub.berkeley.edu/).

How It Works:

1. **Introduce Photovoice:** Explore the power of photography to document human experiences and communicate issues of importance to the photographer. Engage students in examining sample photographs, analyzing how they capture unique perspectives of specific places and times. Ask: What do you believe the photographer wanted to communicate through this photograph? Why?

2. **Practice Ethical Photography:** First review what ethical photography entails, such as not disturbing or interfering with the natural setting and moment being captured. If a photograph includes identifiable persons, permission must be granted. Afterward, engage students in taking photographs on school grounds or in the community. They explore how different techniques can be used to produce unique effects on the viewer.

3. **Initiate the Photovoice Process:** Invite students to take photographs following a prompt such as, "Take photographs showing health in the community." The goal is for students to capture both the strengths and needs of the community in their photos. Using a planning sheet, students may reflect on and organize their approach before taking photographs.

4. **Tell a Story:** Discuss how words and images are interconnected by analyzing a photograph without a caption. Afterward, read the photograph's title and caption. Ask: How do words help tell a more complete story? Invite students to choose a photograph from their collection and narrate a story to include a title, caption, and beliefs about what the photograph represents. Ask students to decide if each photo shows a community strength, a need, or both, and why.

5. **Share and Reflect:** Through a photo exhibition or group discussion, students share their Photovoice projects. Afterward, engage students in reflecting on what they learned about themselves and classmates throughout the Photovoice process.

VALUES, BELIEFS, AND WORLD RELIGIONS

As part of a Grade 7 unit on Values, Beliefs, and World Religions, students were invited to take part in a Photovoice process to identify community strengths and needs. After creating a photo of choice, they developed a title and caption using the questions:

- What is happening in your photo?
- What beliefs and values does it reflect?
- Is this showing a strength, a need, or both, and why?

The aim was for students to connect the ideas of values and beliefs to their community and see how areas of inquiry can come through a process of investigation and reflection. A sample Photovoice image and response is found in Figure 4.15.

Figure 4.15

Edgar's Photovoice: Our Hidden Way of Thinking

Image Title: Our Hidden Way of Thinking

Image Caption: "In this photo there is a pair of glasses looking out over the city, it connects to my belief that everyone has a 'lens' that is shaped by the environment they're in. It also reflects my value for respect because if everyone has a lens it means that they will have different beliefs which you have to accept will not be similar to yours. It also reflects my value of freedom because everyone is free to have their own lenses, it's whether you're allowed to use it or not that matters. A lens gives you strength, it forms you in the way that you are right now, but it also gives needs. You need to accept that others might not agree with your 'lens' and they might try to break it, and that is why you protect it by expressing your ideas and never giving up."

This chapter introduced the Connect phase of inquiry that invites learners to

- *look inward* to develop their self-awareness and perspective consciousness and

- *look outward* to explore the complexity of human perspectives from an individual, community, and systems-level.

In doing so, students develop issue-awareness and go beneath the surface to uncover how multiple perspectives are needed to understand and address global challenges. In Chapter 5, we explore the power of story to communicate, build empathy, and connect with others. Before continuing, reflect on your learning from this chapter and how it may inform your practice.

PAUSE AND REFLECT

- What opportunities do you provide for students to become more self-aware?

- What perspectives are dominant in your curriculum and classroom? Where might there be opportunities to amplify nondominant voices to broaden students' perspectives?

- To what extent are students able to surface and test their assumptions, including biases, about other people and places? How might this be enhanced?

- How does self- and social awareness support students' abilities to confront local, global, and intercultural issues? What might this look like?

CHAPTER FIVE

THE POWER OF STORY TO BUILD CONNECTION

THE STORYTELLING BRAIN

STORIES ARE ALL AROUND US

CONNECTING TO ISSUES USING STORIES

STORIES AS MIRRORS, WINDOWS, AND SLIDING GLASS DOORS

STORIES AS A CATALYST FOR CHALLENGING CONVERSATIONS

THE POWER OF STORY TO BUILD CONNECTION

"We live on stories as much as we live on air and food.

Without them, we are not fully human."

—Paul Salopek, Pulitzer Prize Winning Journalist and Writer

This chapter explores the following Tenets of a Pedagogy for People, Planet, and Prosperity:

- Make authentic links between, across, and beyond disciplines.

- Make use of the power of story to communicate, build empathy, and connect with others.

- Promote perspective-taking, dialogue, and an awareness of self and others.

- Develop intercultural understanding, including a recognition of bias and stereotypes.

Stories Are All Around Us

From bedtime read alouds to conversations between friends, stories are all around us. They are central to the human experience, transcending time, place, and culture (Vaughan-Lee, 2019). Stories shape our attitudes, beliefs, and behaviors. They help us understand ourselves, each other, and our interconnected planet. Intrinsically woven into our human psychology, it is simply impossible to imagine life without stories.

Stories refer to a series of events told through words, images, movement, sound, or other means of communication. They are a socially constructed phenomenon, the content of which are "human lives and mental experiences"

(Siegel, 2012, p. 370). While storytelling is typically associated with the written or spoken word, they can be conveyed in many diverse modalities, such as cartoons, art, dance, film, maps, and photography. Even data can tell a story. In fact, professor of social work Dr. Brené Brown attributes her success communicating research data with diverse audiences to her use of storytelling: "I collect stories; that's what I do. Maybe stories are just data with a soul" (Brown, 2010, 1:13). This is evident in the following Spotlight on Storytelling, which illustrates how data can tell stories that propel social change.

●●● SPOTLIGHT ON STORYTELLING

USING MAPS AND FILM FOR SOCIAL CHANGE

"What kind of stories can we tell that will compel someone to act?"

—Jim Bentley

Jim Bentley is an elementary educator, filmmaker, and National Geographic Explorer who teaches in Elk Grove Unified School District in Northern California. Bentley embraces the power of project-based learning, the National Geographic Geo-Inquiry Process, and storytelling in science and civic education to connect, inform, and empower others to take action. "Students need to be curious, connected, and wonder about what they are learning," he explains. "Using media in teaching and learning, such as film and photography, is powerful to spark an emotional response and the desire to want to learn more."

Figure 5.1

Students Use ArcGIS StoryMaps to Visualize Water Issues

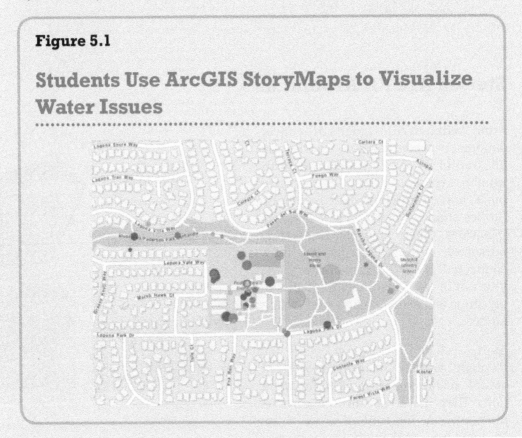

As Bentley integrates the disciplines, his students identify, research, and create solutions to address community issues they care about. As part of the research process, his Grade 5 students collect data in the field using GIS (geographic information system) tools and create StoryMaps (Figure 5.1). A recent project on water availability launched with students reading *A Long Walk to Water* by Linda Sue Park. "Students wondered how accessible water is where we live and how can we make water more accessible in order to reduce plastic waste in our parks and schools?" Bentley shared. Data collection using ArcGIS Survey123 entailed students' uploading images and narratives of decrepit drinking fountains, storm drains, and plastic waste to create a StoryMap. With parents' support, students collected over 152 data points that they then analyzed to identify geographic patterns and make claims about the issue of plastic pollution in their community. Bentley's students presented their data to the local parks and recreation and school district, resulting in the installation of new water bottle refilling stations. See the StoryMap strategy on page 153.

Storytelling and media production are like a freeway with many entry points, be it blogging, infographics, podcasting, or filmmaking, Bentley explains. "Find what works for each student to give them a voice and a platform." Follow Jim Bentley on Twitter at @Curiosity_Films.

The Storytelling Brain

Why are humans so captivated by stories? In *The Storytelling Animal: How Stories Make Us Human*, Gottschall (2013) reveals humans' natural fascination with storytelling. Drawing from history and science, he explains: "We are, as a species, addicted to story. Even when the body goes to sleep, the mind stays up all night, telling itself stories" (p. xiv). The human brain seeks meaning through patterns, from motives found in nature to lyrics in a song. Likewise, stories are recognizable patterns through which we understand the world and how it works. They also activate our emotions and attention, so information learned through stories is more likely to be retained (Schank & Abelson, 1995). In fact, research conducted by cognitive psychologist Dr. Jerome Bruner (1987) suggests we are 22 times more likely to remember information when presented as a story!

As explored in Chapter 4, emotions are integral to learning. This phenomenon is particularly relevant to storytelling in the classroom. When topics and issues are explored through stories that elicit students' emotions, narrative becomes a powerful pedagogical tool. Why? Emotions can change our brain's chemistry, releasing cortisol when experiencing distress and oxytocin when feeling compassion for characters. These hormones can even change our behavior, enhancing one's capacity for trust and generosity, including with strangers (Zak, 2015). Whether authentic or fictional, stories can elicit feelings of sympathy, empathy, and identification with others (Mar, Oatley, Djikic, & Mullin, 2011). They offer pathways for understanding, bridging differences that may traditionally divide. When we construct stories, both brain hemispheres are integrated, enhancing our capacity to perceive one's inner and outer world to become fully human (Easton, 1997). In this chapter, we explore how storytelling offers a unique pedagogical tool for Worldwise Learning: to foster self- and social awareness, to learn about global issues, and to nurture responsibility.

Storytelling as a Pedagogical Tool for Worldwise Learning

The cultural and social act of storytelling is the world's oldest form of education. In schools today, not only do stories transmit knowledge and build students' literacy skills, they help shape classroom climate. Because sharing personal stories fosters connection between the storyteller and listener, storytelling can generate trust and strengthen bonds between teachers and students. Zaretta Hammond (2014) calls the act of storytelling a form of "selective vulnerability" that contributes to building a culture of care. As such, she recommends that teachers weave in personal stories as part of their teaching practice. Similarly, when children feel safe and a sense of belonging, they are more likely to be their authentic selves at school. In this way, storytelling can help students develop their identities and make sense of their lived experiences (O'Bryne, Houser, Stone, & White, 2018). Providing opportunities for students to listen to and share personal stories, such as through Story Circles (see p. 144) or Story Portraits (see p. 145), is integral to creating inclusive classrooms.

As educators, how we select and use stories has the potential to connect and humanize, or to disconnect and dehumanize.

As educators, how we select and use stories has the potential to connect and humanize, or to disconnect and dehumanize. In particular, we must be conscious of how the perspectives and messages we share enable students to feel seen or result in unhelpful oversimplifications. One way to reduce the likelihood of this outcome is by moving beyond the *single story*. In her TED Talk, Nigerian author Chimamanda Adichie (2009) eloquently explains the importance of including a variety of "stories" in the curriculum: "The single story creates stereotypes, and the problem with stereotypes is not that they are untrue, but that they are incomplete. They make one story become the only story" (13:12).

Using diverse stories instead, we can heighten student awareness of different perspectives and build their intercultural understanding. By purposefully choosing stories that reflect different experiences and points of view, students come to see issues as multifaceted and complex.

Stories as Mirrors, Windows, and Sliding Glass Doors

In Chapter 2, we explore how employing an integrated approach entails understanding our students' identities and viewing their unique skills, perspectives, and experiences as assets in the classroom. Global or multicultural literature is a tool that affords the ability to teach children about themselves, as well as other people and perspectives. Coined the "mother of multicultural children's literature," education professor Dr. Rudine Sims Bishop (1990) devised the metaphor of stories acting as *mirrors, windows, and sliding glass doors*. These metaphors provide a visual for understanding the way stories can reflect or help students understand particular experiences.

Stories that reflect students' identities act as *mirrors*. Dr. Sheldon Eakins, Special Education Director and founder of The Leading Equity Center, calls for educators to choose literature that reflects students' cultural identities, assets, and needs. For example, in his context working on a Native American reservation in Idaho, educators should select tribal authors and literature, as opposed to dominant texts like *The Hunger Games* or *Harry Potter*. At the heart of building trusting relationships between teachers and students, he explains, is to honor their lived experiences. Eakins also underscores the importance of choosing *positive stories* of people who reflect students' identities. Often marginalized groups are portrayed in school-selected literature during times of struggle instead of celebrating their contributions or humanity, which shapes how students see themselves (S. Eakins, personal communication, August 17, 2020). *Empowering stories*—those that challenge dominant narratives by including many voices and perspectives—can foster emotional resilience and optimism. The importance of including positive, diverse literature in the curriculum is highlighted in the following Changemaker Spotlight on author and activist Marley Dias.

●●● CHANGEMAKER SPOTLIGHT

MARLEY DIAS, AUTHOR AND EQUITY ACTIVIST

"If we want equity, we need diversity."

—Marley Dias

When she was 11 years old, Marley Dias was an avid reader who became frustrated that all the assigned books at school lacked representation of Black girls. They were

(Continued)

Figure 5.2

Marley Dias

Image shared with permission.

"mainly about white boys and dogs," she complained. She also questioned why award-winning literature like Jacqueline Woodson's *Brown Girl Dreaming* was not part of the curriculum. Marley's mother encouraged her to do something to address the lack of diversity in school books. So she did. Marley founded the #1000blackgirlbooks campaign where she generated a list of 1,000 books where the main characters are Black girls. To date, she has surpassed her original goal by collecting more than 12,000 books! Though the campaign showcases Black and Brown voices, its mission is to create a space for all.

In 2018, Marley authored a personal narrative book, *Marley Dias Gets It Done: And So Can You!* where she explores her activism for equity and inclusion and how to use social media for good, such as to celebrate and advocate for Black authors. She offers recommendations for selecting literature and how to become a lifelong reader. Marley also encourages young people to use their strengths to make positive changes in their communities, just as trailblazers do. Marley cites American librarian and storyteller Augusta Braxton Baker as an "unsung hero in the literary world" as one who inspired her. While working in the NYC Public Library branch in Harlem in the 1930s, Baker located and added children's literature portraying Black characters in a positive light to the library's collection.

Today, Marley uses her voice to make the world a more inclusive place. She is the host of Netflix series "Bookmarks: Celebrating Black Voices" where Black celebrities, authors, and artists read books written by Black authors. "Black girl stories aren't just for Black girls," Marley explains. "They're for everybody." Learn more at: https://www.marleydias.com/

Stories also afford *windows* through which the reader can look to see other worlds, comparing one's life and sociocultural context with another. For example, elementary students learning about how cultural narratives are reflected in sports and games might read *Goal!* by Mina Javaherbin and A.G. Ford. This award-winning picture book celebrates friendship and soccer. Told from the perspective of a young South African boy, the story portrays a group of friends who escape aggressors and life's worries through play: "When we play, / we forget to worry. / When we run, / we are not afraid," he says. The book concludes with a note from the author about the power of soccer to unite players and fans around the world. There are many lists and searchable databases of diverse children's and young adult literature available online, which can help us locate quality books representing a range of genres, cultures, ethnicities, settings, and more. Books may serve as a shared text or as companion texts for guided or independent reading connected to a curricular theme. Access our list of organizations that provide book lists and searchable databases on our companion website.

While selecting diverse stories is an essential first step, Osorio (2018) argues it is equally important to consider *how* the stories are used as a tool to honor students' identities and promote critical consciousness. At UWC Thailand, Grade 3 educator Amelia O'Brien used physical mirrors and windows as a provocation for students to consider the importance of diverse texts (A. O'Brien, personal communication, November 28, 2020). An International Baccalaureate Primary Years Programme school, students analyzed the *form* (What is it like?), *function* (How does it work?), and *connection* (How might it be connected to other things?) of texts as windows and mirrors. Using these key concepts, students identified themes like reflection, empathy, changes in perspective, and sense of belonging (see Figures 5.3 and 5.4). Amelia reflected on the power of this experience for her students saying,

Stories as windows not only expose students to diverse peoples and places, they also highlight our common humanity.

> Because we had invested time in exploring actual mirrors and windows, we understood this idea and could give examples of texts that were mirrors and texts that were windows for us individually. As part of this learning, many realised that the same story can have both elements of self-reflection and insight into

Figures 5.3 and 5.4

Students' Reflections on Texts as Windows and Mirrors

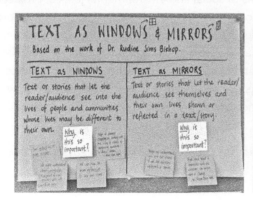

the experiences of others simultaneously. We are now developing identity webs to think more carefully about when and how some texts might be "mirrors" or "windows" for some and not for others.

Multimedia stories, such as documentary films and photo-essays, can also act as *windows*, fostering the intercultural understanding needed to make sense of interconnected issues (Merryfield, 2004). Stories as windows not only expose students to diverse peoples and places, they also highlight our common humanity. In the following Spotlight on Storytelling, we explore the power of storytelling using films and photography available from the Global Oneness Project.

●●● SPOTLIGHT ON STORYTELLING

THE GLOBAL ONENESS PROJECT

Founded in 2006, the Global Oneness Project is a California-based nonprofit organization and multimedia education platform housing award-winning films and photo-essays—highlighting social, cultural, and environmental issues—with companion curricula for elementary to university classrooms. Using storytelling as a pedagogical tool and lens through which to explore our common humanity, Global Oneness Project aims "to plant seeds of empathy, resilience, and a sacred relationship to our planet."

Why are stories so powerful in learning? Cleary Vaughan-Lee (2019), executive director and author, explains that stories evoke a strong emotional response. Without any background knowledge of the individuals or context, we first connect to the human being, whether captured in a still image or film. Our initial interpretations or assumptions about the individuals' lived experiences are then challenged as the story unfolds. By including storytellers who represent a variety of backgrounds and beliefs in the curriculum, Global Oneness Project stories and guided lessons can enhance students' worldviews, broadening their capacity for empathy and for shifting perspective.

Stories also shine a light on world issues and promote responsibility. They afford meaningful connections between the local human experience and broader global meta-level issues, such as climate change, migration, and endangered cultures. Analyzing and comparing human stories helps students uncover concepts and patterns related to universal themes like identity, resilience, and hope. The Global Oneness Project photo-essay titled "The Fall of Flint" by Matt Black (2016), for example, may be used as a case study to examine the intersections of social and environmental justice. Projecting one or more photographs without captions and asking students to make their own predictions about what may be happening first connects students emotionally and intellectually. Exploring deeper into the issue, a teacher may ask a provocative question like "Who is responsible for a community's water supply?" Finally, incorporating related companion texts and stories of youth activists like Amariyanna "Mari" Copeny, also known as Little Miss Flint, inspires students to understand the many ways individuals can raise awareness about issues.

To explore Global Oneness Project stories and lesson plans, please visit https://www.globalonenessproject.org/

Last, stories become *sliding glass doors* when readers become immersed in a new world through their imaginations. This kind of imaginative transportation can foster empathy and shape social perceptions, such as becoming more open to peoples of diverse backgrounds (Djikic & Oatley, 2014). In particular, immersive stories allow students to explore the wider world or visit places that we can only imagine. For example, the Global Oneness Project VR/360 film *The Atomic Tree* by Adam Loften and Emmanuel Vaughan-Lee (2019) takes the viewer to Japan where one meets a 400-year-old Japanese White Pine bonsai that witnessed the 1945 atomic bombing of Hiroshima. Here, one is surrounded by ancient cedar forests and visits Buddhist temples where five generations have nurtured the bonsai. The narrator shares, "The delicate shape of this bonsai contains sacred forests, human family, and deep time, inviting us to reflect on the living strands of kinship that are woven between human and non-human worlds." Use the QR code in the margin to access the film. Note that VR headsets pose health issues to children and are only recommended for age 13 and above. This film can be watched on a desktop using 360 technology. To learn more about using immersive storytelling to *step inside* a life, situation, or issue, please see page 147.

Figure 5.5

The Atomic Tree

Beyond Words: Art, Map-Making, and Data Visualization

In addition to literature and multimedia, **visual storytelling** using art, data, or maps can uniquely contextualize complex issues and perspectives. Because they offer a point of discussion, visuals can provide a catalyst for learning about controversial topics in developmentally appropriate ways. Photojournalism in particular can provide a humanizing entry point for critical analysis and dialogue. One available resource is the Pulitzer Center, a nonprofit that supports quality global journalism and shines a light on underreported stories. Their site offers K–12 lesson plans on issues with articles and multimedia, as well as opportunities to meet journalists in-person or virtually. To launch a unit on biodiversity, for example, a teacher may select a photograph from the Pulitzer Center's Rainforest Defenders Series like "Lilia: Preserving the Amazon River's Fauna is Preserving Planet Earth" (Dalmases & Albarenga, 2020). By removing the caption, students engage their emotions and make connections to prior knowledge and experiences. Students may also use Photographic Storytelling (see p. 151) to tell a visual story representing their unique perspective or place.

Scan this QR code to access the VR film *The Atomic Tree*, or visit globalonenessproject .org/library/films-virtual-reality/ atomic-tree

Storytelling using maps—representations of places, physical features, and other elements—can also foster students' understanding of themselves, other people, and our relationship with the planet. The term *geography* derives from the Greek words *ge* and *graphia*, meaning "Earth-writing." In this sense, information recorded about the Earth using cartography is a form of storytelling.

It tells us about features, interactions, and events on the planet, such as forest coverage, human population patterns, or the location of environmental disasters. Importantly, we distinguish teaching *about* maps and teaching *with* maps. Earlier in this chapter, we highlighted elementary educator Jim Bentley who supported students in map-making to identify problems, notice patterns, and propose changes to their community. Because map-making engages students in spatial thinking, they are able to gain a deeper level of understanding than if they simply viewed a map already created. Such teaching *with* maps enables students to build their **geo-literacy**, the "ability to use geographic understanding and geographic reasoning to make far-reaching decisions" (National Geographic Society, 1996–2020, para. 1). Strategies like StoryMaps (p. 153) and Slow Storytelling (p. 154) engage students in meaningfully documenting the human and environmental features of their local place using a range of tangible and digital tools. Please visit our companion website for resources to support students' geo-literacy skills.

Finally, data visualization is an effective form of storytelling. Traditionally, data have been collected, analyzed, and communicated in STEM fields: the natural and social sciences, computer and information sciences, engineering, and mathematics. How data are often displayed, such as through graphs or tables, leaves many unable to discern the meaning. Integrating visuals and storytelling is an effective way to reach a broader audience and have a greater impact, including in the classroom.

Let's explore an example. With a human population nearing 8 billion, the impacts of our collective consumer habits are difficult to imagine. In fact, research suggests the mind cannot meaningfully conceptualize phenomena at both very small and very large scales (Resnick, Newcombe, & Shipley, 2016). For this reason, visuals are powerful storytelling tools to communicate statistics, especially in the millions or billions, like those related to global consumerism. Photographer Chris Jordan creates large-format prints that translate large statistics into powerful images. His series *Running the Numbers I and II*, explores the consequences of mass consumerism on people, non-human animals, and the environment (Jordan, n.d.). In "Return of the Dinosaurs" based on a painting by John Sibbick, 240,000 plastic bags are shown, equivalent to the number of plastic bags used around the world every 10 seconds! Students can click on the image to zoom in to see individual bags. Seeing individual bags helps make this massive global problem more concrete. To learn more about data storytelling, take a look at the following Spotlight on Gapminder Foundation.

Scan this QR code to view Chris Jordan's images firsthand, or visit chrisjordan.com/gallery/rtn2/#carbon

GAPMINDER FOUNDATION

"Facts don't come naturally. Drama and opinions do.

Factual knowledge has to be learned."

Founded by Ola Rosling, Anna Rosling Rönnlund, and Hans Rosling, Sweden-based Gapminder Foundation is a nonprofit venture that promotes sustainable development by analyzing and communicating statistics and other information through visuals like graphs, photographs, and narratives. Their mission is to foster a "fact-based worldview that everyone can understand" to dismantle common misconceptions about the world. Gapminder tests people's knowledge to identify systematic misconceptions across groups in different countries. Their research shows most people believe the world is poorer, less healthy, and more violent than it actually is.

To address these knowledge-gaps and misinformation, Gapminder creates free teaching material using data visualization methods like graphs showing bubbles in various sizes (where size of the bubbles could be population size, number of children, or any other indicator) and color (often world region) that capture patterns and relationships (see example in Figure 5.6). Due to their interactive nature, Gapminder tools help the user zoom in on one country and learn how it fits into larger global trends. These tools also reveal how averages can hide inequalities that exist between and within countries.

Director and co-founder of the Gapminder Foundation, Ola Rosling explains, "We used to think of progress as if economy, society, and environment were separate spheres . . . in reality, they overlap completely and our mindset is changing" (Gapminder Foundation, 2020, 0:59). Through data presented in a clear, simple way, Gapminder illustrates how issues and solutions are interconnected. For example, improved access to electricity in homes results in increased opportunities to turn on lights to read, enhancing learning that can help children escape poverty in the future.

How can Gapminder be used in classrooms? Mike Hoare is a middle school geography teacher in Birmingham, England, who uses Gapminder to dispel students' stereotypes about other people and places. He launches his first geography unit with the original Gapminder test that covers important areas of global development, such as school attendance, vaccinations, and life expectancy. The results help students become aware of their misconceptions. Because students receive the majority of their news via social media, Mike finds their views are skewed. He challenges students' perceptions using the prompt, "How bad is it really?!" Students research beyond sensational headlines, identifying credible sources and additional data sets. Students also use DollarStreet, a Gapminder project that shows income data as images ordered on a continuum from left to right, representing poorest to richest. Mike finds students are surprised how conditions are better in many places they perceive as impoverished. Using data with visuals has a powerful effect on their understanding of the world, he concludes.

Scan this QR code to learn more about Gapminder, or visit gapminder.org

(Continued)

Figure 5.6

World Health Chart 2019

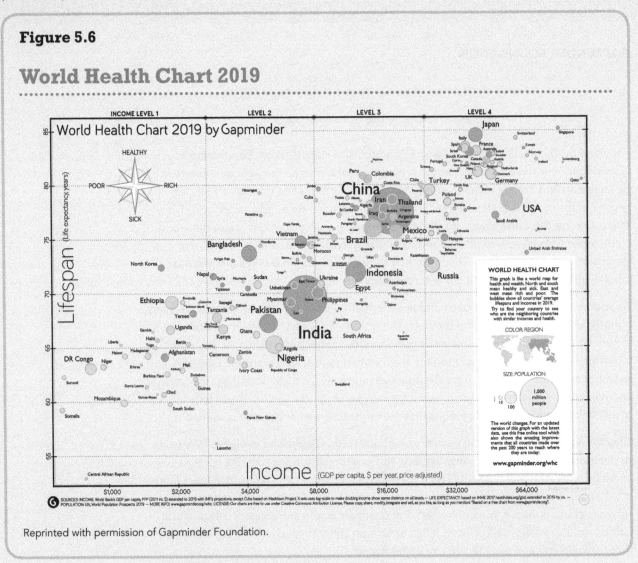

Reprinted with permission of Gapminder Foundation.

Strategies for Storytelling

The following strategies employ the power of story to foster understanding of oneself, others, and complex, interconnected issues. Stories help activate emotions, problematize content, promote dialogue between students, and develop problem-solving skills. By listening to stories, students make connections to their lived experiences, as well as broaden their perspectives and understanding of others. Through creating their own stories, students are empowered to use their voice to make a positive impact. Common elements of storytelling strategies include

- **Promoting Connections:** Paulo Freire (1970) argued that one first "reads the world" before "reading the word." Seek opportunities to connect stories with students' lived experiences, often called *text-to-self connections*. For example, a teacher may ask, "How does this video connect to you? What makes you curious?" Invite students to talk and think about their own experiences as a foundation for critical literacy.

- **Activating Emotions:** As explored in Chapter 4, emotions drive our attention. When choosing a story (in any format), determine the desired emotional response. Do you want students to feel compassion, awe, or wonder? A photograph without captions may draw students in. Do you want students to feel curious and energized to investigate? Reading aloud a current event about a mysterious issue might capture students' attention. Recognizing that emotional states may vary across individuals, teachers can use their knowledge of students to predict how they will respond.

- **Inviting Questions:** Exploring questions about a story provokes perspective-taking and connections between oneself, others, and the world. Questions may be posed by the teacher or generated by students. For example, a teacher may display a photograph as a provocation, asking, "What do you notice? What do you wonder?" During or following a read-aloud or film viewing, the teacher may ask, "What beliefs are revealed by the protagonist in the story? How do you know?" Pulling quotes from a story also invites open-ended questions and personal reflection.

- **Seeking Missing Perspectives:** Promote inclusivity by integrating diverse voices into discussions and story selection. Engage students in identifying dominant structures and systems present in texts (see Chapter 8 for related Critical Literacy strategies). Pay attention to whose viewpoints may be missing or where biases or stereotypes may be reinforced. Seek additional information beyond the text, such as new case studies on issues being investigated to broaden students' worldviews.

- **Challenging Beliefs:** Carefully craft opportunities to explore stories that challenge existing beliefs. For example, a photograph may change how students perceive another part of the world. Going deeper into the context of the story, such as learning about the physical and human geography of a place paired with statistical data, helps students cite reasons why their thinking has changed.

STRATEGIES FOR STORYTELLING

Strategy	Description	Page Number
Story Circles	Students share personal stories and listen for understanding as they witness others' oral stories.	144
Story Portraits	Students create portraits representing aspects of their lives that relate to a given focus or prompt.	145
Immersive Storytelling	Students use multimedia stories to *step inside* a life, situation, or issue.	147
Storypaths	Students participate in a simulated role-play, navigating events, planning cooperatively, and addressing problems strategically introduced by the teacher.	149
Photographic Storytelling	Students use photography to tell a visual story representing a unique perspective or place.	151
StoryMap	Students create a physical or digital map representing human and environmental features in their local place.	153
Slow Storytelling	Students build stories as a record of real-life experiences.	154

STRATEGY FOR STORYTELLING
Story Circles

Best for: Grades K–8

Purpose: Based on the ancient tradition of human storytelling, the Story Circle method was devised by intercultural scholar Dr. Darla K. Deardorff and the United Nations Educational, Scientific and Cultural Organization (UNESCO, 2020). It is a flexible tool that promotes peace, empathy, openness, and intercultural understanding through storytelling and active listening. The following protocol was adapted for K–8 learners with the teacher acting as a facilitator to guide the process.

How It Works:

1. **Form Groups:** Place students in groups of three to four and ask them to sit in a circle. We may introduce this strategy to kindergarteners by asking them to work with a partner. Introduce the story circle process (Steps 2–5). Agree on a nonverbal sign to indicate the end of each person's allotted time to share stories. Choose one timekeeper per group.
   Note: The teacher should avoid participating unless invited to do so.

2. **Become Acquainted:** In each circle, students will take turns introducing themselves in 2 minutes or less, saying one's name, three words or phrases that describe oneself, and why those words or phrases are important to them. Encourage no interruptions, comments, or questions during this process.

3. **Intercultural Storytelling:** Next, in 3 minutes or less, each student describes a personal experience following a teacher-selected prompt, such as "What is one of the most positive interactions you have had with a person(s) who is different from you, and what made this such a positive experience?" For kindergarten to Grade 2 students, we may invite them to tell their story across the fingers of one hand. This helps them sequence their ideas. We may start younger children with a more concrete prompt such as "Tell a story about a positive experience with a neighbor." As before, encourage no interruptions, comments, or questions as each student shares.

4. **Flashbacks:** Afterward, in 15 seconds or less, each student shares a "flashback"—something memorable or impactful—about each story, beginning with the first. Once all participants share flashbacks about the first student's story, continue with the second, and so forth, until all participants share flashbacks about each story. We can invite younger children to use a hand symbol or movement to show they are communicating a flashback (e.g., moving both hands backward next to the face).

5. **Discuss Themes and Reflect:** At the conclusion, ask students to identify themes from across each story. For example, the teacher may ask: (a) What common themes did you hear from the stories?; (b) What surprised you?; (c) What challenged you in the stories you heard? and (d) What did you learn about yourself through this experience? (UNESCO, 2020, p. 72). The teacher may also choose to have students reflect about their experience through writing or drawing.

STRATEGY FOR STORYTELLING
Story Portraits

Best for: Grades K–8

Purpose: Story Portraits is a strategy that allows learners to make personal connections to a topic to share lived stories about it. Depending on the focus of a unit, student portraits will look different. For example, we may ask learners to connect to a specific issue like migration, their culture and heritage, or a place. In the process of creating a portrait that represents how they relate to an issue, students build their self-awareness. Likewise, using portraits as a point of reference, students can share anecdotes from their lives with their peers. Because we ask students to bring together multiple images to make their portraits, we often use physical or digital collage as a technique for these portraits.

How It Works:

1. **Choose Portrait Focus:** Choose a portrait focus that relates to the issue being explored. Make sure the focus directly relates to students' prior life experiences. For example, students learning about animal welfare can create Animal Portraits made up of animals in their lives that they love. Figure 5.7 shows a City Portrait developed by Bernhard, a Grade 3 learner from Berlin Brandenburg International School. The student created his self-portrait using places in Berlin that are important to him as part of a unit on Cities.

Figure 5.7

City Portrait

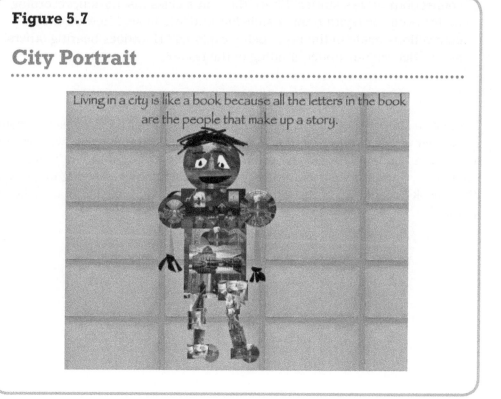

Living in a city is like a book because all the letters in the book are the people that make up a story.

2. **Invite Student Thinking:** Show students a few examples of self-portraits, in particular those that use collage or mosaic. What are they showing and why? How can self-portraits show connections to people, places, things, and issues? Introduce students to the portrait focus and connect it to the wider learning journey. Invite students to brainstorm images, words, or symbols that relate to the prompt. If students require images for their portraits, they can collect them into digital folders or cut them out of magazines and put them into an envelope for later use.

Scan the QR code to access a sample slide deck for introducing Story Portraits in class, or visit **teachworldwise.com/resources**.

3. **Develop Portraits:** Invite students to create their self-portraits using the resources collected. As they work, encourage them to consider stories that live within the portrait. For example, what was the first time they visited a place? Who did they go with? Why is it important to them? If needed, scaffold the digital skills required to make their portraits using technology, as Educational Technology Integrator Aisha Kristiansen did with Grade 3 learners making City Portraits.

4. **Tell Stories:** Once portraits are created, ask students to get into groups of three for sharing. Invite each child to tell one story related to their portrait. Give questions that students can draw from to support their oral storytelling:

   - **Who** was there?
   - **What** were you doing?
   - **When** was it?
   - **Where** were you?
   - **Why** were you doing it? **Why** was it important/meaningful to you?
   - **How** did it happen? **How** did it end?

5. **Make Connections Across Stories:** Encourage students to make connections across stories. Share these in a class discussion, recording patterns on the board or on a slide for students to see. How do these connections relate to the issue being explored? How does hearing others' stories deepen our understanding of the issue?

Extension: Create Analogies

To create a snapshot of their thinking, students can create analogies to accompany their self-portraits (see Figure 5.7). To scaffold the process, we can give a sentence frame related to the prompt, such as "Living in a city is like . . . because . . ." Using this prompt the child artist responded, "Living in a city is like a book because all of the letters in the book are the people that make up a story."

STRATEGY FOR STORYTELLING
Immersive Storytelling

Best for: Grades K–8

Purpose: Using multimedia stories has many benefits, including allowing our students to develop empathy, address stereotypes, increase knowledge of global issues, and make cross-cultural connections. As educators we need to be conscientious about our choice of media and the questions we ask about texts to promote connection and understanding of an issue. Using reputable collections such as the Global Oneness Project, National Geographic Society, or Kanopy enables us to find high quality multimedia resources for our students.

How It Works:

1. **Choose Media:** Choose a film, photo-essay, or other piece of multimedia that reflects the event or issue being explored. Remember the metaphors of mirrors, windows, and sliding glass doors while deciding on a piece of media and how these connect to your aims. Think about how the media chosen provides a new perspective and goes beyond the *single story*.

2. **Set the Stage:** Share the context for the story to be experienced. Ask questions that invite students to make connections to their lives. For example, the short-film *Amar* by Andrew Hinton (2011) shows a day in the life of the 14-year-old and how he balances family, work, and school in a city in India (Figure 5.8). In this case, we may ask students what they do on a typical weekday. They may record when they do certain tasks and for how long on a timeline.

Figure 5.8

A Day in the Life of Amar

Image shared with permission.

3. **Engage with the Story:** As students engage with the story, give them focus questions that draw their attention to certain aspects of the media. We may also give students graphic organizers that help them record specific information related to these questions. For students to become immersed in the story, they may watch or read twice. The first time, students can make observations and connections without focus questions. The second time, students can analyze the film using the focus questions.

4. **Discuss:** After students have had a chance to answer the focus questions and share these in small groups, invite them to engage in a short class

discussion. Ask students to use evidence from the multimedia text to back up their thinking. They can use prompts for this purpose such as:

- **Connection:**
  - o I connected to _____ in the story because . . .
  - o This story is similar/different to _____ because . . .
  - o I think _____ feels . . . because . . .
- **Argument:**
  - o I think this story shows us . . . because . . .
  - o A *big idea* from this film is . . . because . . .

5. **Reflect:** Invite students to reflect on their thinking from the story. This may be through writing or through artistic expression. Younger children may be invited to draw or paint memorable moments or imaginative scenes related to the film given "What if . . ." prompts, for example, "What if none of the redwood trees were cut down?"

Modification: Disrupt Misconceptions Using Provocative Statements

At the beginning of a Grade 6 unit on Human Development, English/social studies teachers use the film *Amar* by Andrew Hinton as an opportunity to disrupt student misconceptions about what poverty looks like. In the film, Amar is fed, clothed, clean, part of a supportive family, literate, and in school. Before watching the short-film, Grade 6 students are asked to read a number of provocative statements about poverty:

- Poverty means a person's needs are not met.
- People who are poor are not educated.
- People are poor because they are not motivated to work hard.
- Children in poverty lack a caring family.

They are invited to record ideas about how strongly they agree or disagree with these statements on a spectrum and engage in small group chats (Figure 5.9). After watching the film, students return to their initial thinking, adding on new ideas or thoughts that emerged. When using provocative statements with students, make sure to address any prejudiced or deficit ideas that persist despite exposure to the multimedia content.

Figure 5.9

Spectrum Statements

Strongly Disagree　　　　　　　　　　　　　　　　　　Strongly Agree

STRATEGY FOR STORYTELLING
Storypaths

Best for: Grades K–8

Purpose: A Storypath is a simulation-like pedagogical approach that uses story elements—characters, setting, plot, conflict, and resolution—as a powerful structure for curriculum integration. In this strategy, students *live* the story. In essence, students create and role-play the characters as they navigate events, plan cooperatively, and address problems strategically introduced by the teacher (Cole & McGuire, 2012). Storypaths engage students in connecting prior knowledge with new experiences using creative problem solving. This experiential strategy develops the self, social, and cognitive dimensions of our students while teaching them an important life lesson: People must work together to solve problems in the community.

How It Works:

1. **Create the Setting or Place:** Introduce the idea of using story as a context for learning. Invite students to co-construct the setting for the story or present one to them that they will design visually. Connect to what students already know by asking questions such as "What does this place look like? What features does it have?" and guide a discussion about the setting. Invite students to then create a visual representation of the place (e.g., mural).

2. **Create the Characters:** Next, ask students to develop realistic characters for the story for later role-play. Using listening, speaking, and writing, invite students to construct the characters' identities and roles in the community. For example, they may write a biography for their character that is both imaginative and believable. The teacher may probe students using questions, such as "What is interesting or important about this character that you want to share? What might they act like and why?"

3. **Build the Context:** Involve students in activities that prompt them to think deeply about the people and place they have created. For example, the teacher can scaffold learning by introducing purposeful investigations to develop knowledge and skills (e.g., if a child is taking the role of a gardener, learning may include plant needs and how to care for them). Students make decisions according to their roles.

4. **Confronting Problems or Critical Incidents:** Strategically introduce realistic problems that the characters may face in place and time. Invite students to role-play their characters and engage in perspective-taking, such as analyzing alternative viewpoints relative to the issue. Students consider what they know about the problem and what new information may be needed to resolve the conflict.

5. **Concluding Event:** In the final stage, students plan and present their solution in diverse ways, such as a community celebration. This brings closure to the Storypath.

MAYBEL THE MAPLE

Early Childhood educator Andrea Morgan at the Berlin Brandenburg International School wanted to deepen her learners' connection to the local forest. On a forest day in September, the children discovered a "fairy house" made of sticks, stones, and leaves at the base of a maple tree in one of their regular play locations. Students' excitement and imaginative play was so palpable, Andrea decided to use the Storypath process to guide their learning. She explains saying, "Initially, the fairies were only planning to send our class one letter, inviting us to observe, sketch, and study the tree. However, the letters from the fairies tapped so deeply into their imaginative play, I later decided all of our learning challenges (as the fairies call them) would be more meaningful if they were sent via fairy letters" (A. Morgan, personal communication, November 8, 2020).

Because the fairy letters encouraged learners to appreciate their forest home, Andrea noticed the children speaking of Maybel with reverence and a level of appreciation they had not previously shown. On one walk to see Maybel, a child said "Did you know it is Maybel's birthday today? We must sing her Happy Birthday." Another week, a child brought in painted leaves as gifts and two other children had written letters to Maybel at home. The class left these at the base of Maybel as an offering to her. These actions showed their enhanced connection to the tree, and more broadly to the forest environment.

Andrea also noticed an increased sense of responsibility from students during this project. She shares, "I am already seeing a deeper appreciation of their role in protecting the forest during their play. Children who previously observed others bending back branches of smaller trees or pulling off bark are now asking peers to change their actions because they could hurt the trees. In a future episode of our Storypath, I intend to place lots of garbage in the children's model fairy houses in hopes to upset them just enough to want to take action when they see trash in their own forest." In the Storypath process, children can be provoked through story to practice an appropriate response to a problem. This allows them to be prepared to act as agents of change when they confront the actual challenge outside school.

Figure 5.10

Kindergarteners Sketch "Maybel the Maple" in a Forest Storypath

STRATEGY FOR STORYTELLING
Photographic Storytelling

Best for: Grades K–8

Purpose: The common refrain "an image is worth a thousand words" reflects the ability of visuals to communicate messages and evoke emotions at a faster rate than narrative text. With half the human brain dedicated to visual processing, it is not surprising that photographs are powerful tools for teaching and learning. Photographic storytelling has the power to promote connection, appreciation, and deeper understanding about diverse people and places. Students can also document their unique and powerful perspectives using photography. The following protocol is from Cleary Vaughan-Lee, Executive Director at the Global Oneness Project.

How It Works:

1. **Choose Compelling Photographs:** Choose one or more photographs aligned with your curricular focus, appropriate to the age and developmental stage of your learners. Photo-essays related to social and ecological issues are available via Global Oneness Project, National Geographic Society, and museum digital collections like the Smithsonian.

2. **Set the Stage:** Introduce the photo-essay and content through discussion and probing questions. For example, if studying the Dakota Access Pipeline, you might ask whether students have heard of it and, if so, what they might know about it. Provide relevant background information.

3. **Read the Photos:** In small groups, invite students to analyze the photographs, recording their observations and wonderings. For younger learners, start with one photograph. For older learners, introduce a group of photographs. Teachers may choose to structure students' close observations using a Project Zero Visible Thinking Routine to focus on specific elements. Ask students to make predictions about what they think photographs are documenting, which can be returned to later. Students can also read the photographer's statement that accompanies a photo to discuss the artist's point of view and purpose.

4. **Delve Deeper:** To explore further, lead a class discussion using a structure such as Socratic Seminar (p. 119) to explore connections students might make to the subject and/or photographer. For example, you might ask students to explore how the photographer's background, culture, and experiences may have shaped their point of view. Alternatively, choose part of the photographer's statement and ask what they think it means or whether students agree or disagree with a certain perspective and why.

5. **Reflect and Project:** Give students a reflective writing prompt to consider the story's broader implications and to integrate their knowledge and ideas from various points of view. Consider introducing secondary sources to provide ways for students to conduct research and compare sources. Students can write responses as short essays, poems, or other forms of media.

Invite students to tell a story by taking a photograph that captures their unique perspectives and lived experiences. For example, the Global Oneness Project Document Your Place on the Planet student photography contest asked students to document their relationship and place on Earth, such as with their family, at home, or in their local ecology. A student example and photographer's statement is found in Figure 5.11. Here she connects to Earthrise, an image captured in 1968 by Apollo 8 astronauts. Earthrise was the first image that captured Earth as a whole and showed the planet surrounded by black space.

Figure 5.11

Document Your Place on the Planet

Cadence Grandell (age 14)—Colorado, United States

Every living thing needs water to survive. The water supply doesn't just come out of nowhere, it is recycled and goes through the cycle again and again. The Earthrise photograph inspired me because it gave humanity a different point of view of the Earth. My photograph is a different view of water.

Especially in this time, people need to know that we are all connected. We may all come from different backgrounds, but we all need water to survive. To take this photo at North Clear Creek Falls in Southern Colorado, I lined up my phone with binoculars to get a good close up on the waterfall. Sometimes you need to look at something from a different perspective to see how beautiful it really is.

STRATEGY FOR STORYTELLING
StoryMap

Best for: Grades K–8

Purpose: A StoryMap "combines maps, text, and other visuals to tell a story about people, places, and events" (Gleeson & D'Souza, 2016, p. 14). Young children can create StoryMaps by hand using photographs and text. Environmental Systems Research Institute's StoryMaps is an online interactive tool that affords more complex storytelling using digital maps, providing an immersive experience and the ability to create your own. StoryMaps help students connect local and global issues and understand the importance of place. They also provide a platform for teaching others and inspiring change. The protocol below is from Jim Bentley, an elementary educator whose students use StoryMaps in project-based learning.

How It Works:

1. **Explore StoryMaps:** Engage students in exploring existing StoryMaps (https://storymaps.arcgis.com/en/gallery) to examine various social and environmental concepts and spatial relationships. How do maps, text, and visuals tell a story about interactions between people and places? Explore geographic features, map symbols, and storytelling elements to determine what makes an effective StoryMap.

2. **Ask Questions:** Invite students to identify a local issue that concerns them. Engage students in generating questions about the issue using various lenses, such as historical, political, or ecological. Model writing a driving question for their project, such as "How can we reduce marine debris entering our oceans?" Afterward, determine what information is needed to act on the issue and how they will collect data, such as through surveys, interviews, and photographic or video data.

3. **Collect Data:** Provide time for students to conduct background research on their issue and determine the scope for data collection (e.g., a neighborhood or radius in square miles). With adult support, students collect data in the field using appropriate tools, such as ArcGIS Survey123. They can also invite others in their networks to participate in data collection such as by sharing a survey's QR code.

4. **Visualize Data:** Next, determine how to visualize the data collected. Ask students, "How can we best use these data to tell a story that will compel someone to act?" Discuss ways to use color, point markers, or other symbols to effectively and accurately visualize the data on a StoryMap. Students then add their data and accompanying photographs, audio or video files, hyperlinks, and text.

5. **Analyze Patterns:** After the StoryMap has been populated, engage students in locating patterns in the data. Ask probing questions like, "What trends do you notice in where water fountains are located in our community?" If students are unable to answer these questions, they may need to collect more data or display it differently.

6. **Take Action:** Once students have completed their StoryMap, discuss how they would like to take action. With whom should they share their story? How? Support students as they create a film, PSA, podcast, or other multimedia presentation to deliver to an authentic audience to affect change.

STRATEGY FOR STORYTELLING
Slow Storytelling

Scan this QR code to learn more about Out of Eden Learn, or visit learn.outofedenwalk .com/

Best for: Grades 2–8

Purpose: Slow storytelling is inspired by National Geographic Fellow Paul Salopek's multiyear, 21,000-mile walk that traced the origin of human migration on foot—a slow journalism experiment called Out of Eden Walk. Modeled after this approach, Project Zero at the Harvard Graduate School of Education designed Out of Eden Learn (n.d.), a global online learning community in which students share stories with other youth around the world. Through slow storytelling, they experience the benefits of slowing down, observing carefully, listening to others, and connecting their lives to the wider world.

How It Works:

1. **Introduce Slow Looking:** Open a dialogue with students on the concept of Slow Looking (see pp. 79–80). What are the benefits of slowing down in our fast-paced world? Relate Slow Looking to mindfulness practice, whereby one observes intentionally with curiosity and attention. Explain that Slow Looking can be applied to our daily lives to enhance understanding of our surroundings.

2. **Provide an Immersive Experience:** Create an opportunity for students to use a Slow Looking practice to observe an object, such as a piece of art or something in nature, they have not yet examined closely. For example, students might go on a walk in pairs and observe a tree. Invite them to observe quietly for at least 30 seconds, recording first impressions. Afterward, encourage students to look more deeply at specific details or notice what is hidden. In journals, students record notes using descriptive language and/or make visual sketches of what they observe.

3. **Share and Reflect:** Following the immersive experience, invite students to share their observations and experiences in small groups. What did they notice through Slow Looking that they might not have otherwise? What discoveries and personal connections did they make? How did the mind and body respond? What do they now wonder? Encourage students to reflect in their journals, which may be through drawing for young children.

Figure 5.12

Students on a Slow Walk

4. **Explore Slow Storytelling:** Discuss how Slow Looking can be a springboard for compelling storytelling using the example of Paul Salopek. In contrast to the 24-hour news cycle, slow storytelling allows the writer to focus, listen, and delve deeply into the content. Read stories from the Out of Eden Walk and analyze the writer's style, discussing how it may have been influenced by the practice of slow walking (https://www .nationalgeographic.org/projects/out-of-eden-walk/).

5. **Create and Share Stories:** Using their observations and notes, students create a story to share with an authentic audience. Storytelling may occur through written or illustrated descriptions, slideshows, videos, visual narrative, and so on. Share and respond to others' stories, comparing and contrasting the storytellers' daily lives and communities.

●●● SPOTLIGHT ON SLOW STORYTELLING

LOKA SCHOOL

Coined a "Small School with Big Dreams," Loka is located along the Punpun River in Bihar, North-India. The school embodies experiential learning and a holistic approach to education that empowers children to change the world. Whether in the classroom setting, on Loka's natural farm, flower gardens, and play fields, or in the community, students engage in deep learning through exploration, dialogue, and reflection. Charlotte Leech, co-founder of Loka School, explains that the school encourages children to be attentive and sensitive, thoughtful, curious, and to find out for oneself, qualities of having a "learning mind."

In 2019, Loka was visited by National Geographic Fellow Paul Salopek on his Out of Eden Walk. Inspired by his work, Loka students joined Out of Eden Learn (OOEL) to share stories with other youth around the world. One recent OOEL learning journey, "Introduction to Planetary Health," engaged students in exploring the connections between environmental changes and human health. It began with slow walking in their neighborhoods, sketching and taking photographs of what they noticed that may impact human and environmental health, as well as questions they wanted to explore.

Students then engaged in digital storytelling with *walking partners*. Reflective prompts invited them to consider how their personal experiences and the place where they live influence their perspectives, as well as how their partners' stories extend their thinking or introduce new perspectives.

Following this experience, students researched specific interconnections between human and environmental health, ultimately informing changes they can make in their daily lives. Through slow storytelling, students not only improved practical skills like writing, but also paid closer attention to the *big things and small things*, including how we are connected to our natural environments and to each other.

To learn more about Loka, please visit https://www.loka.in/

This chapter has explored the power of story as a tool to foster perspective-taking, dialogue, and an awareness of self and others. By selecting stories reflective of diverse identities and lived experiences, students learn what connects us on our shared planet. Whether creating or listening to others' stories, students are reminded of how stories can help us understand with our hearts as well as with our heads. In the next chapter, we look at the Understand phase of Worldwise Learning, where students begin to *zoom out* to the big picture. Chapter 6 focuses on the importance of systems thinking, whereby students come to recognize how systems produce particular behaviors. Leading on from this chapter, systems thinking allows us to move beyond individual stories to tell stories about systems with many parts and interconnections. Before moving on to Chapter 6, we invite you to pause and reflect on your thinking about the power of story.

PAUSE AND REFLECT

- When and how do your students currently share their stories in the classroom?

- How might you avoid the *single story* when selecting literature and other resources for curricular planning?

- What interwoven histories need to be uncovered and acknowledged to create a more equitable, sustainable future?

- How might storytelling lend itself to interdisciplinary, multimodal teaching and learning?

PART III

UNDERSTAND: DEVELOPING "BIG PICTURE" THINKING

Aims of the Phase

- Use systems thinking to recognize interconnectedness within and across issues.

- Develop conceptual thinking that transfers across contexts and situations.

- Form intercultural understanding and an appreciation of diversity.

CHAPTER SIX

SYSTEMS, SYSTEMS EVERYWHERE

SEEING THE FOREST
AND THE TREES

GREATER THAN THE SUM
OF THEIR PARTS

SYSTEMS
SURROUND US

MOVING FROM LINEAR
TO CIRCULAR THINKING

DEVELOPING HABITS
AS SYSTEMS THINKERS

SYSTEMS, SYSTEMS EVERYWHERE

"We ought to think that we are one of the leaves of a tree, and the tree is all of humanity. We cannot live without others, without the tree."

—Pablo Casals, Cellist and Conductor

This chapter explores the following Tenets of a Pedagogy for People, Planet, and Prosperity:

- Provide immersive, whole-body learning experiences, including in nature.

- Make authentic links between, across, and beyond disciplines.

- Develop the ability to *think in systems*.

- Advocate for critical consumerism, extending to media and other sources of information.

- Promote solution-focused thinking, purposeful action, and reflection.

Understanding Issues Using a Systems Approach

We are immersed in systems. Think about where you teach. What makes it a school? Is it the people: the students, the teachers and the parents? Or perhaps the presence of a physical environment, such as classrooms, playgrounds, and cafeterias? What about those intangible elements, like the school culture, the classroom climate, the curriculum, or the use of pedagogies? Do any of these components transform a place into a school? We imagine you'd argue that none of those parts independently makes a school. It is only through the dynamic interaction of these elements that a defining property of schools surfaces: *learning*. For this reason, we can describe schools as complex adaptive systems, where the behavior of individual parts does not represent the behavior of the entire system.

Sir Ken Robinson, in a conversation with HundrEd (2017) elaborates on this notion further saying:

> Education is a dynamic system, not a static one. It's not an impersonal, inert engineering system. It's constantly in flux and changing. It exists in the actions and activities of people every day. So the system is living and constantly changing, and is subject to all kinds of conflicting forces and fluctuations. (para. 3)

We are all part of such living systems, yet are we aware of how they function and how our behaviors contribute to particular outcomes? Are we exacerbating local and global challenges instead of helping improve them? To answer these questions, we need to understand systems. As such, the ability to *think in systems* is an essential attribute of both Worldwise Learners and Educators that this chapter explores.

Every local, global, or intercultural issue is made up of multiple parts that connect, with issues often interrelated at different scales. That trash can in your kitchen, for example, might only collect personal waste, yet is linked to issues such as landfills, unsustainable resource use, and the production of greenhouse gases, like methane, that contribute to climate change at the global level. Unless our students have opportunities to see the big picture, we cannot expect them to understand issues deeply, nor take purposeful action on them. Yet when our students look holistically at an issue, such as the kindergarteners did in the butterfly garden in the following Spotlight, they can see patterns, recognize possible consequences, and act with intentionality.

●●● SPOTLIGHT ON SYSTEMS THINKING

In a kindergarten unit on Pollinators, students focused on understanding the interrelationships that exist between pollinators and other organisms. By taking regular trips to a local butterfly garden, students explored the question, "How do pollinators interact with other living things in a habitat?" They photographed the different animals they identified, such as bees, butterflies, spiders, flies, grasshoppers, caterpillars, lizards, and birds. Spending regular time in the garden space, learners honed their skills of observation and practiced Slow Looking (p. 79). They noticed how lizards and spiders eat insects, as well as how some birds also drink nectar, like bees and butterflies do.

To visualize these connections and show how living things depend on each other, learners chose photos and created a Connected Circle diagram (Figure 6.1). Each photo represented a part of the habitat. Lines across these photos mapped the type of interconnection, allowing for discussions about predator-prey relationships, competition for food, and the concepts of *balance* and *interdependence*. The map also supported learners in exploring "What if . . ." questions such as "What might happen if all the butterflies were gone?" enabling conversations about stewardship behaviors young learners could undertake.

Figure 6.1

Connected Circle of Butterfly Garden

What Is a System, Really?

A **system** is a group of interconnected elements that are organized for a function or a purpose. Some examples are the human body, cities, ecosystems, social networks, governments, and the Earth's climate. System elements, or parts, may be physical or intangible things. Importantly, parts within a

system are interdependent. If one element is changed there is a knock-on effect within the entire system. This means systems are nonlinear by nature: The shape of a system is *round*, not straight. Instead of "A leads to B," A might lead to B, C, and D, but be likewise caused by D and E. For this reason, we cannot predict all changes that will result when systems change, and unintended consequences are likely to occur.

Within complex adaptive systems, the whole is greater than the sum of its parts. This is because elements in a system self-organize, with interactions between parts leading to emergent behaviors. In the human brain, for instance, individual neurons fire, sending signals to other neurons, collectively generating complex cognitive abilities, such as imagination, ingenuity, and reasoning. Another amazing example of emergent behaviors can be found in the humble ant colony. Abilities such as decision making, labor allocation, and communication emerge from interactions among large numbers of individual ant colony members.

SYSTEMS NEST

When we start thinking about how the idea of systems relates to local, global, or intercultural issues, a few key characteristics of systems are important to explore, which connect to the strategies at the end of this chapter. First, we can say that a system has a visible or invisible boundary, surrounded by a broader environment. This means that systems nest, with smaller systems being part of larger systems. For example, a tree is a system made of multiple parts, such as leaves, a trunk, and roots. A single tree can exist as a part of a forest, which is encompassed by an ecosystem that includes other living and nonliving things, such as animals, soil, sunshine, and water. Figure 6.2 illustrates how these systems nest.

Scan this QR code to download an editable version of Figure 6.2, which can be used to encourage students to think about how other systems nest, or visit **teachworldwise.com/ resources**.

As explored in Chapter 4 on perspective-taking, our perceptions often dictate how we interpret an issue. For instance, in North America and Europe, fir, pine, and spruce trees have been plagued for years by bark beetles. Bark beetles are a natural part of the forest life cycle, yet in the past two decades the scope and intensity of the damage caused to trees is unprecedented. Since 2000 alone, bark beetles have devastated 85,000 square miles of forest in the United States, an area the size of Utah (Katz, 2017). Where do we draw the imaginary line around this issue? Should we stop at individual trees? Should we include the forest system? Should we zoom out even more? Because some of the main contributors to this issue are rising temperatures and drought, unless we look at this issue from the planetary level and consider the role of

Figure 6.2

Systems Nest

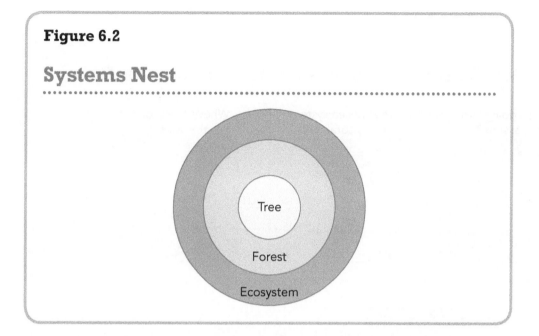

human behavior in climate change, we cannot adequately begin to solve the plight of these trees. In this case, local solutions are like Band-Aids, which don't truly address the root causes that allow the beetles to thrive in the first place. As we investigate issues with our students, we need to consider from which *systems perspective* we might meaningfully develop understanding to produce informed student action. This requires the ability to see *in wholes* and recognize when boundaries are artificially drawn.

INFLOWS, INTERACTIONS, AND OUTFLOWS

Another important aspect of systems is the presence of **inflows** and **outflows**, known collectively as **flows**. Inflows are what go into a system, whereas outflows are what are produced from interactions within the system. Flows establish dynamic equilibrium within a system. They can also produce changes to systems at different rates. For example, to understand how coral bleaching affects global warming, we need to understand how the algae found in healthy reefs absorb carbon dioxide (inflow) to support photosynthesis (interaction), resulting in the production of oxygen (outflow). Coral bleaching is caused by increased temperatures, overexposure to sunlight or pollution, and reduces the number of these algae. This consequently reduces the amount of carbon dioxide a reef is able to absorb from the atmosphere, limiting its ability to mitigate climate change. An inflow and outflow of this system can be seen in a middle school student's simplified Stock and Flow diagram in Figure 6.3. See this tool in detail on p. 186.

FEEDBACK LOOPS

A final key attribute of systems we'd like to explore is **feedback loops**. As mentioned previously, systems are cyclical. System parts are often connected to each other in a loop, where they influence each other. Feedback loops are structures that show how parts influence each other. They tell the story of an issue or event by allowing us to see how the dynamic relationships between system parts contribute to particular behaviors. Feedback loops come in two forms: balancing loops and reinforcing loops.

As we investigate issues with our students, we need to consider from which systems perspective *we might meaningfully develop understanding to produce informed student action.*

Figure 6.3

Stock and Flow Diagram: Coral Reef Inflow and Outflow

What's going into the system?

The chosen system (e.g., coral reef)

What's going out of the system?

Carbon Dioxide → **IN** → Coral Reef → **OUT** → Oxygen

BALANCING LOOPS

Balancing loops *stabilize* systems. One way to think of a balancing loop is that the parts of the loop work to cancel themselves out. Let's look at a concrete example. In ocean ecosystems, sharks eat fish. An increase in the population of fish will lead to more sharks, because sharks will have more to eat. This is represented using the plus sign on the arrow connecting these elements (Figure 6.4). However, an increase in the shark population will lead to a decrease in the fish population. This is represented by a minus sign. In this way, the number of fish and the number of sharks balance themselves out, with neither member dominating the ecosystem. If we were to graph the relationships between fish and sharks, it would look like equilibrium or like oscillation up and down within a given range. This pattern is common across predator-prey relationships. Learning about human population growth provides another excellent way for students to learn about balancing loops. The following Spotlight on Population Education, the only U.S. K–12 education program focusing on human population growth, demonstrates how an understanding of the human population is vital for sense making about local, global, and intercultural issues.

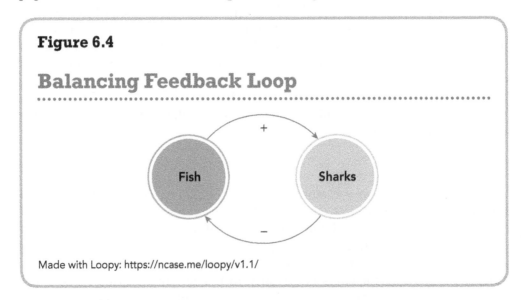

Figure 6.4

Balancing Feedback Loop

Made with Loopy: https://ncase.me/loopy/v1.1/

Reinforcing loops, on the other hand, *accelerate* conditions. They show how the relationship between parts produces more of the same action, resulting in growth or decline. So what might this look like? Let's think about our oceans and how they interact with the climate system. As greenhouse gases in the atmosphere have increased, so has the atmosphere trapped more energy from the sun. This has led to the ocean absorbing more heat. In fact, independent analyses have shown that the amount of heat stored in the ocean has increased considerably since the 1950s (United States Environmental Protection Agency, n.d.). Warming oceans cause ice sheets to melt, releasing stored methane into the atmosphere. As greenhouse gases increase, so does ocean heat. Yet warming oceans also contribute to increasing greenhouse gases (like methane). This is shown with the plus signs on each arrow (Figure 6.5). Reinforcing loops, when graphed, show themselves as exponential growth or decay, often through a hockey stick–shaped line. Reinforcing loops can show decline with the use of minus signs on each arrow.

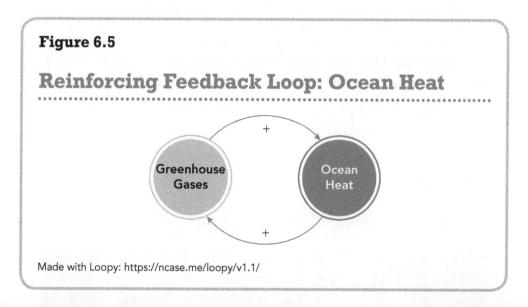

Figure 6.5

Reinforcing Feedback Loop: Ocean Heat

Made with Loopy: https://ncase.me/loopy/v1.1/

●●● SPOTLIGHT ON POPULATION GROWTH

POPULATION EDUCATION

"It is inspiring to help students recognize that they are part of something larger than themselves. For students to know they matter in that larger system and that they have an impact on it."

—Carol Bliese, Senior Director of Teacher Programs

Population Education (PopEd), a program of Population Connection, is the only U.S. K–12 education program focusing on human population growth. Founded in 1975, PopEd has reached thousands of educators through its unique curriculum and hands-on

(Continued)

(Continued)

professional development. The PopEd tagline, "It's all about people – how many of us there are, how we shape the world, and how we interact with each other," captures well its integrated approach to bringing human population issues into classrooms through experiential learning and "learning by doing," such as simulations, role-play, games, concrete representations of data, scientific inquiry, and more.

Human population issues typically fall into two overarching themes: environmental and societal. Within these themes are numerous related concepts in disciplines like life and Earth sciences, civics, geography, and mathematics. Because global issues are naturally interdisciplinary, PopEd resources typically align with two or more subject areas, affording educators flexibility as they incorporate them in their curriculum. Carol Bliese, Director of Teacher Programs, explains that

[n]o issue exists in a vacuum. For example, if studying river pollution, it's critical to analyze the impact of this pollution on the community. Everything is interconnected. We want students to understand how they are connected to the world around them: from their home, classroom and school communities to the global community. We use authentic data, stories, and case studies to show a topic's relevance, to bring real issues to life. (C. Bliese, personal communication, August 5, 2020)

Figure 6.6

Students Explore Polluted River Water

Because large numbers (such as a world population of 7,800,000,000 and counting) can be challenging to conceptualize even for adults, population issues can be scaled for diverse ages and learners. A classroom, for example, can represent a "population" to explore a host of global issues with children, such as resource use, that can be scaled to national or international levels. Interactions in this microcosmic system of the classroom not only involve tangible materials like desks and pencils, but also relationships. How we work together (or not) to solve problems affecting the system has significant impacts on individuals, communities, and ecosystems. A popular lesson is "Who Polluted the Potomac River?" that uses an interactive story and simulation to demonstrate how increasing human populations have polluted local waterways. Importantly, the lesson's discussion questions encourage students to consider why prevention is more beneficial than cleanup.

To integrate population issues in the curriculum, Carol Bliese recommends that educators reflect on two key questions as related to their content or process standards:

1. Does the number of people (in terms of their behaviors or interactions) in a system, process, or issue matter?

2. Does changing the number of people affect the outcomes in that system, process, or issue?

If the answers are yes, teachers can then explore how to make human population issues more intentional and explicit in their curriculum and instruction, and PopEd resources aim to help. To learn more about PopEd and to access their K–12 educational materials, please visit https://populationeducation.org/.

A summary of the attributes of systems we have explored can be found in the Frayer Model (Figure 6.7). The Frayer Model, a strategy for conceptual thinking, is discussed in detail in Chapter 7 on page 206.

Developing Systems Thinkers

Local, global, and intercultural issues are *complex*. Understanding them deeply requires both a shift in thinking and a shift in behavior. It no longer works to say that "A causes B" when we live in a networked world where social, economic, and environmental factors intermingle. Mass migration, which at first glance appears to stem from unemployment, may have also been caused by an ongoing drought, farmers' low crop yields, and high levels of crime. Systems thinking refers to "the ability to recognize and understand relationships, to analyze complex systems, to perceive the ways in which systems are embedded within different domains and different scales, and to deal with uncertainty" (United Nations Educational, Scientific, and Cultural Organization, 2018, p. 44). In other words, systems thinking is the ability to see the trees *and* the forest at the same time, toggling between the parts and the whole to understand how systems work. We can describe this as taking a holistic approach.

It no longer works to say that "A causes B" when we live in a networked world where social, economic, and environmental factors intermingle.

Figure 6.7

Frayer Model of a System

Frayer Model

Definition	**Characteristics**
A system is a group of interconnected elements that are organized for a function or a purpose.	• Systems have elements or parts. • Parts interact and connect. • Relationships are nonlinear. • Systems self-organize, leading to emergent behaviors. • Systems change can produce unintended consequences. • Systems have boundaries. • Systems include inputs and outputs. • Feedback loops reinforce or balance relationships.
Examples	**Non-examples**
• Ecosystems • Cities • Schools • Body systems • Waste production and management • Food production • Social media	• Processes, like directions given by GPS • Mechanisms, such as a pulley • Isolated objects, like a water bottle

Concept:

System

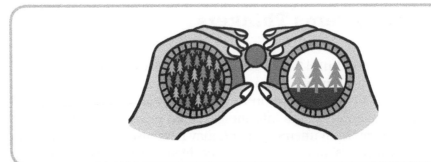

Interestingly, humans have a natural propensity to understand how systems work. As Hammond (2014) shares in *Culturally Responsive Teaching and the Brain*,

> The brain tries to understand how things are organized into a system. Is the object, concept, or event part of a larger system or pattern? Is it a smaller part of the whole or is the whole made up of smaller parts? (pp. 132–133)

The human brain also tries to understand how events, objects, and concepts are connected. In other words, systems thinking is not a fad. It is part of what it means to be human.

Systems thinking encompasses both a way of seeing the world as well as a set of tools and strategies. It is a mindset we adopt to better understand the complexity of the world around us. Some theorists have previously believed that children cannot be systems thinkers until adolescence, but this has been proven false. Children are natural-born systems thinkers (Clapp, Solis, Ho, & Laguzza, 2020). However, we would expect children across the K–8 spectrum to present different thinking skills as they engage with systems. Linda Sweeney (2015) shares that kindergarten to second-grade students can identify parts of a system and how they work together. Third- to fifth-grade students can understand that the whole can carry out functions that the individual parts cannot and look at the interaction among the parts. Sixth- to eighth-grade students can begin to explore how systems interact with other systems.

Systems thinking is not a fad. It is part of what it means to be human.

So what are the advantages of systems thinking, and why would we seek to develop these skills in K–8 students? Donella Meadows (2008), in her seminal book *Thinking in Systems*, describes the goals of systems thinking, stating:

The systems-thinking lens allows us to reclaim our intuition about whole systems and

- hone our ability to understand parts,
- see interconnections,
- ask "what-if" questions about possible future behaviors, and
- be creative and courageous about system redesign.

Then we can use our insights to make a difference in ourselves and our world. (pp. 6–7)

This last aspect, the ability to use insights to take purposeful action in the world, is an important one. In Western thought in particular, there are some dominant assumptions that drive the way we address issues in the world:

1. Every issue has a solution, which we can determine by breaking down a problem into its parts.

2. Issues can be solved linearly, in a step-by-step way.

3. We can address issues by viewing them in isolation.

4. Remaining objective and rational is possible and necessary to understand an issue.

Yet as we have explored, these assumptions do not hold water. "Solutions" can lead to more problems. For instance, antibiotic use (a solution) has led to antibiotic resistance (a problem). Systems are more than just a number of parts; they are networks of relationships. This means systems are linked to other systems, and therefore cannot be separated from their contexts to understand them. Likewise, we can balance rationality with intuition, bringing together the left brain with the right to understand the world deeply. We need to help our students let go of these assumptions, which lead to reductionist, linear thinking, and develop new habits. We need to couple systems thinking with strategic, critical, and creative thinking to develop sustainable, long-term solutions that address root causes. As Linda Sweeney (2017) asserts:

> If we raise young people to have a concept of the whole—of how systems work—they will be geared toward seeing the systems around them and will not, by nature or training, see things in isolation. They will not stand for silos but will reach out over silos because they know better. They will be indignant when conversations become narrowly linear and will look for a wider variety of causal connections. (p. 153)

This is particularly true if we want students to recognize and dismantle systems of oppression that enable socially and ecologically unjust ends. As we work toward becoming anti-racist and anti-bias educators, systems thinking enables us to understand how the structure of a system can produce inequity at the societal level.

By supporting our students to develop a number of systems thinking habits, such as "Seeing the Big Picture" or "Changing Perspective to Increase Understanding," they can approach problem solving with understanding and intention. Figure 6.8 shows the Habits of a Systems Thinker from the Waters Center for Systems Thinking. These habits highlight the mental processes that underlie systems thinking. They articulate the behaviors we would like to see students engage in as they investigate local, global, and intercultural issues and develop into systems thinkers. These habits are available as cards, which include a description of the habit as well as a set of related reflective questions.

Strategies for Systems Thinking

The following strategies enable our learners to see interconnectedness and develop the skills to think holistically. As with any strategy we use with our

Figure 6.8

Habits of a Systems Thinker

Image reprinted with permission from the Waters Center for Systems Thinking (2020).

students, our questioning and scaffolding is paramount to helping students access deeper levels of understanding. To facilitate systems thinking, we:

- **Question With Intention:** Knowing that we want to move away from reductionist, linear thinking, we intentionally ask questions with the attributes of systems in mind. For example, "What caused this?" tacitly communicates to students that there is a single cause, whereas "What factors contributed to this?" allows students to search for multiple causes. We need to be mindful how our use of language, especially through our questioning, might reaffirm dominant assumptions. Sample guiding questions can be found on page 173.

- **Take the Helicopter View:** Thinking holistically means being able to zoom out to a macro-perspective and see things from above. By getting "above an issue," we are able to identify links between parts of a system and across systems. We may ask students questions about the purpose or structure of a system to encourage them to take a similar perspective, for example, "What is the purpose of this system? How do the parts connect to meet this purpose?"

- **Be a Pattern Seeker:** Systems thinking is about learning to recognize the web of relationships that exists within a system. By using questions such as "What's this got to do with that?" we can nudge students to probe deeper as they investigate relationships.

- **Question Boundaries:** As previously explored, systems nest and are part of larger systems. In particular when exploring issues, problematize how people label them and invite students to look for broader connections. For example, is childhood obesity caused by individual genetics? The family and its habits? As families live within communities, what role might they play in providing access to nutritious, healthy food?

Systems thinking strategies are opportunities to visualize and create what Donella Meadows (2008) calls "systems pictures" (p. 5). Because of the high degree of interaction within systems, many of the strategies included invite students to map connections in nonlinear ways. They ask students to look below the surface of the Iceberg Model (p. 110) to locate patterns of behavior, the structure of a system, and underlying mental models. Important to note is that all systems thinking tools will create models, which are simplifications of the real world. That said, many systems thinking tools support students in creating nonlinguistic representations as "thinking-process maps," an instructional strategy that positively affects student achievement (Marzano, 2010).

As we introduce systems thinking tools to younger students, we may need to introduce students to age-appropriate versions of some terms (e.g., a system's *purpose* might also be called its *job*) and likewise ensure students apply tools to relevant, developmentally appropriate case studies that they understand deeply and can analyze for parts and relationships. A number of lower elementary examples are shared throughout the rest of this chapter to help contextualize these ideas.

STRATEGIES FOR SYSTEMS THINKING

Strategy	Description	Page Number
Guiding Questions	Students consider a range of questions to explore the parts, relationships, and purpose of a system.	173
Physical Models	Students create models using divergent materials to understand how a system functions.	174
Behavior-Over-Time Graphs	Students chart an aspect of a system over time and look for patterns.	177
Connected Circles	Students create a map to visualize relationships between parts within a system.	180
Causal Maps	Students chart cause and effect relationships and feedback loops within a system.	183
Modified Stock and Flow Diagrams	Students identify inflows, interactions, and outflows within a system.	186
Cause and Consequence Mapping	Students consider the multiple causes and effects of a single event or situation.	188
Root Cause Trees	Students consider the symptoms and root causes of an issue.	191

STRATEGY FOR SYSTEMS THINKING
Guiding Questions

Best for: Grades K–8

Purpose: Guiding questions can be used in a variety of ways to promote systems thinking. They can be used to structure learning engagements, including stopping points for read alouds. Likewise they can support student discussion and reflection. The questions have been designed using the levels of the Iceberg Model, shared in Chapter 4. As we move from behaviors to structures to mental models, the questions likewise deepen and represent areas of higher leverage for systems change. Where necessary, simplify or rephrase the questions for kindergarten to Grade 2 students.

Identifying the System:
- Is it a system or a group of unconnected parts?
- What's the purpose of the system?
- Is the whole greater than the sum of its parts?
- What are the parts and how do they connect?

Looking at Behaviors
- What is happening in this system? What patterns do you notice?
- What behaviors emerge from the connection between parts?
- How might we graph the behavior of this system over time?
- What patterns can we find about how this system behaves over time? Do these patterns remind you of another situation you've experienced or learned about?

Looking at Structures
- What's going into and out of the system?
- How do parts balance each other or reinforce behaviors (balancing loops and reinforcing loops)?
- What happens when a part of the system is missing or is added?
- What intended and unintended consequences might come from changing the system? Which of these might be delayed and only emerge over time?
- How might this system be related to other systems?

Looking at Mental Models
- From whose perspective is the story written? How do you know?
- What are the boundaries of this system? Who decides this?
- What do people think about this system? Why do they think this?
- How might altering our perspective make us see this system differently?

STRATEGY FOR SYSTEMS THINKING
Physical Models

Best for: Grades K–8

Purpose: In this strategy, students playfully combine research and building to create their own physical models of systems. In doing so, learners identify the parts, purpose, and interactions that exist between system parts. This strategy is particularly helpful for introducing students to the concept of *systems*.

How It Works:

1. **Research the System, Its Parts, and Interactions:** Before building models, students learn about a system, for example, through mini-case studies. This could be through a video, short reading, or outdoor experience. If they are using media resources, engage students in watching and/or reading multiple times. Each time they can read for a different purpose. The first time can be to gain an understanding of the system's purpose. Next, they can read and make a list of the parts of the system. Last, they can read a third time, thinking about connections between parts.

2. **Build a Model:** Next, invite students to create their own model of the researched system in small groups (3–4 students) using divergent parts. Include a range of traditional and unconventional materials, such as LEGO bricks, magnetic tiles, wooden blocks and arches, tissue paper, colored felt, shells, pine cones, and stones. Ask students to refer back to their notes to ensure they include the system parts and interactions between them. In Figure 6.9 students construct a beehive system using recycled black packaging foam, magnetic tiles, and LEGO bricks.

Figure 6.9

Students Create Models From Mini-Case Studies

3. **Annotate the Model:** At this point, students should be ready to annotate their models. The purpose of this step is for students to articulate how they have represented the connections between parts and explain how the system functions. Younger children can do this by taking a photo of their model and creating a screencast to discuss it. Older children can write on sticky notes and place these directly on the model as is seen in Figure 6.10 showing a middle school model of the river system.

4. **Share and Discuss:** Invite students to take a gallery walk to see other students' models and reflect on questions such as those shared in the Guiding Questions strategy. For example, ask them to reflect on the shape of each system (e.g., are they linear or round and why?). Because there are multiple models to compare, this is also an excellent opportunity to discuss what makes a strong model and how we can represent our thinking using objects. This modeling activity can be built on using other systems thinking strategies, such as Connected Circles (p. 180), Causal Maps (p. 180), or Stock and Flow Diagrams (p. 186).

Figure 6.10

An Annotated Model of the River System

Modification: Making Games

Best for: Grades K–8

Games provide immersive, interactive opportunities to experience systems. They place players within constructed, complex worlds, which can be viewed as systems. As participants interact with the set of rules that makes up the simulation, they see how individual and group decision making leads to particular outcomes. In particular, Gee (2007) claims that games are powerful tools to develop "embodied empathy" about systems. This means that players develop an understanding about how systems work as they experience relationships between system parts.

When students make their own games, they construct rules and anticipate the ways these rules will lead to particular outcomes. As Matthew Farber (2019) from University of Northern Colorado shares, "While playing games can reinforce systems thinking literacy, the act of making games can teach systems fluency" (para. 10). Although there are many opportunities to create digital worlds, students can also construct physical games using cardboard and other materials. As students construct their own simulations and games, we can encourage them to think in systems by integrating the five principles of game design as system elements:

1. **Space:** How the game space looks and feels (e.g., maze-like, open).

2. **Goal:** How the game is won.

3. **Components:** What is used to play the game (e.g., extra lives, points, enemies).

4. **Mechanics:** What actions are performed in the game (e.g., collecting, running).

5. **Rules:** What the rules of the game are.

Figure 6.11 shows an example of a student-created game from Kris Leverton's Grade 4 class at United World College South East Asia. Learners created games to reflect their understanding of body systems, in this case the digestive system. By developing games, students considered the system's function and parts, how parts interact, and what occurs when there is a problem with a part.

Figure 6.11

Student-Created Game Showing the Digestive System

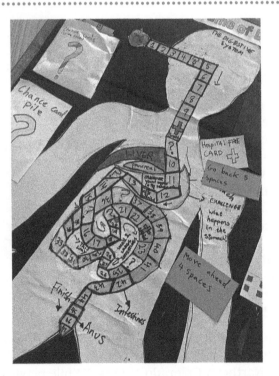

STRATEGY FOR SYSTEMS THINKING
Behavior-Over-Time Graphs

Best for: Grades K–8

Purpose: Displaying information using graphs can make it easier to interpret data, see patterns, and form connections. Graphing also provides an opportunity for meaningful interdisciplinary learning. Especially in elementary school, we see students graphing data they have no need to interpret: their classmates' favorite colors or the price of different items in the supermarket. Taking the time to look for authentic contexts to collect and graph data strengthens learning in both mathematics and the discipline from which data is drawn. Behavior-Over-Time Graphs are a form of graph that allow students to see how variables change within a system over time. A variable is represented on the y-axis with time represented on the x-axis. This strategy enables students to think about patterns that exist as a system changes and how these are represented graphically.

How It Works:

1. **Research the System:** Ensure that students have sufficient prior knowledge about the chosen system before creating Behavior-Over-Time Graphs. For example, students should be able to describe the purpose of the system and how it works. They may gain this knowledge experientially (e.g., by spending time in a school garden, through interviews, or by accessing forms of media).

2. **Choose a Variable to Represent:** In this first step, we ask students to consider what important elements of the system change over time. For example, students learning about gardening may choose variables such as temperature, plant height, soil quality, or number of pests. Because only one variable is represented on the y-axis of our graph, we may choose multiple variables that small groups of students can graph separately.

3. **Gather the Data:** Provide opportunities for students to gather the data related to their variable. In the gardening example, students may collect the data over a number of weeks, as they engage in gardening activities. Help students reflect on the accuracy of their data. Resources, such as Our World in Data (https://ourworldindata.org/), can be used as alternative sources of data where it cannot be measured through hands-on activities. If need be, teachers can collate the data for students to graph.

4. **Chart it Graphically:** Using the data collected, invite students to create their Behavior-Over-Time Graphs. Be sure to discuss where on the y-axis their graph should start with reference to their data, as well as what labels the y-axis and x-axis would be given. Model this as a mini-lesson, so students have a sense of how to proceed in small groups or independently.

5. **Predict Future Behavior:** At this point, ask students to use the shape of the graph to predict what would happen in the future. How would the line continue? The present can be marked on the graph through the use of a dotted line such as that found in Figure 6.12. Encourage students to use patterns found in the data to support their hypotheses.

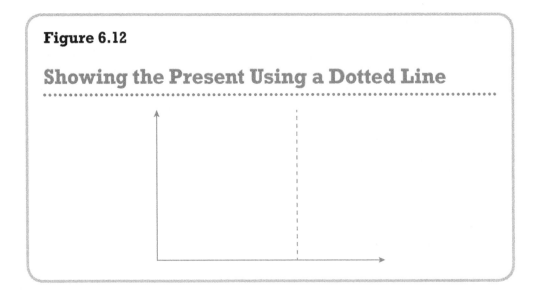

Figure 6.12

Showing the Present Using a Dotted Line

5. **Discuss:** We may choose to ask questions such as:

- How has ____ changed over time? Why?
- What is the shape of the graph (e.g., line curving up, curving down, oscillating)? What does this tell us about how the variable changes over time?
- What changes may happen in the future based on this pattern? What makes you say that?
- What new questions does this graph make you have about the system?

If multiple variables were graphed separately, ask students to look for relationships across them. For instance, if the temperature over time in an ecosystem is represented on one graph, whereas the number of births of animals is represented on another, what interdependencies can they see between the variables? "What if . . ." questions are also excellent prompts to use at this point that ask students to change their time horizon and think about possible futures.

Modification: Graphing Emotions, Qualities or Skills Over Time

Behavior-Over-Time Graphs can also be used to chart individual or group emotions, qualities, or skills over time, enabling teaching into the skill of retelling. For example, students studying leaders may graph how an individual's courage, integrity, or determination changed over time as different life events occurred. This same strategy can be applied to map a character's emotional journey in a picture book. Figure 6.13 shows the changes to Greta Thunberg's feelings of loneliness over time using the picture book *Our House is On Fire* by Jeanette Winter. Note that the *y*-axis charts her level of loneliness, while the *x*-axis marks life events as she gets older and establishes her identity as a changemaker. In this case, multiple lines are drawn, showing the discussions and conclusions of individual groups of students. This could also be done as a whole class as part of a read aloud experience.

Figure 6.13

Using Behavior-Over-Time Graphs for Character Development

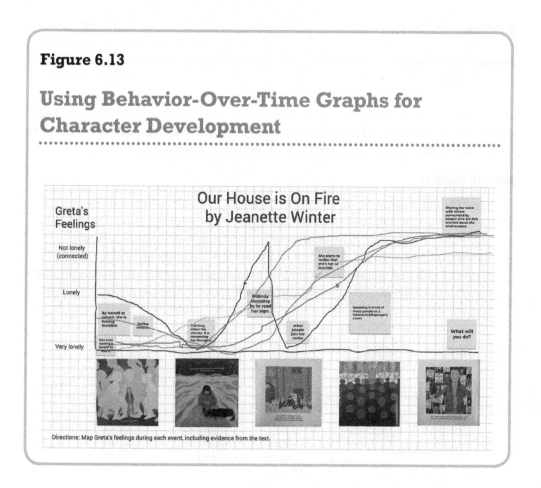

STRATEGY FOR SYSTEMS THINKING
Connected Circles

Scan this QR code to access an editable Connected Circles template, or visit **teachworldwise .com/resources**.

Best for: Grades K–8

Purpose: Connected Circles is a strategy for students to trace and visualize relationships between parts of a system, allowing them to see the interdependence of parts as well as how the connections between parts produce particular behaviors. It works best accompanied by student research into an issue, event, or situation, where students can draw from their factual knowledge to justify the connections they are making between system parts.

How It Works:

1. **Identify the Issue:** First, decide what issue, event, or story will be mapped. It may be a situation taken from a newspaper article, an issue experienced firsthand on a field trip, an event encountered in a storybook, or an overarching topic being researched. Figure 6.14 shows a Connected Circle mapping golf ball pollution caused by coastal golf courses, as part of a unit on Systems Thinking & Sustainable Development. The case study focused on Alex Weber, a Californian teen who collected more than 50,000 golf balls off the coast in various states of decomposition.

Figure 6.14

Students Map Golf Ball Pollution

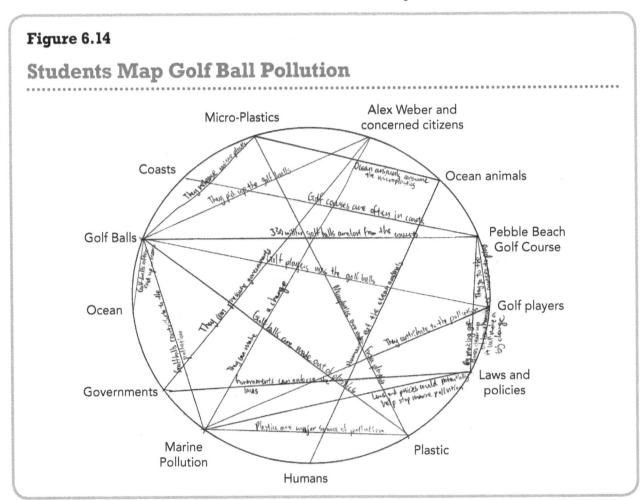

2. **Identify System Parts:** Name system parts using nouns or noun phrases. Place these around the circle. Keep the number of elements under 15, and use even fewer for younger children. Remember the goal is to identify relationships and accompanying behaviors, so we are looking to include the most significant system parts. Students can participate in identifying some of or all the parts in this step. They can do this as part of a class discussion or in small groups. Remember that elements can be tangible (e.g., *Golf Players*) or intangible (e.g., *Laws and Policies*).

3. **Introduce the Tool and Its Purpose:** Introduce the purpose of the Connected Circles tool as a way to visualize a system and its parts. Review the characteristics of systems, such as those shared earlier in this chapter, and provide a guiding question or prompt to students, for example, "Today we'll explore relationships between parts of golf ball pollution and how we might begin to identify solutions related to this issue."

4. **Chart Relationships:** Students work in partners or small groups to chart relationships between parts. They should have the article, story, video, or their notes open to access during the activity to ensure their connections are accurate. Emphasize that parts may connect to multiple elements. Ask students to write the relationship or relationships between parts on the line that connects them, for example:

Golf players ------ contribute to ------> Ocean pollution

Younger children can take a photo of their map and create a screencast, identifying the connections between parts orally. Give sample verbs to help them make connections, if required. For example:

Increases	Decreases	Produces	Consumes
Leads to	Grows	Reduces	Uses
Causes	Drives	Shapes	Spreads

5. **Zoom in on Feedback Loops:** Next, ask students to review their maps and zoom in on language they used on their lines that describes change. This will help them identify feedback loops. Ask students to *close the loop* for any of these links. For example, can students identify a line that suggests change (e.g., using the verb *increases*) and then link back to the original part with a new line? Invite students to trace each loop in a different color, so feedback loops stand out from other connections.

6. **Discuss and Reflect:** Engage the class in a discussion using some of these reflective questions or those shared in the Guiding Questions strategy on page 173:

   • Which parts have many connections going to them? Why? What would happen if it were missing from the system?

   • What is the significance of an element that has no connections? Might it be indirectly related to other system parts?

   • What does it mean when connections go away from and lead back to the starting part? What is happening in that feedback loop?

   • What does this diagram tell us about how the system behaves? Which parts might act as leverage points for changing the system?

Modification: String Game

Instead of creating a model on paper, the String Game creates a physical model with connections between system parts represented by yarn or string. In this version, each student represents one part of the system. For example, in a forest system there may be the sun, water, pine trees, bees, beetles, frogs, mice, squirrels, foxes, deer, wolves, and so on. To know who represents which part, children can hold a card with a photo or draw a picture to represent the element. These can also be made into necklaces and hung around children's necks. Make sure to review each part of the system before beginning to ensure accurate connections are made. Any participant may start the web by making a connection using the frame:

I am a ___ and I connect to ___ because . . .

The child then passes the yarn to the element mentioned. Repeat multiple times until there is a dense web of connections across the elements. Students should hold the yarn with enough tension that they can feel the interconnectedness of elements. Next, point to one of the parts and announce that it has been removed from the system. In the case of organisms, this may be due to disease, hunting, or lack of food and/or water. The individual holding that card then tugs on the strings to show which parts would be affected by its removal. Repeat as required with different elements. As a class, discuss how different events can affect the system. What would happen if multiple parts were removed at the same time? When might this happen in real life? How might adding an element change the way the system worked? Figure 6.15 shows the String Game in action with Grade 4 students in Kris Leverton's class. As system elements, children represent the 17 Sustainable Development Goals to see how they connect and rely on each other to be accomplished.

Figure 6.15

Grade 4 Students Play the String Game Using the Sustainable Development Goals

STRATEGY FOR SYSTEMS THINKING
Causal Maps

Best for: Grades K–8

Purpose: All natural and human systems are composed of interacting feedback loops, either balancing or reinforcing loops. Causal maps show multiple cause and effect relationships within a system. As a result, they often chart feedback loops between system parts. Causal maps allow us to see the dynamic interactions that exist within a system, giving us clues as to where there may be leverage points, or possible points for change. Understanding causal relationships and the nuanced effects of feedback loops is critical to solving global challenges, such as climate change. This is illustrated in the Changemaker Spotlight on Swedish climate activist Greta Thunberg below.

How It Works:

1. **Identify an Issue, Problem, or System:** Depending on the context for learning, introduce students to the issue, problem, or system to be mapped. Although this strategy works well for issues in need of improvement, it can likewise be used to understand a system better. This is evident in Figure 6.16, which shows a kindergarten causal map for a butterfly garden (see the Connected Circle strategy also used in this unit on p. 180).

2. **Brainstorm Parts to Map:** Identify the most important parts of the issue, problem or system. Causal maps can quickly get messy and complex, because they have so many arrows going between system elements. We recommend keeping the number of parts to 10, with even fewer for younger children. The kindergarten example uses six elements. Parts can be brainstormed as a class, or shared with students, depending on their age and familiarity with the context. If this strategy is being used to unpack an issue, avoid using language such as "fewer" or "less" in front of parts (e.g., fewer fish). These details will be represented using words and symbols on the line later in the strategy.

3. **Add Arrows and Words:** Invite students to draw arrows between elements that seem related and to add words on the line that describe the relationship. The direction of the arrow is important and these should be kept unidirectional. Two arrows should be used to show different impacts experienced between two parts. For example, in the kindergarten example, this is shown with:

   Bees -------- Pollinate --------> Flowering Plants (+)

   Flowering Plants --------- Provide Nectar --------> Bees (+)

4. **Identify Feedback Loops:** Once arrows and words are written to describe relationships, students can find feedback loops. Here they are looking for how changes to one system element, such as an increase or

decrease, impact another system part. In essence, feedback loops tell the story of a system. Because kindergarten students focused on the concept of *balance* in natural systems, the language of the question in Figure 6.16 was modified to support sense making. Children considered, "How do living things give to and take from each other in a habitat?" Remember, not all causal maps will have feedback loops. If students cannot find any feedback loops, encourage them to think if an important system part was left out or if a loop was missed.

Figure 6.16

Kindergarten Causal Map of a Butterfly Garden

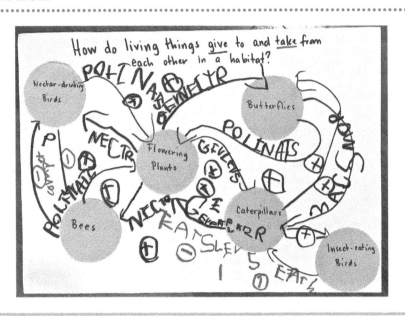

5. **Add Signs:** Students add plus and minus signs to show relationships within a feedback loop. These can be represented in different colors, such as plus signs in blue and minus signs in red. Having different colors on the map can help students more easily find balancing and reinforcing loops.

6. **Discuss:** After students have created their maps, encourage them to reflect using a number of questions that ask them to *read* their maps. This also provides a moment for students to consider leverage points, or places to intervene in the system to produce change. Note that it may not always make sense to discuss leverage points, as is evident with the kindergarten example shared. To prompt reflection, we may ask:

- What relationships do you see in your causal map?

- What feedback loops do you see in your causal map? Describe them.

- In what ways do these feedback loops balance each other out (balancing loops)? In what ways do these feedback loops multiply or accelerate actions (reinforcing loops)?

Optional:

- What leverage points might exist within this issue or problem on your map?

- What might you change to tackle this issue or problem based on those leverage points?

●●● CHANGEMAKER SPOTLIGHT

GRETA THUNBERG

"You must take action. You must do the impossible.

Because giving up is never an option."

As an introverted young student in Stockholm, Greta Thunberg felt invisible. For several years, she sank into a depression, refusing to speak or even eat. Concerned for her well-being, her family sought medical care for Greta and learned that she has Asperger's syndrome, characterized by difficulties in social interaction and nonverbal communication. Greta's diagnosis also bore gifts: the capacity for hyperfocus and persistence to accomplish goals. At age 15, she became deeply concerned about climate change, spending countless hours researching its causes and effects on Earth's ecosystems and living creatures. Greta decided to raise awareness by protesting in front of the Swedish Parliament House every Friday holding a sign that read "School Strike for Climate." Soon she was joined by other Swedish students, and eventually young people around the world in an international climate movement known today as Fridays for Future.

Greta's activism led to speaking to world leaders at the 2018 United Nations climate summit in Poland where she spoke about climate justice and the power of people working collectively. "If solutions within the system are so impossible to find," she said, "maybe we should change the system itself. . . . The real power belongs to the people." This talk resulted in 200 nations agreeing to rules governing the Paris Agreement on climate change that aim to limit warming to 1.5°C over pre-Industrial levels to avoid irreversible effects of climate change: coral reef extinction, rising sea levels, and deadly storms, droughts, and heatwaves.

Greta has since spoken throughout the world to create awareness about the need to cut our global carbon emissions. At the 2019 United Nations Climate Action Summit, she warned about "irreversible chain reactions beyond human control" that will occur if we do not take immediate action. As one who demonstrates the habits of mind of a systems thinker, Greta understands how interdependent feedback loops and continuous, incremental changes create disruptions in fragile climate systems that humans may be unable to counter once tipping points are reached. To learn more about the youth-led climate movement Greta inspired, visit https://fridaysforfuture.org/.

STRATEGY FOR SYSTEMS THINKING
Modified Stock and Flow Diagrams

Best for: Grades 2–8

Purpose: Modified Stock and Flow Diagrams allow students to recognize the inflows and outflows of a system (flows) that affect a system. It enables students to inquire into what occurs when the rate of an inflow or outflow changes within a system (e.g., increases or decreases). Normally Stock and Flow Diagrams contain variables and feedback loops within them. To simplify this for Grades 2 to 8 learners, this modified version invites students to focus on how things come into and go out of a system and how this affects the system and its interactions. This is a useful strategy for helping students see how systems exist within an environment, which affects how they function.

Scan this QR code to access an editable version of Figure 6.17 to use in your classroom, or visit **teachworldwise.com/ resources**.

How It Works:

1. **Choose a System or Part of a System:** Identify the system or part of a system (remember, systems nest) to chart. Place this in the middle box of the Modified Stock and Flow Diagram template, as seen in Figure 6.17.

2. **Research How the System Works:** Engage students in learning about how the system functions. As students read or watch media related to the system, ask them to consider the questions, "What's going into the system?" and "What's going out of the system?" Students can then record inflows and outflows of the system on two colors of sticky notes or annotate texts using two colors of highlighters. This helps students draw out the most relevant information for the diagram.

3. **Consider Inflows and Outflows:** Invite students to complete the diagram by adding inflows and outflows to their diagram. Are there any relationships between inflows and outflows? What are these?

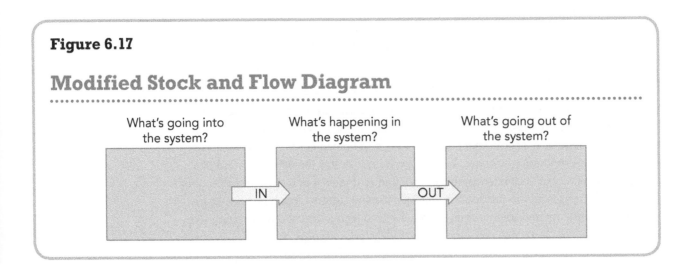

Figure 6.17

Modified Stock and Flow Diagram

What's going into the system?

What's happening in the system?

What's going out of the system?

IN

OUT

4. **Discuss:** At this point, facilitate a discussion about what students found out about the flows of the system. Make sure to highlight the role of the environment surrounding the system in shaping how it works. A nesting systems diagram, such as that shared earlier in this chapter (Figure 6.2) can help students understand how the system in question relates to other systems. Here we may ask students to reflect on questions such as:

- What happens to the inflow once it enters the system?

- What occurs within the system to produce the outflow?

- What happens to the outflow once it exits the system?

- What might happen if the rate of the inflow coming into the system increased or decreased? What makes you say that?

- What might happen if the rate of the outflow being produced or leaving the system increased or decreased? What makes you say that?

- What larger systems is this system connected to?

STRATEGY FOR SYSTEMS THINKING
Cause and Consequence Mapping

Best for: Grades K–8

Purpose: Cause and Consequence Mapping looks to make a model of a situation or event to explore causes and consequences that emerge from system behaviors. To do so, students begin with a *starting point*, which is the current state. Then they work forward and backward from this starting point. Using this strategy, students come to realize how situations often have multiple causes and produce multiple consequences. Likewise, they can see how meaningful systems change can only occur by addressing root causes, instead of the immediate causes of an issue.

How It Works:

1. **Choose an Event or Situation:** Choose an event or situation based on the local, global or intercultural issue being studied. Students can engage in this strategy after reading an article, watching a news report, or experiencing an issue firsthand.

2. **Identify the Current State and Immediate Causes and Consequences:** Using the graphic organizer shared in Figure 6.18 (available as a template using the QR code), place the current situation in the middle box. Engage students the following questions to identify the Before and After:

   • What came directly before that caused this situation?

   • What consequences will occur immediately as a result of this situation?

Scan this QR code to download an editable version of Figure 6.18 to use in your classroom, or visit **teachworldwide.com/resources**.

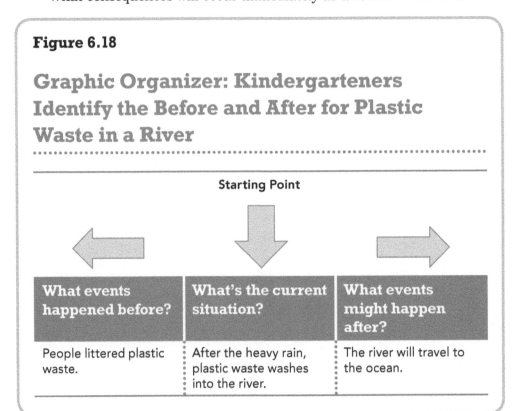

Figure 6.18

Graphic Organizer: Kindergarteners Identify the Before and After for Plastic Waste in a River

Starting Point

What events happened before?	What's the current situation?	What events might happen after?
People littered plastic waste.	After the heavy rain, plastic waste washes into the river.	The river will travel to the ocean.

3. **Identify Causes that Came Before:** Having identified the events that occurred directly before and after the current situation, students work backward to reach root causes. Here we prompt students asking, "What happened before that?" and invite them to record each of the causes on a card. Using different colored cards for the causes and consequences can help students see the relationships between causes, situations, and consequences. Note that students do not need to work linearly forward and backward. They may identify multiple causes and consequences that produce configurations such as that found in Figure 6.19. We continue working backward until we reach the root causes of an issue. In the kindergarten example above, students stopped at the root cause that "Single-use plastic is used to make things."

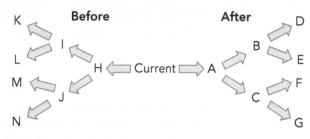

Figure 6.19

Identifying Multiple Causes and Consequences

4. **Identify Consequences that Come After:** Now that students have thought back in time, they start extrapolating out to the consequences of a situation. Here we ask the question, "What might happen after that?" Important here is that students are using research to back up their thinking. For example, kindergarten students were able to successfully predict that "fish and other ocean animals might eat the plastic and get sick" only because they had done previous learning around this topic. They created their maps as paper chains, linking their cards together to show connections (Figure 6.20).

5. **Discuss and Reflect:** Once students have identified multiple causes and consequences, invite them to reflect using a number of questions, such as:

   - What causes were identified? How did each of those causes have a cause?

   - What consequences emerge from this event or issue? How did some consequences become causes of other consequences?

   - What does this activity tell you about what causes an issue or event?

   - What root causes were identified? What might it look like to address these root causes to produce change?

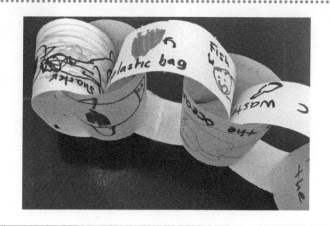

Figure 6.20

Cause and Consequence Paper Chain for Plastic Waste in a River

HOW WE MAKE STUFF

A collaboration between the Ellen MacArthur Foundation and children's book author Christiane Dorion, the interactive website *How We Make Stuff* provides a number of relevant early years case studies that show how our use of resources produces multiple consequences for humans and the environment. Based on a children's book of the same name, *How We Make Stuff* showcases everyday products, such as a bar of chocolate or rubber duck, and how they are made using a linear "take, make, use, throw" mindset that produces waste. Promoting circular approaches where goods are created using the Earth's natural cycles, including integrating waste products into the manufacturing process, the stories on the website illustrate how system overhauls are required for large scale change. Check out *How We Make Stuff* at https://www.made2bmadeagain.org/.

Figure 6.21

How We Make Stuff

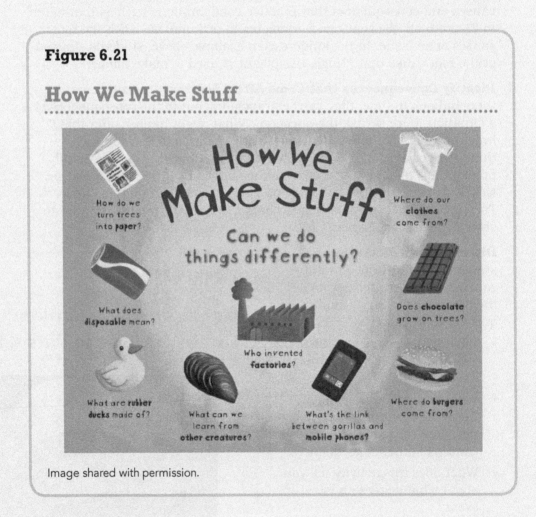

Image shared with permission.

STRATEGY FOR SYSTEMS THINKING
Root Cause Trees

Best for: Grades K–8

Purpose: Root Cause Trees allow students to look for root causes to issues, enabling them to begin to design sustainable actions and solutions (see Chapter 8). This strategy is similar to Cause and Consequence Mapping, yet is built around the ideas of root causes and symptoms of a problem. These ideas are represented symbolically using the visible leaves and branches (symptoms), the tree trunk (the problem), and the invisible roots (root causes).

Scan this QR code to access an editable Root Cause Tree template, or visit **teachworldwise.com/resources**.

How It Works:

1. **Review Language:** Before introducing this graphic organizer to students, review the language of root cause, problem, and symptom. A root cause is the initial cause of a condition. Root causes are under the surface and largely invisible. Symptoms, on the other hand, are the visible manifestation of a problem. For example, headaches might be a symptom of too little sleep.

2. **Identify a Problem or Issue:** Choose the problem or issue to represent on the Root Cause Tree. For example, Figure 6.22 shows a Root Cause Tree by middle school educator Julia Fliss focusing on the lack of healthy food on campus. Depending on the age of students and context for learning, students may be working on the same or different problems in small groups.

3. **Brainstorm Symptoms:** Invite students to brainstorm symptoms of the problem based on their research and experience. These may be, for instance, statistics, observations, or feelings. Ask students to record these ideas in the foliage of the tree. Symptoms recorded by Julia's students included being tired after lunch and a decrease in mental health.

4. **Research Root Causes of Symptoms:** Based on the problem and symptoms, students will likely need to return to their research at this point to identify how the symptoms were caused by particular root causes. What causes lie under the surface and produce these symptoms? The 5 Whys questioning technique developed by

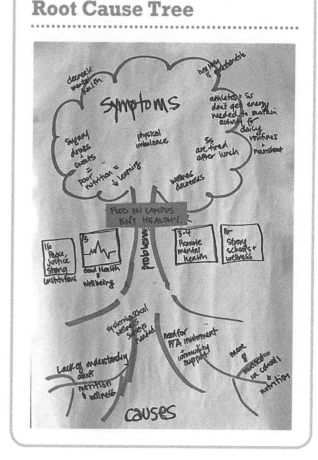

Figure 6.22

Root Cause Tree

Japanese innovator Sakichi Toyoda can guide this process. By repeating the question "Why?" five times, Toyoda believed one can drill down to reveal the root causes of a problem. For example, using the above issue that "Food on campus isn't healthy," the first question might be "Why isn't food on campus healthy?" *Because there is lack of sufficient funding dedicated to nutrition in schools.* "Why is that?" and so forth, until "why" has been asked five times. Note that to reveal multiple root causes, the technique will need to be repeated down each main *root* of the tree.

5. **Prioritize Root Causes:** After identifying the root causes, invite students to prioritize them and record the most significant root causes underneath the ground on their chart. These can then be used to ideate potential solutions and sustainable actions. For strategies to accompany the development of solutions, see Chapter 8.

In this chapter, we've explored the power of systems thinking as a way to look at and understand the world. Both a mindset and a set of tools, systems thinking asks students to challenge their assumptions and question seemingly simplistic solutions to complex problems. If a solution seems too good to be true, it probably is! Systems thinking is a core component of the Understand phase of the Worldwise Learning Cycle, allowing students to zoom out and think holistically. Chapter 7 continues to expand on the Understand phase of the Worldwise Learning Cycle. It focuses on an important sidekick to systems thinking: conceptual thinking. Conceptual thinking enables students to view their learning about issues as illustrative case studies, drawing transferable concepts from them that can apply to situations now and in the future. Before moving to Chapter 7, take a moment to pause and reflect on your learning about systems thinking.

PAUSE AND REFLECT

- How might systems thinking help your students better understand issues and the world around them?

- Think about the units you teach your students. Which of these might contain opportunities for the development of systems thinking? What might this look like, given the age of the children you teach?

- Systems thinking is both a mindset as well as a set of sense-making tools. How might you foster a systems thinking mindset while students engage in these strategies?

- What evidence might you look for to determine if your students were thinking in systems?

CHAPTER SEVEN

UP TO THE CONCEPTUAL LEVEL

A COGNITIVE SUPERPOWER

STUDENTS OWNING THEIR THINKING

MENTAL CONSTRUCTS THAT TRANSFER

CLEARING ROADBLOCKS
TO CONCEPTUAL THINKING

SCAFFOLDING THINKING
USING CASE STUDIES

KNOWLEDGE
SKILL LEARNING

CONCEPTUAL
UNDERSTANDING

UP TO THE CONCEPTUAL LEVEL

"When spider webs unite, they can tie up a lion."

—Ethiopian Proverb

This chapter explores the following Tenets of a Pedagogy for People, Planet, and Prosperity:

- Use real-world issues as organizers for learning.

- Design inquiry-based experiences for the application of learning, such as projects.

- Use a case study approach.

- Scaffold conceptual thinking that transfers.

Conceptual Thinking to Understand Complexity

To help our students see patterns and make connections between their learning and the world at large, we need to take their thinking *up* to the conceptual level. In Chapter 1, we explore the need to move away from the "inch deep, mile wide" curriculum to a three-dimensional model that includes concepts to ensure intellectual rigor. In Chapter 3, we consider how interdisciplinary learning can support *up and out* transfer. By *up*, we refer to our desire to take learning up to the conceptual level by inviting students to construct their own conceptual understandings. By *out*, we mean that students should have opportunities to apply learning to situations across disciplines and beyond classroom walls. This means using their learning in a new context for a *purpose*. By mobilizing their learning within complex, novel situations, students make choices about how to use their learning and grapple with the unknown. As shared in the Introduction, this supports the development of global competence. What exactly do we mean by conceptual thinking? Erickson, Lanning, and French (2017) describe it this way:

> Conceptual thinking requires the ability to examine factual information critically, relate new learning to prior knowledge, see patterns and connections, draw out significant understandings at the conceptual level, evaluate the truth of these understandings based on the supporting evidence, transfer the understanding across time or situation, and, often, use the conceptual understanding to creatively solve a problem or create a new product, process, or idea. (p. 23)

In other words, conceptual thinking consists of forming an understanding of *individual* concepts, making connections *between* concepts using evidence, and *transferring* concepts to new situations and contexts. Forming, Generalizing, and Transferring are the three levels of conceptual thinking, which we explore in this chapter (see Figure 7.2).

Conceptual thinking is a cognitive superpower. It is a super strength for an age in which we are inundated with information. The World Economic Forum (2019) estimates that by 2025, 463 exabytes of data will be created each day globally. That's the equivalent of 212,765,957 DVDs packed with data each day! As teachers, we know how limited the time is with our students. We simply cannot teach them everything. And we need to make sure what we teach our students can be used *flexibly* and *creatively*. Developing students' conceptual thinking as they acquire knowledge and skills has the following benefits:

- Improves the acquisition and retention of knowledge by making it connected.

- Supports intentional skill use.

- Facilitates the application and transfer of student learning.

- Future-proofs learning by allowing students to recognize new examples of concepts now and in the future.

By promoting conceptual thinking, we can equip learners with the skills they need to make sense of real-world issues we have not yet encountered. Yet unlike the superpowers found in comics or films, conceptual thinking is a learned skill we can nurture and grow in our classrooms.

Over the course of this chapter, we look specifically at the three areas of conceptual thinking shared above and how they relate to each other. At the end of the chapter, we share a number of classroom strategies to build these aspects of conceptual thinking along with examples from issues-focused units. This chapter draws heavily on *Concept-Based Inquiry in Action* (Marschall & French, 2018), which is a great resource to pick up if you want to take a deeper dive into classroom strategies and examples of conceptual thinking in action. The following Spotlight provides an illustration of students as they describe and sort examples to develop individual concepts.

Unlike the superpowers found in comics or films, conceptual thinking is a learned skill we can nurture and grow in our classrooms.

SPECTRUM SORT

Grade 7 learners at UWC South East Asia *tune in* to the context of a unit on Systems Thinking & Sustainable Development by exploring the concepts of *human environment* and *natural environment*. To do so, students engage in an inquiry-based strategy, working in small groups to sort a number of photos along a spectrum. These show different environments around the globe such as

- rice terraces,

- igloos in the tundra,

- megacities, and

- forests adjacent to farmed fields.

As students place examples on the spectrum, they make choices about the extent to which human activity is present in the image. Students look for evidence of settlements or ways that humans modified the environment. Some students rightly share that the presence of images themselves suggest that all these places are at the very least within human reach. At the end of this learning experience, students are given a photo of a context not yet explored as an exit ticket: "Is it an image that shows the human environment, the natural environment, or somewhere in-between? What makes you say that?" Students record their answer on the back of the photo and use evidence from the Spectrum Sort to justify their thinking. The Spectrum Sort, as a concept formation strategy, is outlined on page 210. This lesson was followed by an examination of Critical Questions, a Critical Literacy strategy, which can be found on page 253.

Figure 7.1

Spectrum Sort for Human and Natural Environment

Levels of Conceptual Thinking

As shared in Chapter 1, concepts are mental constructs drawn from a topic or a process that transfer to new situations and contexts (Erickson, Lanning, & French, 2017). They

- are one to two words (nouns) or a short phrase;

- abstract (to different degrees), timeless, and universal;

- have examples that share common attributes;

- transfer across new situations and contexts; and

- can be micro (specific to a discipline) or macro (broad and interdisciplinary).

Let's look at an example: the idea of a *family*. Families have existed as long as humans have been on the planet. Stories, recorded in ancient texts and oral traditions across cultures, tell of relationships and interactions between family members. That is, the idea of a family is both timeless and universal. Although it feels less abstract as a concept, it has many different examples that share attributes. Whether a child lives in a family with a single parent, extended relatives, or adoptive parents, each of these families has commonalities. Families have their own culture, with a set of customs and traditions practiced. Families often have a strong commitment to each other, support each other in meeting their needs, and express affection. Understanding the idea of a family can help students recognize new instances of the concept that they may encounter now or in the future. It allows them to both reduce the complexity of the world and transfer their understanding to new situations.

Level 1: Concept Formation

Acquiring individual concepts, also known as **concept formation**, is the initial stage of conceptual thinking. It consists of describing, comparing, and categorizing examples and non-examples to develop understanding of an individual concept (Gagné, 1965; Taba, 1965). The brain is a pattern lover. Our desire to understand the world by recognizing and naming patterns we see around us is how we learn from birth. As students engage in concept formation, they explore the boundaries and dimensions of a concept, like what makes a *habitat* different from an *ecosystem*. Concept formation strategies help students develop an initial understanding of a concept. This understanding becomes refined as students investigate factual examples in a unit, such as case studies. To move students to more complex, sophisticated levels of conceptual thinking, we must first form their understanding of *individual* concepts (Figure 7.2). This level provides the solid foundation for other, more complex forms of conceptual thinking to occur. If we jump over this initial level of conceptual thinking, we run the risk that students maintain misconceptions or construct inaccurate conceptual understandings during a unit.

Figure 7.2

Levels of Conceptual Thinking

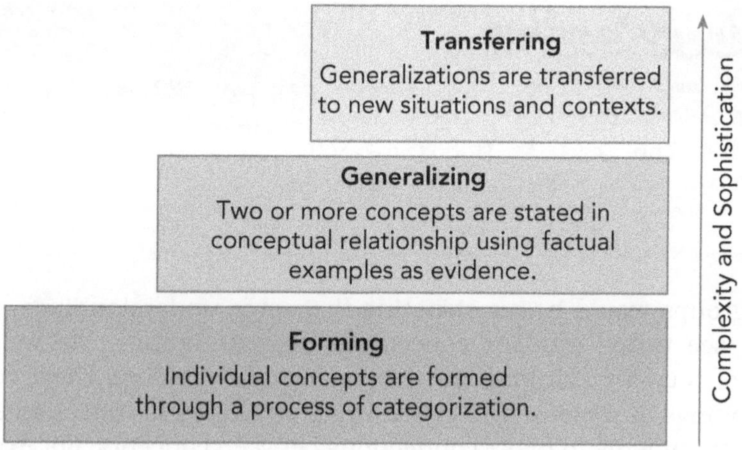

Transferring
Generalizations are transferred to new situations and contexts.

Generalizing
Two or more concepts are stated in conceptual relationship using factual examples as evidence.

Forming
Individual concepts are formed through a process of categorization.

Complexity and Sophistication

Reprinted with permission by Marschall and French, 2018.

Level 2: Generalizing

Once students have a strong understanding of individual concepts, we can invite them to form relationships between two or more concepts and state these as generalizations. As described in Chapter 1, we also refer to these as *conceptual understandings* or *big ideas*. Because they do not reference a specific time, place, or situation, conceptual understandings transfer. They describe our learners' most important takeaways from a period of learning. For example, Figure 7.3 shows a conceptual understanding at the end of a unit on World Religions. Here learners create a *conceptual snapshot* of their learning with the intention of carrying it with them into an unknown future. Strong conceptual understandings, which are precise, true, and transferable,

- are written in active voice (e.g., "determines" instead of "is determined by");

- are written in present tense (e.g., "causes" instead of "caused");

- are written in third person (e.g., no I, we, me, or us);

- are value and judgement free (e.g., avoid "should" or "must");

- include two or more concepts (e.g., <u>Misunderstanding</u> can lead to <u>conflict;</u> concepts underlined);

- use qualifiers as needed (e.g., may, often, can);

- are supported with evidence from prior learning; and

- can follow the phrase "Students will understand that. . . ."

In the planning process, we intentionally articulate conceptual understandings to guide our teaching (see p. 203). That said, because individual students

Figure 7.3

Student Conceptual Understanding

<u>Understanding</u>:

We now understand that religion does not necessarily unite or divide people — it does both. Different values and beliefs can lead to conflict, but religion forms strong communities with unbreakable bonds.

or small groups would be constructing their own understandings, we would expect to see varied student conceptual understandings. We welcome the diversity of student thinking as they share and discuss their conceptual understandings as a class. The generalizing strategies in this chapter provide scaffolds for students to make connections between concepts. For example, we may use conceptual questions, sentence frames, or structured activities that facilitate abstract thinking.

Level 3: Transferring Understanding

Once students have constructed understandings, they can transfer these to new situations and contexts. In Chapter 8, we advocate for students to test drive their understanding of an issue by taking action. That said, we can also support students in transferring their understanding within the classroom environment. By presenting new case studies, discussing relevant current events or engaging students in projects, we can strengthen our learners' ability to transfer their thinking to new contexts. Because taking action closely relates to the transfer of learning, we recommend looking at Strategies for Developing Solutions and Taking Action in Chapter 8 to complement the strategies for transfer shared in this chapter.

Clearing Roadblocks to Conceptual Thinking

We can only counter the "inch deep, mile wide" curriculum by coupling knowledge and skill learning with intellectually rigorous conceptual learning. Depending on our school context, curricular standards are written in a variety of ways. As described in Chapter 1, many of these standards are articulated as verb-driven statements, which name what the student should know or be able to do. If we want to take students' learning to the conceptual level, these standards may feel like a roadblock. However, seeing conceptual connections is a skill that we can develop and refine as educators. As we have explored earlier in this chapter, concepts are written as nouns or short phrases. We can *mine* our standards for concepts, allowing us to organize student learning around big ideas. In other words, no matter what content or skills we have to cover, teachers hold the power to design learning experiences that promote conceptual thinking.

Let's take a look at a Grade 1 example (Figure 7.4). Imagine we are designing an interdisciplinary unit about animal welfare, where Grade 1 learners will read and write opinion pieces about community issues such as stray dogs. To plan for conceptual understanding, we need to extract concepts from standards and articulate them as conceptual understandings. These understandings name the conceptual learning we seek to develop in students, in addition to knowledge and skills typically named in standards. Figure 7.4 shows concepts found within Common Core English Language Arts standards and possible conceptual understandings we could articulate using them to guide literacy teaching in the animal welfare unit (concepts underlined). We can see how these conceptual understandings reflect the skill learning from the standards.

Mandated standards may feel like a roadblock when we are trying to take student learning to the conceptual level. However, we can mine our standards for concepts—written as nouns or short phrases—and organize student learning around these big ideas.

Figure 7.4

Unpacking Concepts From Standards (Grade 1)

Standards	Extracted Concepts	Possible Conceptual Understandings
Identify the main topic and retell key details of a text.	Main Topic/Idea Key Details Text	<u>Readers</u> use <u>key details</u> to explain the <u>main idea</u> of a <u>text</u>.
Identify the reasons an author gives to support points in a text.	Reason Author Points Evidence* Text	<u>Authors</u> state an <u>opinion</u> and use <u>evidence</u> to support <u>reasons</u> for their <u>opinion</u>.
Write opinion pieces in which they introduce the topic or name the book they are writing about, state an opinion, supply a reason for the opinion, and provide some sense of closure.	Opinion Introduction* Reason Closure/Conclusion	<u>Authors</u> structure their opinion writing using an <u>introduction</u>, <u>body</u>, and <u>conclusion</u>.

*Although support and introduce are used in the standards as verbs, we can infer that the concepts of *evidence* and *introduction* are important to understanding. We refer to these as *implicit concepts*.

By adding a question starter, we can *flip* conceptual understandings into strong conceptual questions (Figure 7.5). These conceptual questions can then structure literacy learning in an inquiry, be shared with students, and frame generalizing strategies. Although we could construct multiple conceptual questions from one understanding, we've attempted to simplify this process by showing direct connections between them. So what do we do with these questions? Take a look at the Conceptual Questions strategy (p. 214), which provides a number of ways that we can use these supercharged questions. Generally, we would have one to three conceptual questions for each conceptual understanding. Figure 7.5 shows how we can flip the conceptual understandings from Figure 7.4 into conceptual questions that ask students to make connections between concepts. Note that the questions use *authors* instead of *this author* to make them transferable.

Figure 7.5

Flipping Understandings Into Questions

Conceptual Understanding	Related Conceptual Question
Readers use key details to explain the main idea of a text.	How do readers explain the main idea of a text?
Authors state an opinion and use evidence to support reasons for their opinion.	How do authors back up their opinion?
Authors structure their opinion using an introduction, body, and conclusion.	How do authors structure an opinion in writing?

Developing Conceptual Understanding Through Case Studies

Although we've discussed the many benefits of thinking at the conceptual level, we want to reiterate the importance of grounding conceptual thinking in knowledge and skill learning. Conceptual understandings emerge from and reflect real-life contexts. If students have insufficient knowledge or skill learning under their belt, they struggle to think abstractly about it. To put it metaphorically, imagine you are getting ready to sing a solo in a concert. You haven't warmed up your voice yet, and the concert leader wants you to practice the parts with high notes right away. Your voice cracks: You simply aren't ready for the difficulty of what's being asked of you. Developing students' knowledge and skills in a unit is like warming up the voice, setting the stage for the challenging work to come.

For this reason, we use a case study approach, which invites students to learn relevant knowledge and skills for a given conceptual understanding. Here we choose case studies that best reflect unit conceptual understandings. A case study approach has many benefits, such as allowing us to

- show examples of conceptual understandings in context;

- connect to local and global people and places;

- provide mirrors, windows, and sliding glass doors into the racial, cultural, and linguistic backgrounds of our students;

- facilitate dialogue on challenging issues like discrimination and racism using real-world examples;

- foster intercultural sensitivity and understanding, including appreciation of human diversity;

- provide student choice and personalize learning; and

- create inquiry-based experiences driven by teacher and/or student questions.

An important consideration when using a case study approach is ensuring students are exposed to a range of examples. If we only use one case study, for example, a single mentor text for the opinion writing unit in Grade 1, students may overgeneralize, stereotype, or develop inaccurate understandings. This is similar to Chimamanda Adichie's idea of the "single story" shared in Chapter 5. We want to move students away from the notion of the single story becoming the *only story*. Although we may start with the most obvious example, we look to build nuance and sophistication using multiple case studies (see p. 83 for examples). Particularly when focused on diverse peoples and places, case studies in the form of literature, film, and immersive stories offer a range of perspectives and human experiences. Such case studies help students go beyond the single story and strengthen their intercultural understanding.

Building on methods for perspective-taking and storytelling in Chapters 4 and 5, this chapter explores ways to develop transferable conceptual understandings in students, supporting their ability to solve problems in the face of increasing complexity and uncertainty. Our choice of case studies can enable students to develop awareness of the cultural practices, beliefs, and values of diverse peoples or places, while simultaneously connecting to the overarching concepts of a unit. For example, an integrated science, social studies, and

language arts unit focuses on the interconnectedness of culture, language, and the environment. Case studies include the stories of indigenous peoples, such as the Anishinaabe of Canada and the Sápara of Ecuador, and their critical roles protecting 80% of the world's biodiversity through nature-based solutions (Raygorodetsky, 2018). By analyzing ancestral values and their intimate connection to the natural environment as reflected in their Indigenous languages, students develop the conceptual understanding: _Language reflects the values, beliefs, and shared experiences of a cultural group, including interactions with the local environment._ Although the primary aim of this chapter is to explore the power of conceptual thinking for our learners, we can leverage case studies as a way to both stretch students' worldviews, as well as build deep understanding.

Strategies for Conceptual Thinking

Becoming a Worldwise Learner means being a critical thinker who can take purposeful action within a community. If we want to make this vision a reality, students' thinking needs to belong _to them._ As we support students in developing and articulating their understanding, we reflect on how we can promote student agency. One of the ways we do this is through an **inductive approach**. In the inductive approach, students explore factual examples, look for patterns across them, and then form generalizations to synthesize their thinking (Figure 7.6). In doing so, learners construct _their own_ understandings. This kind of learning is extremely agentic, because students experience high levels of ownership and autonomy over their thinking. Notably, inquiry is one of our primary mechanisms for supporting inductive learning, for example, through use of teacher and/or student questions (see Conceptual Questions on p. 214).

This counters to the **deductive approach**, where teachers give students the big ideas of a unit, before factual examples have been explored. As students explore factual examples, they validate the _teacher's_ ideas. Although this may be more time efficient, it does limit diverse ideas and students' ability to view themselves as conceptual thinkers. That said, we use a deductive approach more frequently in concept formation activities by giving learners a concept definition before sorting examples and non-examples. In both inductive and deductive approaches, **synergistic thinking**—the interaction between factual and conceptual levels of thinking—is required to reach deep understanding (Erickson & Lanning, 2014).

Aligning to the Stages of Conceptual Thinking shared in Figure 7.2, the following strategies are categorized as strategies for concept formation, generalizing, or transfer of conceptual understanding. As mentioned, unless students have a strong understanding of individual concepts and acquired knowledge and/or skills that reflect conceptual relationships, we cannot expect them to construct their own conceptual understandings. Chapter 8, with its focus on the application of learning through action, builds on the strategies for transfer found in this chapter.

Figure 7.6

Inductive and Deductive Approaches

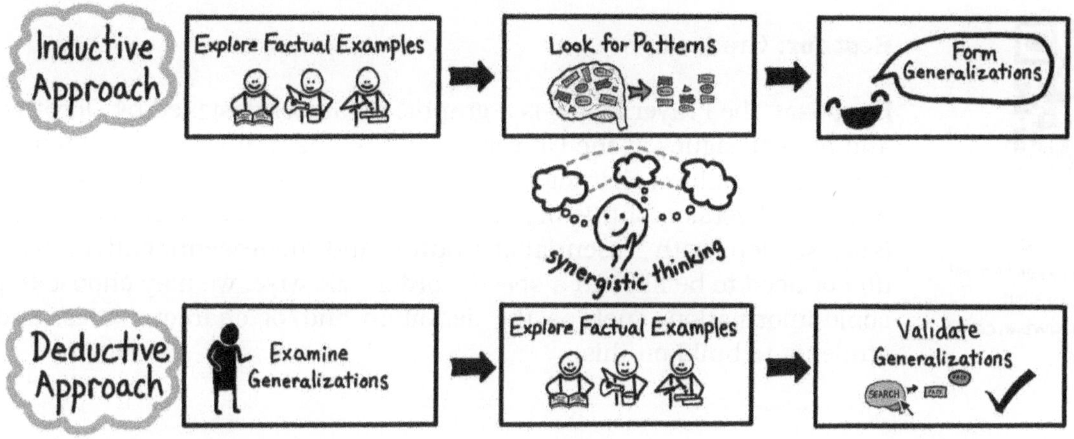

Reprinted with permission by Marschall and French, 2018.

STRATEGIES FOR CONCEPTUAL THINKING

Strategy	Description	Page Number
STRATEGIES FOR CONCEPT FORMATION		
Frayer Model	Students use a graphic organizer to chart a concept's definition, characteristics, examples, and non-examples.	206
Is/Is Not	Students sort examples and non-examples to understand a concept.	208
Spectrum Sort	Students analyze examples of a concept and order them along a conceptual scale.	210
All, Some, None	Students use what they notice about all, some or none of the examples of a concept to draw out essential attributes.	212
STRATEGIES FOR GENERALIZING		
Conceptual Questions	Students ponder questions, moving their thinking from the factual to conceptual level.	214
Connect 4	Students use a graphic organizer to uncover similarities and differences between case studies.	217
Hexagon Connections	Students group and connect hexagons to reflect conceptual relationships.	219
Corner Connections	Students draw connections across and between corners to articulate conceptual relationships.	221
STRATEGIES FOR TRANSFER		
Stress-Testing Generalizations	Students test their understanding using new case studies provided by peers or the teacher.	223
How Does It Connect?	Students respond to questions about how a factual case study connects to a conceptual understanding.	224

STRATEGY FOR CONCEPT FORMATION
Frayer Model

Scan this QR code to download an editable Frayer Model template, or visit **teachworldwise.com/ resources**.

Best for: Grades K–8

Purpose: The Frayer Model is a graphic organizer designed by Dorothy Frayer and her colleagues at the University of Wisconsin. It enables students to consider the definition, characteristics, examples, and non-examples of a concept. A modified version of this organizer can replace the definition and characteristics sections with "essential attributes" and "nonessential attributes." Boxes do not need to be filled in a specific order. Likewise, we may choose to provide some information, such as the definition and/or characteristics, and invite students to build on this.

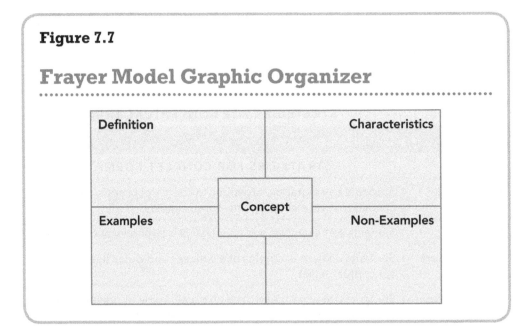

Figure 7.7

Frayer Model Graphic Organizer

Definition	Characteristics
	Concept	
Examples	Non-Examples

How It Works:

The Frayer Model is a flexible graphic organizer that can be used in a number of ways. Here are a few ideas for how to use it with students.

Pre-Assessment: To engage and activate students' prior knowledge, students can use the Frayer Model to record their initial thinking without a formal definition or set of characteristics. This can provide us with useful assessment data about their current understanding that can inform planning. Students can revisit their Frayer Models during or at the end of a unit, adding on to the organizer to show new learning.

Wall Chart: We can create wall-sized Frayer Models that can be added to over the course of a unit. This can allow students to move or change information as they develop their understanding. Depending on the age of students and complexity of the concept, we may choose to complete part of the Frayer Model for learners to refer to as a scaffold. In Figure 7.8 we can see how teacher Kris Leverton chose to co-construct all parts of the model with his Grade 4 students. The Examples and Non-Examples parts of this wall chart also show possibilities for dialogue and debate. Thinking about a number of businesses, Grade 4 students needed to determine whether they were sustainable or not. For this reason, the bottom section of this wall model is more like a spectrum than two clear sections. There was disagreement among groups after they engaged in research on each company, which provided a future opportunity to return to the organizer later in the unit.

Figure 7.8

Frayer Wall Chart for Sustainable Business

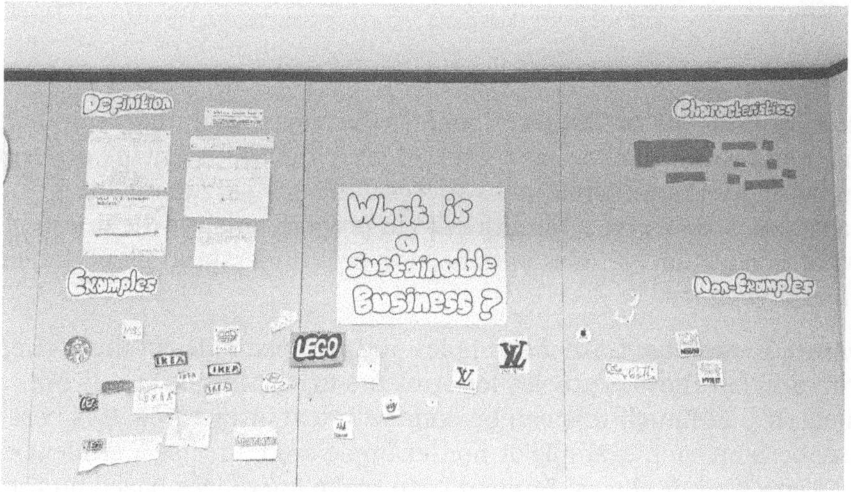

STRATEGY FOR CONCEPT FORMATION
Is/Is Not

Best for: Grades K–8

Purpose: The Is/Is Not strategy is a targeted approach to solidify knowledge and understanding of an individual concept. In the strategy, students sort examples and non-examples of a concept. *Is* means the example does show the concept. *Is Not* means the example does not show the concept. To develop true and transferable conceptual understandings that relate to the wider world, students need to leverage their understanding of individual concepts. The following protocol was adapted from Marschall and French (2018) by Laura Montague, a Grade 2 teacher at the Avenues: The World School in New York, New York.

How It Works:

1. **Identify Concept to Target:** Consider the conceptual understandings and guiding questions in your unit. Identify the unit's driving concepts students need to understand to successfully navigate the guiding questions. For example, for students to properly answer the question "What is biomimicry?" students need to first understand plant and animal *physical features*.

2. **Collect Examples:** Gather examples and non-examples of the concept. Print and cut these examples for students to sort into *Is* and *Is Not* categories. Although this can be done with text or pictures, it is best to have both on each example or non-example card, in case a student does not know what it shows. Students can make inferences based on the appearance of the picture and/or morphemes within the word(s).

3. **Introduce the Sort:** Sit students in a circle on a carpet or in seats. Introduce the activity and discuss and model what small-group collaboration should look and sound like.

4. **Sort in Small Groups:** Group students in pairs or trios. Prompt students to collaboratively organize the cards into *Is* and *Is Not* categories. Younger children can use a T-chart as an organizer to support them in this step. A photo of students' *Is/Is Not* sort for Physical Features can be found in Figure 7.9. As students sort, take anecdotal notes of understandings and misconceptions to be discussed during the class reflection.

5. **Reflect:** Once finished, use a practice such as a gallery walk, digital sharing, or group presentations to elicit students' reasons for the placement of their examples and non-examples. Give them a chance to talk through any particularly challenging cards. Use this time to clarify misconceptions, highlight successes, and invoke wonderings.

Figure 7.9

Grade 2 Is/Is Not Sort on Physical Features

STRATEGY FOR CONCEPT FORMATION
Spectrum Sort

Best for: Grades K–8

Scan this QR code for an editable version of this spectrum, or visit **teachworldwise.com/ resources**.

Purpose: The Spectrum Sort is a strategy that works well for concepts that have examples of varying degrees. In this strategy, students develop their understanding of a concept by sorting along a spectrum of *least* to *most* (Figure 7.10). The strategy can also be modified by changing the scale and having two opposing concepts on either end of the spectrum. We can see an example of this in Figures 7.11 and 7.12 where Grade 3 students thought about how the *natural environment* (at one end of the spectrum) slowly turns into the *built environment* (at the other end). This was part of a unit on Cities. This strategy is shared with permission from *Concept-Based Inquiry in Action* (Marschall & French, 2018).

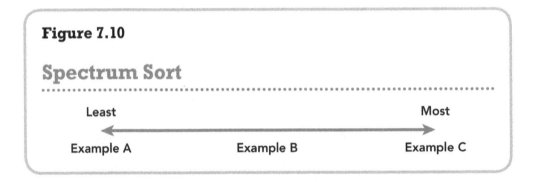

Figure 7.10

Spectrum Sort

Least   Most

Example A   Example B   Example C

How It Works:

1. **Define the Scale:** Define the scale by choosing an adjective related to the concept being investigated. For example, the concept of *health* would have the scale "least to most healthy."

2. **Introduce the Activity:** For students new to this strategy, model two or three obvious examples on the scale. Explain that this activity is not about having right answers, but about justifying thinking. Encourage students to compare examples as they place them and provide reasons for their thinking. For example, is eating a piece of fruit healthier than eating a sandwich? Here we can provide the following sentence frames to support students in articulating their ideas:

   • **Justifying Thinking:** I think ____ belongs here on the spectrum because . . .

   • **Comparing Examples:** I think ____ is more/less (scale adjective) than ____ because . . .

3. **Sort Examples:** Invite students to work in pairs or small groups to place examples along the spectrum. Non-examples are placed off the spectrum to show they do not fit in the set. This sorting activity can be done with words, picture cards, photos taken by students, or physical objects, depending on the concept and the age of the students.

4. **Ask for Justification:** When engaging students in the Spectrum Sort, ensure that they can justify the placement by giving reasons. How do students make a decision about where to place a new example, if some are already ordered on the line?

5. **Discuss:** Bring groups together to discuss their findings as a class. If students have little prior experience with the concept, highlight the ends of the spectrum, for instance, what examples ended up being on the *most* side. Be sure to discuss examples that students felt were the most challenging to place. Why might this be?

6. **Record Ideas:** In this step, record student thinking about the target concept. For instance, ask the question, "What is common to examples on the *most* side? What is common to examples on the *least* side?" and record attributes. Invite students to come up with their own examples, which can be added to the class chart.

Figures 7.11 and 7.12

Spectrum Sort for the Built Environment (Cities)

STRATEGY FOR CONCEPT FORMATION
All, Some, None

Best for: Grades K–8

Purpose: All, Some, None enables students to explore the essential and non-essential attributes of a concept. In this strategy, we ask students to either identify attributes of a concept from a number of factual examples or sort attributes using a placemat showing sets (such as that shown in Figure 7.14). This strategy is modified with permission from *Concept-Based Inquiry in Action* (Marschall & French, 2018).

How It Works:

Here is one way to use All, Some, None:

1. **Collect Examples:** Before engaging learners in this strategy, collect a number of examples and non-examples of the concept. Include a number of obvious examples that will allow students to easily identify the concept's attributes, along with a few less prototypical examples.

2. **Provide the Focus Concept and Factual Examples:** Discuss the concept students should be thinking about as they look at factual examples. For example, we may say, "All these are examples of advertising. What can we find that is present in all, some, or none of these examples?" Ask students to record ideas as they look at the examples, for example, on a whiteboard.

3. **Identify Characteristics:** Here we ask the questions, "What is the same across *all* the examples? What was common across *some* of the examples? What is in *none* of the examples?" and record student thinking. At the end of this step, we should have a list of characteristics for the concept. Make sure to prompt students if they seem to hold any misconceptions.

4. **Write a Definition:** Using the characteristics from the previous step, co-construct a definition for the concept. For example, Figure 7.13 shows the thinking of the Grade 3 class after they compared and contrasted their Spectrum Sorts to think about the built environment (see p. 210 for previous strategy). Here we asked the question, "Looking across your sorts, what do we notice might be present in many cities?" Note that the word *many* was intentionally used as attributes across global cities may vary.

Modification: Attribute Sort Using a Placemat

A Google Slide version of this placemat, which you can modify, share, and/or print for students is available using this QR code, or visit **teachworldwise.com/resources**.

Instead of providing examples, give students attributes of the target concept and an All, Some, None placement (Figure 7.14). In this example, students sort attributes of religion such as "Has a moral code" or "Has a place of worship." During their sort, they consider the question, "Are these evident in *all* organized religions, *some* organized religions, or *no* organized religions?" Use the ideas generated in small groups to develop a class definition for the concept or compare thinking with another definition (e.g., from a dictionary or an organization).

Figure 7.13

All, Some, None for the Concept of City

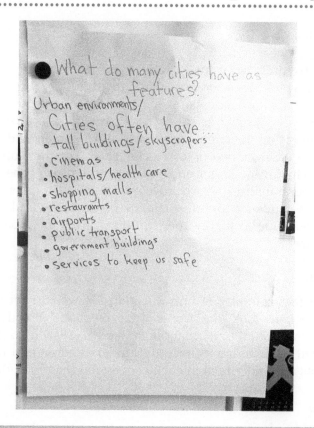

Figure 7.14

All, Some, None Placemat for the Concept of Religion

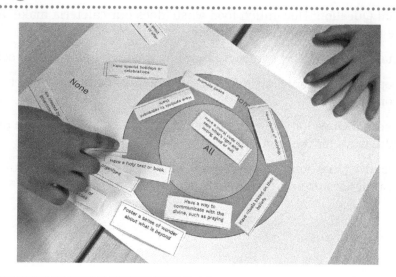

STRATEGY FOR GENERALIZING
Conceptual Questions

Best for: Grades K–8

Purpose: In any unit, we want to have a range of guiding questions that allow us to engage different levels of students' thinking: factual, conceptual, and provocative. Factual questions support the acquisition of knowledge and skills, while also providing the evidence required to answer conceptual questions. Conceptual questions, written in third person and present tense, ask students to connect two or more concepts. They are one of our most important tools in our toolkit for encouraging students to construct their own conceptual understandings. Provocative questions, also known as *debatable questions*, invite students to take a stance on an issue and use their prior knowledge or learning to justify their thinking. They may be conceptual or factual in nature.

How It Works:

Let's look at a few examples of unit questions so we can get a feel for what conceptual questions look like. Conceptual questions directly relate to and "unpack" unit conceptual understandings. For this reason, each example will be accompanied by a sample conceptual understanding and unit organizing issue. Concepts are underlined in each conceptual understanding.

Kindergarten

Unit Organizing Issue: Waste Management

Conceptual Understanding: How a <u>community</u> manages its <u>waste</u> can harm or protect the <u>environment</u>.

- Factual Question: What waste do we make at break and lunch time in the classroom?

- Factual Question: How much food waste does our cafeteria make, and where does it go when it is produced?

- Factual Question: How can we reduce our waste at home and at school?

- Conceptual Question: How might waste practices harm or protect the environment? Why?

- Conceptual Question: How can communities manage their waste in less harmful ways for the environment?

- Provocative Question: Whose responsibility is it to ensure community waste practices protect the environment?

Grade 4

Unit Organizing Issue: Human Development

Conceptual Understanding: Human <u>modifications</u> to the <u>physical environment</u> can produce <u>intended</u> and <u>unintended consequences</u>.

- Factual Question: What evidence of human modification can we find in our immediate surroundings? For example, sidewalks, construction, bridges, parks, and so on.

- Factual Question: What might be the intended and unintended consequences of these modifications in our community?

- Conceptual Question: Why might humans modify the physical environment?

- Conceptual Question: What happens when humans modify the natural environment?

- Conceptual Question: How can human development take into account the needs of both humans and the rest of the natural world?

- Provocative Question: What knock-on effects might occur if people decided to build a new road or shopping center? Explain.

Grade 8

Unit Organizing Issue: Ecosystem Collapse

Conceptual Understanding: <u>Organisms</u>, and <u>populations</u> of organisms, depend on <u>interactions</u> with other <u>living beings</u> and <u>nonliving factors</u>.

- Factual Question: What organisms live within our local coastal ecosystem? (Case study would be dependent on location of school, interest of students, and curricular standards.)

- Factual Question: How do organisms depend on each other and on nonliving factors in this ecosystem?

- Factual Question: What would happen if we removed this organism from the ecosystem? Why?

- Conceptual Question: What interdependent relationships exist within ecosystems?

- Conceptual Question: How might an ecosystem's resources determine the growth of organisms and populations?

- Provocative Question: How important is biodiversity to ecosystems? Why?

Conceptual questions can be used in a number of ways in the classroom to support students in constructing their own conceptual understandings. Figure 7.15, shared with permission from *Concept-Based Inquiry in Action* (Marschall & French, 2018), offers a variety of tips for how to scaffold thinking using conceptual questions:

Figure 7.15

Using Conceptual Questions

Use Conceptual Questions to . . .	How to Use
Design focus questions	Develop more specific conceptual questions that can be used at the lesson level, for example, "How do goods and services fulfill needs and wants?" may become "How do goods and services support personal health?"
Frame a lesson	Review the conceptual question at the beginning and end of a lesson.
Construct learning intentions	Tell students, "By the end of this lesson, you will be able to answer the question . . ."
Label graphic organizers	Place a conceptual question at the top of a graphic organizer to focus thinking.
Organize student sharing	Collect student thinking related to a conceptual question over time, for example, as students investigate different case studies.
Create an exit ticket	Ask students to write a response to the conceptual question at the end of a lesson.
Design an assessment	Design formative and summative assessments using conceptual questions.

STRATEGY FOR GENERALIZING
Connect 4

Best for: Grades K–8

Purpose: Connect 4, co-developed by Nancy Fairburn and Carla Marschall, is a strategy to locate patterns across factual case studies. This strategy requires students to synthesize information to generalize. The organizer is broken into five sections. Four sections are for recording information related to the case studies investigated. A fifth section, in the middle of the organizer, includes a conceptual question or sentence frame that asks students to generalize based on their findings. The conceptual question, showing what the class should be able to answer after using the strategy, is placed at the top of the organizer (Figure 7.16). This strategy is shared with permission from *Concept-Based Inquiry in Action* (Marschall & French, 2018).

Scan this QR code to access an editable Connect 4 template, or visit **teachworldwise.com/resources**.

Figure 7.16

Connect 4 Placemat

Connect 4 Placemat   Conceptual Question: How might humans value natural resources in different ways?

Example 1: The way humans adapt to their natural environment

Summarize the case study:
└ larger hearts & lungs to adapt to the higher altitudes
- domesticated birds who fished for them

In what way(s) do humans value natural resources in this example?
— They value the natural food chain and use it to there advantage.
-

Example 2: the way humans have changed/modified the environment

Summarize the case study:
— when g humans want to settle in the area, often leads to deforestation.

In what way(s) do humans value natural resources in this example? — They value the the wood & space of their environment

Based on the case studies, how might humans value natural resources?
— Humans value natural resources for their own needs & wants. Either treat them with respect or harm. Humans also learn from the environment and base their lives around it. Nature comes into everyone's daily basis and provides what we need to survive. Humans depend on natural resources. for farming and domestication

(side notes: Connecting to God, materials, food)

Example 3: The way humans live with/alongside nature

Summarize the case study:
- the Amazon rainforest provides the Kayapo people with their daily needs
- the forest has also taught them to recognize different beneficial plants.

In what way(s) do humans value natural resources in this example?
- For daily needs, food, water, shelter, etc.
- They learn from nature and base their lives around it.

Example 4: The spiritual & beliefs system have in regard to their environment.

Summarize the case study:
- only eat halal meat
— have a little respect for animals

In what way(s) do humans value natural resources in this example?
— They value living organism in regard to their beliefs of halal & the muslim religion.

How It Works:

1. **Introduce Conceptual Question:** Frame the lesson around a conceptual question, such as "How might humans value natural resources in different ways?" Present this question before showing the organizer.

2. **Model Using the Organizer:** If using this strategy with placemats, it is important for students to understand that (1) each person in their group of four must use a different case study and (2) information recorded should relate to the headers in each box. For our question on resources, we ask for a short summary of the case study and how humans value natural resources in that particular example. Show what this may look like with a sample case study so students see the thinking involved. For younger students, this template can become a class chart and the teacher can be the scribe. The class may investigate four case studies over time, filling in details in the chart when appropriate.

3. **Seek Out Patterns:** Once students have filled in their individual part of the placemat, they engage in conversation. Their goal is to identify similarities and differences across case studies. To facilitate this, we can provide talk prompts such as "I notice that _____ and _____ are similar because . . ." or "Across all four case studies. . . ." This primes students for generalizing in the next step, which may or may not occur in the same lesson.

4. **Create Conceptual Understandings:** In the middle box of the organizer, students construct conceptual understandings that reflect the patterns they have identified. This box can include sentence stems to scaffold student thinking such as "Humans value natural resources for. . . ."

5. **Collect and Synthesize Ideas:** Once all groups have created conceptual understandings, discuss them as a class. What commonalities seem to exist across the conceptual understandings? Could they be combined in any way? Small-group understandings can then be turned into class conceptual understandings that reflect common thinking. Be sure to prompt students if any misconceptions are evident in small-group conceptual understandings. For example, we may ask, "Is that true in all situations?" or "Did any group have a case study that refutes that statement?"

STRATEGY FOR GENERALIZING
Hexagon Connections

Best for: Grades K–8

Purpose: Hexagon Connections encourages flexible and creative thinking as students form conceptual understandings. Using a number of paper hexagons, with a single word or short phrase in the middle, students group concepts that reflect their understanding in a unit. Because hexagons have six sides, each hexagon can connect to multiple concepts.

Scan this QR code to access our template for creating these cards, or visit **teachworldwise.com/resources**.

How It Works:

1. **Choose Concepts:** Considering the unit choose a maximum of 10 to 15 concepts (fewer for younger children) for students to connect. These

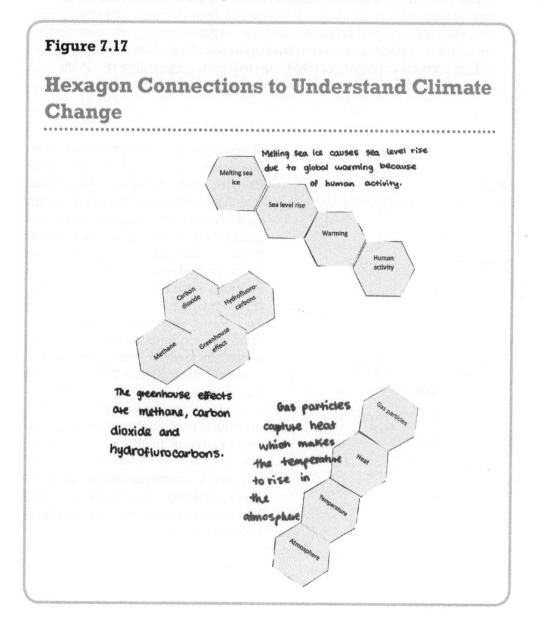

Figure 7.17

Hexagon Connections to Understand Climate Change

should come from unit conceptual understandings. Remember that concepts can also be unpacked from state or national standards.

2. **Create Cards:** Create hexagon cards with a concept on each card. For kindergarten to Grade 2 students, we may choose to add a picture to each of these cards to support comprehension.

3. **Introduce the Task:** Share the goal of the activity with students, which is to use the cards to come up with big ideas they're drawing from the unit. Encourage them to have a conversation about the cards to determine which may best go together. These can then be placed in different configurations on the paper.

4. **Connect and Generalize:** Invite students to discuss, group, and place their hexagons on a piece of paper. These can be glued down when they are satisfied with their placement. After hexagons are glued down, students can annotate next to each of their clusters and write conceptual understandings. Figure 7.17 shows a sample Hexagon Connections activity from a Grade 7 unit on Climate Change. Notice that because both concepts and other nouns (e.g., methane and carbon dioxide as types of gases) were given to students, not all their sentences are conceptual understandings. However, ideas such as _Gas particles_ capture _heat_ which can make the _temperature_ rise in the _atmosphere_ would be a transferable idea (concepts underlined).

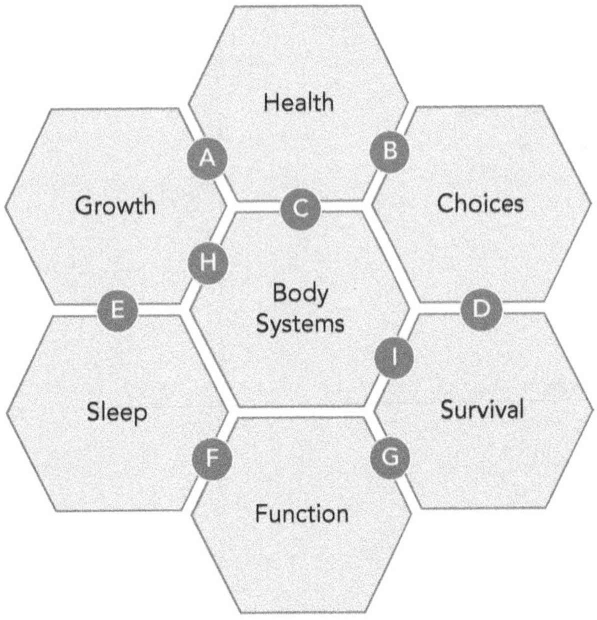

Modification: The Honeycomb

This modification, designed by Andrew McCarthy, comes from Geraldine Brogden, Primary School Instructional Coach at United World College South East Asia, Dover Campus. Instead of giving students free choice about how to place and group hexagons, create a honeycomb-shaped template that includes seven important unit concepts. Include letters or numbers on the border between two concepts. Then ask students to write individual sentences to show how those two concepts connect. Figure 7.18 shows an example from a Grade 4 Body Systems unit. Here students were asked to articulate relationships between concepts such as health and growth or choices and health. From this, they developed understandings such as _Body systems_ can support _growth_ by giving parts of the _body nutrients_ (Connection H).

Figure 7.18

The Honeycomb

STRATEGY FOR GENERALIZING
Corner Connections

Best for: Grades K–8

Purpose: Corner Connections provides a playful, generative way to support students in constructing their own conceptual understandings. As students make connections, they draw from their prior learning and justify their thinking. It is a conceptual thinking *warm-up* that encourages students to search for possibilities.

How It Works:

1. **Engage in Case Studies:** Before students think about the chosen concepts, ensure that they have had sufficient opportunities to explore both case studies related to them and have a deep understanding of each of the concepts individually. Students are encouraged to use notes, graphic organizers, or class charts to support their thinking.

2. **Choose Concepts:** Choose up to four concepts, which are placed in the corners of a piece of paper or chart paper, mini whiteboard, or, for older students, a digital format. Make sure that the four concepts chosen can be brought together to make a single conceptual understanding. Figure 7.19 shows an example for a Grade 7 unit on Climate Change. Learners articulated relationships between parts of the climate system using this strategy. For younger learners, we may choose to accompany each concept with a photo.

Figure 7.19

Corner Connections for the Climate System

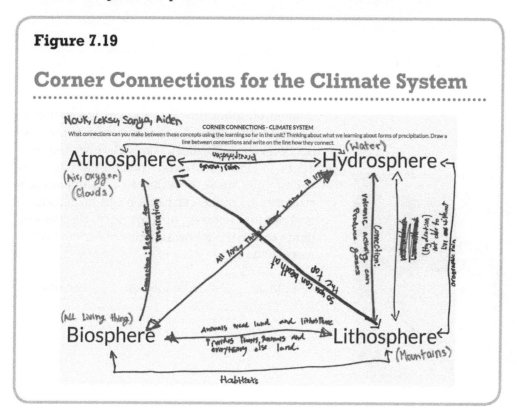

3. **Invite Connections:** Invite students to make connections between the concepts in each of the corners using lines, arrows, and words. Important is that students justify their thinking about why two concepts connect. They can also write down related case studies that show the relationships they have articulated.

4. **Articulate Understandings:** After students have charted their connections, ask them to put the concepts in a sentence that represents how they are connected. Remember, we want this statement to go beyond individual case studies. As such, encourage students to write their statement in third person, present tense using a strong verb. Below their statement, students can mention particular case studies that support their understanding. Figure 7.20 shows a sample student understanding developed using this strategy. Case studies are referred to below their conceptual understanding.

Figure 7.20

Student Understanding Using Case Study Examples as Evidence

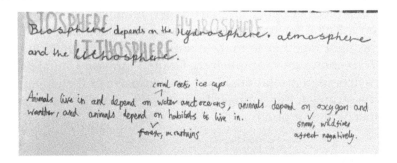

Figure 7.21

Concept Roles

Modification: Concept Roles

Instead of doing this through writing, students can take the role of a concept and make connections through discussion. Here we ask students to first go around their circle clockwise before they make crosslinks. This encourages students to make connections to all concepts, and not just between obvious ones. We ask students to use the following sentence frame in this modification:

- I am a ___, and I connect to _____ because . . .

STRATEGY FOR TRANSFER
Stress-Testing Generalizations

Best for: Grades K–8

Purpose: In this strategy, students transfer their understanding to new case studies to see how well their thinking matches a new context. When students generalize, we expect them to provide evidence of their understanding using one or more case studies. Considering new factual examples encourages students to revise their thinking. Let's say students construct a conceptual understanding that is locked in time, place, or situation. We may introduce a new case study, so students consider the transferability of their understanding. Stress-testing can take place immediately after the conceptual understanding is formed or in a follow-up lesson. This strategy is shared with permission from *Concept-Based Inquiry in Action* (Marschall & French, 2018).

How It Works:

The teacher can prompt students a few ways in this strategy:

1. **Invite Discussion:** Invite the class to support or refute a conceptual understanding using known case studies to justify thinking. The conceptual understanding may be from an individual, small-group, or the whole-class. Once students have taken the time to view and discuss the understanding with a partner, we ask a range of questions: Is this conceptual understanding always true? Can anyone think of a case study that does not fit this idea? How would we change the understanding to represent all the case studies we have researched? At the end of the discussion, we revise the statement so it better reflects our collective thinking. Encourage students to reword the conceptual understanding, explaining their choices along the way.

2. **Compare Examples:** Pair students who can challenge each other's ideas with the case studies they have investigated. Can they combine their ideas to form a new conceptual understanding? This strategy works especially well when using a case study approach where students study a range of case studies individually or in small groups. Imagine, for example, that students research a range of individuals in a unit on exploration, such as Marie Curie, Mae Jemison, and Zheng He. We may pair up one student who investigated scientific exploration with one who researched geographic exploration so they can build on each other's thinking.

3. **Introduce a New Case Study:** Introduce a new case study, intentionally selecting one that will encourage students to rethink their ideas. For example, let's say a group of students studying migration generalize that *Migrants* seek new *opportunities* and better *living conditions*. In this case, we may expose students to slavery and other examples of forced migration. Then we would ask students to adjust their conceptual understanding to fit all case studies explored. In some cases, this may be as simple as adding a qualifier such as *often* or *sometimes*.

STRATEGY FOR TRANSFER

How Does It Connect?

Best for: Grades K–8

Purpose: This strategy provides an opportunity to understand new case studies, while returning to previously developed conceptual understandings throughout the year. It helps students connect units, see relevance in current events, and apply their learning flexibly. This strategy is shared with permission from *Concept-Based Inquiry in Action* (Marschall & French, 2018).

Figure 7.22

How Does It Connect?

How It Works:

1. **Present a New Case Study:** Share a new case study with the class that relates to previously developed conceptual understandings. This could be a news article, video, personal anecdote, or current event.

2. **Make a Connection:** Pose the question that asks students to compare the new case study with previous case studies: How does it connect? The question invites students to connect two case studies using a concept or conceptual understanding (see Figure 7.22). We can leave the prompt open or be more specific by directly referencing a concept or conceptual understanding we would like to assess.

3. **Students Respond:** Students may share thinking in a variety of ways: in pictures or diagrams; through small-group or whole class discussion; using art or drama; or in a short, written statement or essay. However, it can be as simple as writing a response on a sticky note and sharing with a peer!

4. **Promote Use of Evidence:** Look for evidence of synergistic thinking, where students move between factual and conceptual levels of thinking. What evidence do students provide for their thinking?

In this chapter, we've explored the role of concepts and conceptual understandings in promoting transfer of learning to novel situations and contexts. This enables learners to make sense of current and future issues they encounter and builds their global competence. By identifying concepts and conceptual understandings that reflect knowledge and skill learning in our unit planning, we ensure our students' learning is future-proofed against the current exponential development of information. In the next chapter, we consider how students can become global citizens who take action on issues. Student action represents one of the most powerful forms of transfer of learning. It also helps students develop their identities as changemakers, who can make a tangible difference to local and global communities.

PAUSE AND REFLECT

- How can conceptual thinking allow students to deeply understand current and future issues?

- How might you be able to determine transferable concepts and conceptual understandings from your curriculum to include in unit planning?

- How might you promote conceptual thinking as students engage in factual or skills-based learning? Where might there be natural stopping points in a unit to encourage synthesis of learning?

PART IV

ACT: PARTICIPATING AS GLOBAL CITIZENS

Aims of the Phase

- Nurture global citizenship identities.
- Critically evaluate texts to advocate for social change.
- Develop, implement, and reflect on solutions in partnership with others.

CHAPTER EIGHT

CITIZENSHIP WITHIN AND BEYOND THE CLASSROOM

LIVING MULTIPLE CITIZENSHIP IDENTITIES

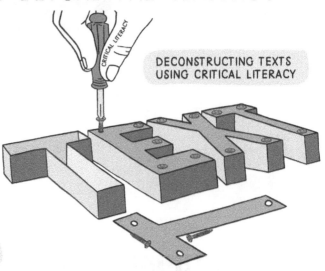

DECONSTRUCTING TEXTS USING CRITICAL LITERACY

DEVELOPING INFORMED SOLUTIONS

Who is impacted by this issue in our community and around the world?

What and where is the greatest need?

What action has been taken on this issue that we could connect to or learn from?

What are the intended and unintended consequences this action could have?

What does success look like, and how will we evaluate it?

FOSTERING AUTHENTIC PARTICIPATION

ADVOCATING FOR NATURE

CITIZENSHIP WITHIN AND BEYOND THE CLASSROOM

"One day I will be an ancestor and I want my descendents to know that I used my voice so that they could have a future."

—Autumn Peltier, Chief Water Commissioner for Anishinabek Nation

This chapter explores the following Tenets of a Pedagogy for People, Planet, and Prosperity:

- Engage students in shared decision making.

- Design inquiry-based experiences for the application of learning, such as projects.

- Promote global citizenship to extend to all living beings.

- Advocate for critical consumerism, extending to media and other sources of information.

- Promote solution-focused thinking, purposeful action, and reflection.

In Chapter 2, we discuss the importance of creating democratic classrooms that build values such as inclusion, respect, voice, and participation, as well as concepts core to citizenship, like rights, responsibilities, peace, and conflict. We also argue that we should view the classroom as a microcosm of society and allow our students to experience firsthand what makes a just community through their actions within it. Yet in line with our aspiration for students to transfer their learning *up and out* to the wider world, citizenship in the classroom needs to be coupled with citizenship *beyond* it. As the following Spotlight demonstrates, students can create ideas of value and take meaningful action as part of the learning process.

●●● SPOTLIGHT ON GLOBAL CITIZENSHIP

SDG PROJECTS AT XI'AN LIANGJIATAN INTERNATIONAL SCHOOL

Founded in 2004, "To provide a non-profit education focused on enabling confident, open-minded global citizens through life-long learning and a sense of community,"

(Continued)

(Continued)

Xi'an Liangjiatan International School in China has made the United Nations Sustainable Development Goals (SDGs) an embedded part of the secondary school. Through regular engagement and discussion about the goals in project-based learning time, students understand their personal responsibility in helping the world meet the 17 SDGs by 2030. To this end, Middle Years Programme (MYP) 1–4 students (12–16 year olds) are involved in interdisciplinary SDG Projects every year. For 1 week, mixed-age groups of 8–10 students tackle specific aspects of an SDG of choice through student-led projects. The week culminates in a summit where students hear about and from their peers about their research. Of the projects, Secondary Principal Daun Yorke says, "Students put their minds and hearts into these ungraded projects that have become part of the fabric of our secondary school culture. This is student agency in action."

A key focus of the week is considering root causes of issues and potential sustainable solutions that address them. For example, Jarry Liu and a team of students investigated SDG #7 Affordable and Clean Energy, looking into how renewable energy can be generated through bicycle use. They considered ways that mechanical energy can be turned into electrical energy by adding generators to a bicycle's back wheel. Jarry's passion has led him to look for local solutions to reduce energy use, such as having bikes available in school, where students and staff members can both exercise and generate energy to charge devices at the same time. The SDG Projects encourage students to use learning from across the disciplines flexibly. They allow students to view themselves as capable and competent in affecting change as global citizens.

Figure 8.1

MYP Students Investigate How Bicycles Can Generate Electricity

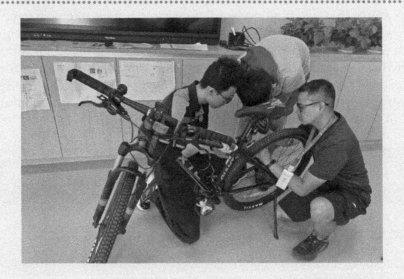

Big Ideas of Global Citizenship

Citizenship derives from the Latin word *civitas* meaning *city* and represents a conception of citizenship from the past, where individuals identified more as members of a city than a country or territory. It reflects an historical worldview smaller in scale, zoomed in tightly on a physical location. This contrasts to the globalized, highly interconnected, and networked nature of the world today. We are connected to places out of reach or even to places that only exist virtually. Through everyday choices we make from transport to diet, our behaviors as citizens extend beyond the local scale to affect others around the globe.

Understanding that the impacts of world's gravest problems are experienced *across* places, a **global citizenship** stance empowers our learners to think critically to understand issues and ideate creatively to improve them. This means that learning for global citizenship develops students' capacity to become entrepreneurial and generate new ideas of value. Yong Zhao, educator and distinguished professor from the University of Kansas, stresses the importance of school in nurturing students' entrepreneurial thinking saying,

> We need to create opportunities for children to exercise their creativity, to refine their creativity, by creating things that matter to other people to make lives better for others, to better the world, to pursue a purpose bigger than themselves. (as cited in Richardson, Henriksen, & Mishra, 2017, p. 3).

As our students become global citizens, they develop the language and toolkit for pursuing their purposes and passions. In doing so, they build a more just, sustainable world.

So what might global citizenship look like in the classroom? Drawing from the United Nations' definition for global citizenship, we have identified some *big ideas* and associated behaviors that can shape how we approach citizenship learning with our students (Figure 8.2). These big ideas are further elaborated on as sections within this chapter.

What Global Citizenship Is Not

It is also important to consider what global citizenship is *not*. Based on people's prior experiences and familiarity with the term, there are a number of assumptions we could make about what global citizens look like and do. In addressing these assumptions head-on, we frame the rest of this chapter and the beliefs that have gone into its construction:

1. Global citizenship is not helping others far away, while being unaware of the effects of one's actions locally. Instead, global citizens reflect on their beliefs and behaviors and the impacts these make on their immediate communities.

2. Global citizenship is not charity, which perpetuates stereotypes and oversimplifies complex issues, while allowing learners to think they have

Figure 8.2

Big Ideas of Global Citizenship

Because . . .	In the classroom, our students . . .
Global citizens develop global citizen identities.	Co-construct understanding about what it means to be a citizen at different scales.
	Value diversity and develop their intercultural understanding.
	Participate as a citizen in the classroom, school, and wider community.
Global citizens interrogate and draw connections between the structures, systems, and perspectives that underpin issues, including at different scales.	Become knowledgeable about local, national, and global systems and structures (e.g., government, climate).
	Critically read media for perspectives, biases, and underlying assumptions.
	Draw connections between and across issues at different scales.
Global citizens engage in purposeful, informed action with others.	Collaboratively develop solutions, which address authentic needs and reduce inequity.
	Are self-aware and reflect on how ethically responsible their behaviors are.
	Plan for, engage in, and reflect on the impact of their actions.

made a difference. Instead, global citizens seek out diverse perspectives and think in systems to understand an issue *before* taking action.

3. Global citizenship is not addressing symptoms of a problem, instead of root causes, because challenging dominant beliefs and values is *uncomfortable.* Instead, global citizens are self-aware and willing to name, question, and challenge inequitable social and political structures that exist.

4. Global citizenship is not applying *one size, fits all* solutions to unique geographical and cultural contexts. Instead, global citizens use their intercultural understanding to develop and test solutions in partnership with the people who are most affected by and knowledgeable about an issue.

5. Global citizenship is not playing the hero and expecting recognition for one's actions. Instead, global citizens feel a sense of personal responsibility and commitment to others, which drives their actions.

Big Idea #1: Global citizens develop global citizen identities.

Social-emotional learning underpins the development of cultural values, global awareness, and a global identity (Singh & Duraiappah, 2020). Through perspective-taking and empathy-promoting experiences (Chapters 4 and 5), Worldwise Learners come to understand who they are, where their beliefs and values originate, and how these apply to situations in the world. An understanding of one's identity is an important precursor to developing a global identity. For this reason, we must provide our learners with experiences that ask them to stretch their conceptions of self. Through our use of discussion and issues-focused learning, teachers can foster the development of an inclusive global identity that exists in harmony with students' other multiple identities. Teachers can also include explicit instruction in identity development that promotes positive self-image as citizens, such as using Strengths Inventories (p. 247) or Changemaker Identities (p. 249). Overall, "the more teachers talk and teach about the world, the stronger the students identify themselves with the world and global activities" (Rapoport, 2020, p. 16). Using a global lens across our curriculum, for example, in our choice of case studies (pp. 83–86), is an easy and practical way to enhance students' global identities.

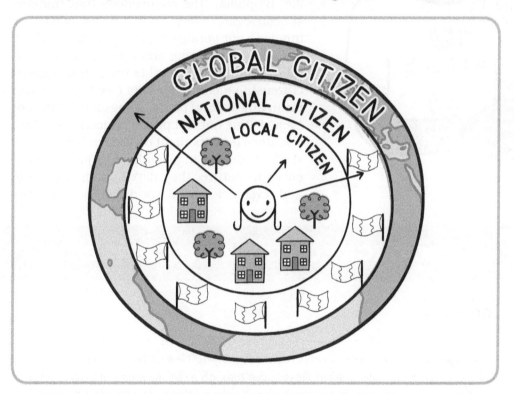

Developing global citizenship identities requires that students consider what it means to be a *planetary* citizen, committed to both social and ecological justice. As David Orr (2004) suggests, "The ecological emergency is about the failure to comprehend our citizenship in the biotic community" (p. 32). Because a traditional view of citizenship focuses on rights and responsibilities within *human* communities, we have engaged in actions without considering the detrimental impacts they have on ecosystems. These actions have in many cases brought our planet's life systems to the precipice. We have forgotten that we are a part of ecosystems and rely on them for essentials like water, food, medicine, and air. Unless we interrogate the idea that we are separate from the natural world, we perpetuate the myth that our planet is inexhaustible. Just as we cannot participate meaningfully in national elections if we do not understand how our government systems function, understanding natural laws and planetary limits are requisite learning for any global citizen. We recommend the Cloud Institute's Education for Sustainability Standards and Performance Indicators as essential student learning in this area (https://cloudinstitute.org/cloud-efs-standards).

We have an obligation to teach our students how to advocate for both human *and* non-human beings. This ecological aspect of global citizenship starts by nurturing our students' connectedness to nature. From birth, children are naturally drawn to the living world: They find worms, spot grasshoppers, or watch birds as they create mesmerizing flocking patterns. These are signs of biophilia, or our love of life. Biophilia, "the connections that humans subconsciously seek with the rest of life," is innate to our youngest learners (Wilson, 1999, p. 350). Appreciating and connecting to natural environments is vital to promoting a global citizenship identity. For city dwellers, this can mean time in local parks, going on field trips, or even visiting natural places remotely as citizen scientists (see Spotlight on Citizen Science). As students engage in playful, imaginative experiences in nature, they develop empathy, awe, and reverence for the world and its creatures.

●●● SPOTLIGHT ON CITIZEN SCIENCE

ZOONIVERSE

Zooniverse, a collaboration between organizations, universities, and the Adler Planetarium in Chicago, is a citizen science portal, home to nearly 100 live citizen science projects. Volunteers can contribute to scientific research through a diverse range of projects that includes counting penguins in remote regions (Penguin Watch), locating and drawing around the center of organelles affected by disease (Science Scribbler), and identifying asteroids in Hubble Space Telescope images (Asteroid Hunter). Zooniverse grapples with the issue of what scientists should do with large data sets by inviting interested volunteers to participate in the research process. Far from an isolated, intellectual exercise, Zooniverse projects have deepened our understanding of the planet, and beyond, and even led to concrete policy changes. For example, research from Penguin Watch has helped set the boundaries for protected areas for penguins to fish in the Southern Ocean.

Citizen science builds students' identities as global citizens by allowing them to think at multiple scales and often about faraway places, changing their perspective about the world around them. Tracking the movement of thousands of animals migrating on the Serengeti, for instance, can allow a child to develop a connection to a place never visited or inspire a range of questions that lead to independent inquiry. Importantly, this sense of connection is coupled with an authentic purpose, drawn from project aims. As founder of Zooniverse, Chris Lintott explains, "Citizen science allows all of us as citizens of the world to contribute to our understanding of it" (C. Lintott, personal communication, August 5, 2020). Promoting access and inclusion, Zooniverse encourages scientific engagement with the world regardless if a volunteer is 5 or 95.

Using a platform like Zooniverse promotes both playful and slow interactions by students. The process of unhurried observation of data-rich images brings enhanced awareness, where students can pay individual attention and allow themselves to be surprised. For example, when categorizing animals in Snapshot Serengeti, students may come to notice patterns about which animals are visible in the morning, middle of the day, or evening. As students immerse themselves in a project's data, they begin to generate hypotheses about what they are seeing. As Chris Lintott shares, "There's a big difference between the textbook exercise and 'Here are 50 galaxies that no one has ever seen before. What do you see?'" Because there are no right answers, shifting the role of the teacher from a repository of information to a co-collaborator is vital when participating in citizen science.

How might citizen science support a range of learning aims in the classroom? In addition to building knowledge and understanding related to a specific area like ecosystems, projects can be used to develop

- **Numeracy** through application and consolidation of counting strategies
- **Data literacy** related to data interpretation, sample size, and scientific disagreement. Specific classroom resources to engage learners in discussing uncertain data are provided by Zooniverse
- **Scientific literacy** related to the process of hypothesis generation and the nature of evidence

Scan this QR code to learn more about Zooniverse, or visit zooniverse.org

---

Figure 8.3

An Image From Zooniverse's Penguin Watch

Reprinted with permission from Zooniverse.

Big Idea #2: Global citizens interrogate and draw connections between the structures, systems, and perspectives that underpin issues, including at different scales.

Becoming globally minded requires that students can toggle out and engage in *big picture* thinking, for example, by using systems thinking (Chapter 6) and conceptual thinking (Chapter 7). Being globally minded also means students must become *critically literate* and learn how to read texts for perspectives, biases, and underlying assumptions. This includes identifying how believable a text is by considering its credibility and reliability (e.g., the ability to trust the *who* and *what* of a source). In doing so, students can see how concepts of power and control apply to the construction of texts and to realities in the world more broadly.

We use the word *text* as a catch-all for any form of media, such as a picture book, newspaper article, photograph, artwork, map, advertisement, or film. As we advocate for use of multiple forms of media when exploring issues, we view critical literacy practices as deeply intertwined with media and digital literacy. Critical literacy enables students to identify structures and systems, which advantage or disadvantage particular backgrounds, identities, and ways of thinking. By understanding the way that texts influence beliefs and behaviors, students can develop solutions, which "contribute to changing inequitable ways of being and problematic social practices" (Vasquez, Janks, & Comber, 2019, p. 307).

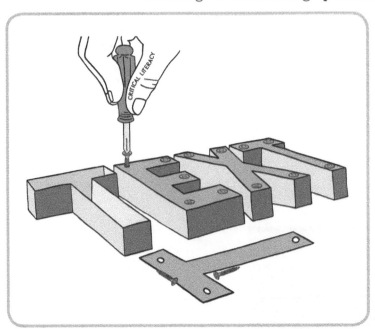

With the core belief that all texts are socially constructed, **critical literacy** is the practice of *deconstructing* a text. Critical literacy is like a screwdriver, enabling us to dismantle the language, structure, and perspective of a text just like we would the parts of a home appliance. In doing so, we can identify underlying messages. These may be a text's bias or the way a text promotes certain power structures, such as affirming stereotypes or cultural norms. Through critical literacy practices, students become aware of messages in a text, reflect on whose voice is being heard or silenced, examine how social and political structures may promote inequity, and use language to advocate for social change. Lewison, Leland, and Harste (2015) refer to these as four dimensions of critical literacy: disrupting the commonplace, considering multiple viewpoints, focusing on the sociopolitical, and taking action.

A key understanding our students gain through critical literacy practices is that texts are *never* neutral. They reflect perspectives held by the author, which can be transferred to the reader. Because texts can influence us, it is vital to move beyond superficial messages to ask questions about the deeper structural levels of a text. Let's look at a quick example using two map projections (Figures 8.4 and 8.5). Although they are both political maps that show the borders between countries, they differ vastly in the way they represent space. Just like the portrait can never fully represent the portrait sitter's three-dimensional face, maps always have distortions formed by the way cartographers choose to represent space.

The first map uses the Mercator projection and the second reflects the Gall-Peters projection. The Mercator projection notably distorts the sizes of land masses as they move away from the equator, meaning Northern Hemisphere continents take prominence. In reality, South America is nine times larger than Greenland, but they are represented as nearly the same size on the Mercator projection. Drawn by Flemish cartographer Geradus Mercator in 1569, the Mercator map was created with reference to colonial trade routes. Designed to help European sailors navigate the globe, imperialism and colonialism are etched into this projection. The Gall-Peters map, although not without its own controversies, stretches continents to give them a proportionally accurate amount of space. Comparing Greenland with South America, we can now see that its actual area is much smaller than the southern continent. If you're interested in learning more about the size of countries or continents in relation to each other (or inviting students to explore this), we highly recommend The True Size (https://thetruesize.com).

By inviting our students to ask questions such as "Who made the map? Who was it made for? Why was it made?" we can better understand how a map-maker's choices shape the representation of space. We can identify perspectives

Figures 8.4 and 8.5

Mercator and Galls-Peters Map Projections

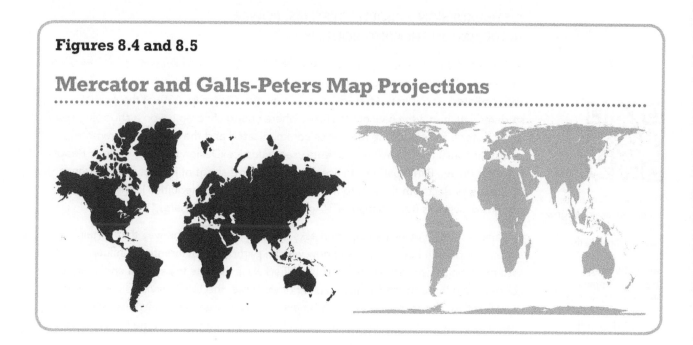

about which countries or places are deemed more important for particular audiences. These perspectives often reflect dominant groups around the globe, because the ability to produce media often comes with power and authority. As educators, we must view students' interactions with texts as opportunities to critique established realities and conscientiously choose texts for them to examine. We recommend seeing how other educators are using critical literacy to engage in anti-racist and anti-bias teaching. Check out #DisruptTexts on Twitter and the thought-provoking work of co-founders Tricia Ebarvia, Lorena Germán, Dr. Kimberly N. Parker, and Julia Torres at https://disrupttexts.org/.

Just as texts are socially constructed from particular perspectives, so are the ways we read them. Because we read texts using our prior knowledge and experiences, the process of making meaning from a text is shaped by our beliefs and values. Beliefs and values act as subconscious filters of information. Using tools such as the Ladder of Inference (p. 113), we can encourage students to reflect on their beliefs and slow the process of drawing conclusions. This is particularly important when students read information from multiple competing points of view. The Waters Center for Systems Thinking calls this "going down the ladder," providing useful metaphorical language that can remind students to consider their mental models. Critical literacy practices can be transformative for our students, allowing them to reimagine texts to promote a more socially just world. The following Spotlight using a Project Zero JusticexDesign thinking routine illustrates the power of critical literacy for students.

●●● SPOTLIGHT ON CRITICAL LITERACY

JUSTICEXDESIGN'S PEOPLE, SYSTEMS, POWER, PARTICIPATION THINKING ROUTINE

A Grade 4 class was learning about sustainable businesses and consumer choices. As a case study, the class investigated the toy system: how toys are designed, manufactured, and marketed to children. After creating Connected Circles (p. 180) of the system, students watched a *toy haul* on YouTube, where young children go on a shopping spree in a toy store. To unpack the messages communicated and the way these promote particular consumer behaviors, students used a JusticexDesign thinking routine: People, Systems, Power, Participation. JusticexDesign is an off-shoot of Project Zero's Agency by Design project with the aim to help learners "recognize inequities in the everyday designs of systems they encounter" (Agency by Design, n.d., para. 1).

People, Systems, Power, Participation asks learners to identify the way that certain systems or people have power and how we can participate differently to influence systems. Using this strategy, students identified ways that the toy system encourages consumption through media influencers. For example, the toy haul video consistently used positive language. The word no is never heard, nor are any questions asked by parents. There is no discussion between children and parents about the materials or

Scan this QR code to access JusticexDesign's People, Systems, Power, Participation thinking routine, or visit agencybydesign .org/sites/default/ files/People_Systems_ Power_Participation_ AbD%20Tool.pdf

manufacturing of toys as children put them into the cart. At the end of this routine, students concluded that *not* engaging in behaviors, for example not watching influencer videos or not buying particular toys, can also change systems to make them more sustainable. Access JusticexDesign's People, Systems, Power, Participation thinking routine by scanning the QR code. A Google Doc template of this protocol, with simplified questions and explanations of types of power for elementary learners, can be found on our companion site.

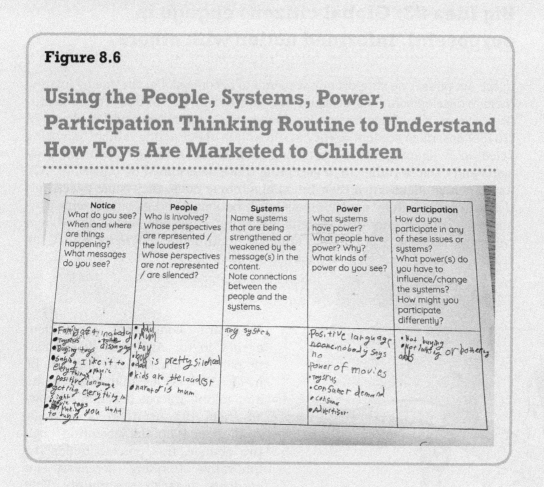

Figure 8.6

Using the People, Systems, Power, Participation Thinking Routine to Understand How Toys Are Marketed to Children

Notice	People	Systems	Power	Participation
What do you see? When and where are things happening? What messages do you see?	Who is involved? Whose perspectives are represented / the loudest? Whose perspectives are not represented / are silenced?	Name systems that are being strengthened or weakened by the message(s) in the content. Note connections between the people and the systems.	What systems have power? What people have power? Why? What kinds of power do you see?	How do you participate in any of these issues or systems? What power(s) do you have to influence/change the systems? How might you participate differently?
• Family of 4, nobody • Toyrus, some • Buying toys disagree • Saying I like it to everything physic • positive language • getting everything in sighte • movie toys • thinking you want to buy?	• dad • mum • boy • boy • dad is pretty silenced • kids are the loudest • narator is mum	toy system	Positive language noone nobody says no power of movies • toysrus • consumer demand • consumer • Advertiser	• Not buying • Not looking or bothering ads

While the free flow of information is essential to a democratic society, we live during a complex era flooded with advertisements, propaganda, and misinformation. Given our hyperconnected world, the World Economic Forum (2013) argues that misinformation can spark "digital wildfires" that cause havoc in the world. From seeding hate to influencing ballots cast around the world, misinformation is pervasive. It is a threat to shaping local and global citizens who act with agency. The ability to locate and access relevant and accurate information is critical to becoming media-literate. All students must learn how to locate and recognize credible, reliable information.

Evaluating sources is also an essential life skill. By teaching how to separate fact from fiction, students develop higher-order thinking skills that allow them to make informed decisions as citizens and consumers. For the purposes of this chapter, we *zoom in* on strategies that allow students to deconstruct texts for underlying messages. For an excellent resource for evaluating sourcing, we recommend Stanford History Education Group's Historical Thinking Chart. Supporting students with sourcing, corroboration, and contextualization of a text through guiding questions, this chart can be used across the curriculum and not only for history units. You can access it using the QR code in the margin.

Scan this QR code to access Stanford History Education Group's Historical Thinking Chart, or visit sheg .stanford.edu/ history-lessons/ historical-thinking-chart

Big Idea #3: Global citizens engage in purposeful, informed action with others.

In the Act phase, we support our students to become global citizens by inviting them to develop solutions to issues and take action. Key to this process is student agency. The Organisation for Economic Co-operation and Development (2018b) describes student agency stating, "It is about acting rather than being acted upon; shaping rather than being shaped; and making responsible decisions and choices rather than accepting those determined by others" (p. 32). As we help students turn their intentions into actions, they come to see how they can meaningfully contribute as local, national, and global citizens. This approach runs counter to a "citizens-in-waiting" conception of childhood, recognizing the capacity of children to make an authentic difference *now* (Cook & Beer, 2018).

FOSTERING AUTHENTIC PARTICIPATION

A central component of student agency in the Act phase is authentic participation. Children want to be involved in issues that affect them, and taking informed action empowers them. Because there is no single *right answer* in implementing positive change, this process builds the innovative thinking necessary for students to tackle uncertainty. That said, we cannot ask our students to devise solutions for issues they care about and then provide little space or time to make these a reality. In doing so, we communicate that their ideas matter little outside the confines of the classroom. Instead, we involve students in making decisions about their intended actions using a democratic classroom approach (Chapter 2).

Here students shape the development of actions rather than be shaped by the teacher's preconceived ideas about what solutions should look like. In this model, we think differently about the power we have as adults. We must recognize our inherent "power to" as educators: *power to* give students a voice, *power to* help students find an audience, *power to* highlight students' capabilities as instruments of positive change. This may be a support role, but it comes with immense responsibility. So what does authentic participation look like as students develop solutions (Figure 8.7)?

Figure 8.7

Authentic Student Participation in Solution Development

Authentic participation involves:

- A relevant issue being explored by students, where they have the capacity to make a measurable difference

- Clear co-constructed goals and targets (e.g., *What will we achieve? How will we know?*)

- Students' views being valued and respected

- Honesty and openness from the educator, which enables students to make informed choices

- Shared decision making between educators and students

- Child-friendly language and structures for developing and discussing solutions

- An active stance to inspire change and move away from "slacktivism"

- Adequate time and resources for implementing and reflecting on solutions

- Adult support, where required

We must recognize our inherent "power to" as educators: power to give students a voice, power to help students find an audience, power to highlight students' capabilities as instruments of positive change.

DEVELOPING INFORMED SOLUTIONS WITH STUDENTS

Although we share decision-making power with our students, it is important that potential solutions to issues are purposeful and informed. We want to encourage students to develop and implement solutions that go below the surface to address root causes. The Institute for Humane Education (2020) calls these "solutionary solutions." From their Solutionary Guidebook, a solutionary solution:

- Reflects a deep understanding of the complexities of the problem, its causes, and the underlying systems that perpetuate it

- Strives not to harm people, animals, or the environment and seeks to avoid unintended negative consequences

- Works to positively transform the underlying systems that perpetuate the problem. (p. 19)

Recognizing that learning across the K–8 continuum looks very different, we lay out what this might look like for children of different ages and developmental stages (Figure 8.8). Note that we have intentionally chosen issues that have been explored in other chapters.

Figure 8.8

Example Solutions Across the K–8 Continuum

Age of Students	Issue	Root Causes Identified by Students	Solution
Kindergarten	Pollinators	Pollinator habitats are being destroyed due to development and urbanization. Pollinators that migrate need host and flowering plants to survive and reproduce.	Students create a pollinator garden with host and flowering plants on school grounds, taking into account the needs of local species. They make a plan for taking care of the garden after it is planted.
Grade 3	Migration	Migration often occurs when individuals are pushed or pulled toward better life conditions. Push factors include war, lack of safety, or famine. After arrival in a country, they can face many barriers such as prejudice.	Students interview migrants in the local community and use them to create picture books for younger children in the school. Telling the story of each migrant interviewed, they promote understanding and compassion for their circumstances to reduce prejudice in society.
Grade 7	Ocean Plastic Pollution	Single-use plastic and littering directly into local waterways contributes to plastic pollution in the ocean.	Students create a "No Single-Use Plastic" Pledge, which is signed by students, teachers, and family members. People who sign the pledge commit to small actions, such as bringing a reusable water bottle with them and saying no to plastic straws and cutlery.

Scan this QR code to access an editable version of the reflective question graphic organizer, or visit **teachworldwise .com/resources**.

It is important to note that students must have a deep understanding of an issue to develop solutions that address root causes. As students apply perspective-taking and systems thinking tools to issues (Chapters 4 and 6), they can identify meaningful *ways in* to improve a situation. We also ask students to research what has already been done to solve the issue locally and globally and consider their constraints (e.g., time, money). To ensure that these actions benefit communities with the fewest unintended consequences, we encourage students to engage in partnerships with those affected and underpin their actions with honesty, humility, critical thinking, and reflection. These ideas are summarized as reflective questions in Figure 8.9. These questions are also available as an editable graphic organizer using the QR code in the margin. The following Spotlight elaborates on the importance of solutionary solutions and developing students who view themselves as capable and competent changemakers.

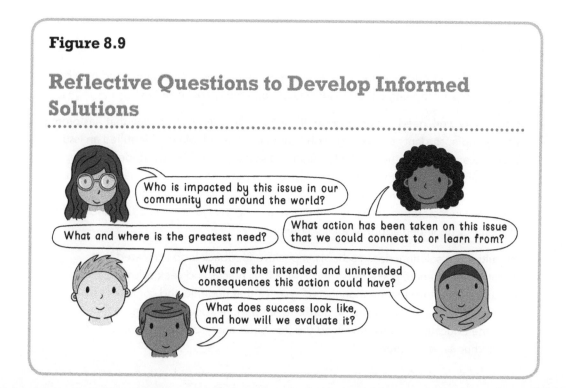

Figure 8.9

Reflective Questions to Develop Informed Solutions

Who is impacted by this issue in our community and around the world?

What and where is the greatest need?

What action has been taken on this issue that we could connect to or learn from?

What are the intended and unintended consequences this action could have?

What does success look like, and how will we evaluate it?

●●● SPOTLIGHT ON INFORMED SOLUTIONS

AN INTERVIEW WITH ZOE WEIL FROM INSTITUTE FOR HUMANE EDUCATION

Solutionary [sul-LOO-shuh ner-ee]

A person who identifies inhumane, unsustainable, and unjust systems and then develops solutions that are healthy and equitable for people, animals, and the environment.

Co-founded by Zoe Weil, the Institute for Humane Education is a nonprofit organization that works to create a just, humane, sustainable world through education. In her 2010 TEDx Talk, "The World Becomes What You Teach," Weil called for the revisioning of the purpose of schooling. Because the education system underpins all other social, economic, and environmental systems, Weil suggests that it is critical to prepare students with the knowledge, motivation, and skills to be "conscientious choice-makers and engaged changemakers for a restored and healthy and humane world for all." Such individuals are *solutionaries*.

What distinguishes solutionary work from other types of problem-based learning or philanthropic action, such as fundraising to support a cause? While Weil emphasizes that supporting students in humanitarian work is valuable and needed, solution-seeking typically ends at that step. In other words, it does not address the root causes of the problem so that it is solved. Solutionary work, however, aims to address *solvable problems* at the causal level to develop *solutionary solutions*. Broad, complex issues like climate change or poverty can certainly be examined for their root causes and possible

(Continued)

(Continued)

solutions, but individuals or groups of students cannot solve them alone and may be more successful tackling a local manifestation of a big global problem.

Solutionary work need not be original. It can include scaling up an idea that has promise. For example, students at Deering High School in Portland, Maine, identified an issue that concerned them: their school's punitive disciplinary policy. The students analyzed the systems that perpetuate the school-to-prison pipeline and researched solutions that were effective elsewhere. They created an alternative disciplinary process for their school grounded in restorative justice with the goal to help everyone succeed in school. The students' school then adopted their solution!

By cultivating solutionaries in schools, a positive feedback loop is created that encourages others to make *most good* (MOGO) choices and seek solutions that positively transform the interconnected systems that underlie and contribute to the problems that affect all life on Earth. To learn more about the Institute for Humane Education and to download the free Solutionary Guidebook, visit https://humaneeducation.org/

TYPES OF ACTION

As students come to develop their solutions, we introduce them to the four action types described by Berger Kaye (2010) and explain how each type meets different community needs. These are direct action, indirect action, advocacy, and research for action. Definitions and examples for each of these action types can be found in Figure 8.10.

The four types of action provide useful, common language to help students justify why particular solutions might be better than others. For instance, imagine a community is a *food desert* with limited access to healthy and affordable food. Individuals living in such communities can become undernourished as well as obese, because fast food restaurants and convenience stores are the only accessible food options. Some students may argue that they could use indirect action to try to improve this issue, donating and sending fresh food to the community on a regular basis. This might bring temporary relief, but the larger question would be whether it produces sustainable, long-term change. Such action would likely not address root causes. Instead, students might choose to meet the needs of the community by coupling advocacy and direct action. By raising awareness of food deserts as an equity issue and helping community members grow their own food in a community garden, students might be able to affect more lasting change.

That said, action should not always happen external to oneself. A critical part of being a conscientious citizen is recognizing our complicitness in unsustainable systems, whether they be connected to people, planet, or prosperity. We need to ask ourselves: What should we continue doing? What should we do differently? How should we think differently? What do we need to let go of? For example, in the Spotlight of Grade 4 students exploring the toy system

Figure 8.10

Actions Types and Examples

Described by Berger Kaye (2010) as Service Learning Types

Direct Action: Acts of service that directly involve the recipient or environment. **Examples:** • Composting food waste • Planting along a riverbank • Reading to younger children • Boycotting unethical products	**Indirect Action:** Working through an intermediary, such as an aid organization. **Examples:** • Holding a fundraiser for an NGO • Conducting a food or clothing drive for hurricane victims • Collecting school supply donations for less fortunate families
Advocacy: Raising awareness about a particular issue to build support or change behavior. **Examples:** • Creating an online petition calling for legislation on pesticide use • Developing and holding an exhibition or a performance on the right to play • Holding a film screening on water scarcity • Writing letters to local government officials about the need for community bicycle lanes	**Research for Action:** Processing and representing information; further self-initiated research. **Examples:** • Undertaking a local biodiversity survey • Mapping the local community to understand access for people with mobility issues • Contributing to a community of research, such as Frontiers for Young Minds, where scientific research is peer reviewed by 8 to 15 year olds: https://kids.frontiersin.org/

(p. 238), children identified the need to stop watching influencer videos that could promote their own consumption. Unless our students can change their thinking, habits, and behaviors to reflect their learning, we cannot expect others to do the same. Change starts from within.

Strategies for Global Citizenship

The following strategies support learners to build their citizenship identities, engage in critical literacy, and develop solutions to issues. They build on strategies in prior chapters, where learners connect to and deeply understand an issue. As students create solutions in the Act phase, we ask them to build on their learning in the Connect and Understand phases. For example, they may use ideas recorded in graphic organizers, such as the Sustainability Compass (p. 116), Connected Circles (p. 180), Root Cause Trees (p. 191), to brainstorm appropriate actions. Remember that many of the strategies in Chapter 2 related to co-planning can also be modified to support the planning of student-led action. While reading through the strategies in this chapter, reflect on the way that strategies in other chapters may complement them.

STRATEGIES FOR GLOBAL CITIZENSHIP

Strategy	Description	Page Number
STRATEGIES FOR CITIZENSHIP IDENTITY		
Strengths Inventory	Students identify personal character strengths and give examples of actions that demonstrate them.	247
Changemaker Identities	Students uncover qualities of changemakers and reflect on their own identities.	249
Circles of Compassion	Students widen their circles of compassion, reflecting on how compassion can spark action.	251
STRATEGIES FOR CRITICAL LITERACY		
Critical Questions	Students explore critical, multilayered questions that promote perspective-taking, empathy, and understanding about people, places, and events.	253
Close Read Analysis	Students engage in multiple readings of the same text to deconstruct it.	255
Paired Texts	Students compare and contrast two texts to identify the messages each may contain.	257
Frames	Students explore how the framing of an image changes its meaning using paper frames.	259
STRATEGIES FOR DEVELOPING SOLUTIONS AND TAKING ACTION		
Focused Observation	Students gather data from and about a community through focused observation.	261
Rapid Prototyping	Students develop prototypes, get feedback, and revise their possible solutions.	264
Artivism	Students create artwork and/or performances to advocate for change related to an issue.	267
Reflection on Action	Students reflect on the outcomes of their action and set goals for future solution development.	269

STRATEGY FOR CITIZENSHIP IDENTITY
Strengths Inventory

Best for: Grades K–8

Purpose: Character strengths are "pathways to greater self-awareness and confidence" (VIA Institute on Character, 2020, para. 1). When these strengths are recognized, individuals feel a sense of ownership and authenticity in who they are, the desire to display and apply their strengths, and choose activities that revolve around them (Seligman, 2002). Strengths-based learning also cultivates both individual and collective well-being and promotes culturally sustaining practices in schools (Paris, 2012). The following protocol is from Michael Fauteux, Executive Director and Co-Founder of GiveThx, a research-based curriculum and app for schools that strengthens well-being and social-emotional skills using gratitude science.

Scan the QR code to learn more about Give Thx, or visit givethx.org

How It Works:

1. **Explore Character Strengths:** Introduce the concept of *character strengths*. The VIA Institute on Character site outlines 24 strengths categorized by

   - **wisdom** (creativity, curiosity, judgment, love of learning, perspective);

   - **courage** (bravery, perseverance, honesty, zest);

   - **humanity** (love, kindness, social intelligence);

   - **justice** (teamwork, fairness, leadership);

   - **temperance** (forgiveness, humility, prudence, self-regulation); and

   - **transcendence** (appreciation of beauty and excellence, gratitude, hope, humor, spirituality).

   Identify character strengths that are appropriate for your students' ages and background knowledge. For Grades K–5 students, literature like *True You: Authentic Strengths for Kids* by Fatima Doman (2018) can introduce these concepts. Students ages 10 to 14 may self-assess their character strengths using the YIA Youth Character Strengths tool (https://www.viacharacter.org/professionals/youth).

2. **Peer or Group Gratitude Practice:** Engage students in recognizing character strengths in peers by writing individual gratitude notes. Model this practice using sample prompts like, "Thanks ___for___. It was helpful because ___." If using GiveThx, students may tag their gratitude note by character strength.

3. **Reflect:** Invite students to reflect on the personal character strengths noticed by others by answering the following:

   - **Strengths:** Look at your gratitude notes. What is a top reason people are grateful for you?

   - **Evidence:** What behavior best shows this strength in action?

- **Impact:** What did you do? How did the person benefit and/or feel?
- **Self:** How does being recognized for this strength make you feel? Any surprises?

Emphasize student agency over their actions and their impact on others.

Extensions:

- **Share Out:** Presenting to a partner or the class can be powerful.
- **More Evidence:** Require multiple gratitude notes and/or past reflections as evidence.
- **Growth Areas:** Change the activity to identify a growth area.
- **Student-Led Conference:** This is a great task to share at parent meetings.

Strengthening Teacher-Student Relationships Through Gratitude Practice

When noticing that his adolescent students struggled with their identities, Grade 7 teacher Donovan T. Hall from Impact Academy in California introduced gratitude practice as a way to recognize character strengths and to build stronger teacher-student relationships. He explains that "many students hold the unconscious belief that their teachers value them only when they do well academically. I use gratitude statements to connect students and teachers on a deeper level, creating feelings of safety and inclusion for everyone."

To introduce gratitude practice, Hall presents the following formula:

I am so grateful for (person) for (action they took) because (impact it had on them).

With practice, students expand on this sentence frame. For example, one student wrote to him:

I am very grateful for you because you understand students' needs and don't get frustrated. When I ask questions in class, I feel like I can ask any clarifying questions whenever I need to, not worrying about what others think. This makes others feel free to ask questions and makes their work turn out better. Thank you.

Donovan explains that when gratitude is reciprocated between teachers and students, each member of the learning community is able to analyze the positive impact they have on others.

STRATEGY FOR CITIZENSHIP IDENTITY
Changemaker Identities

Best for: Grades K–8

Purpose: The primary purpose of this strategy is to help students see what makes a changemaker and relate this to their identities. By learning about historical and contemporary changemakers, both those within the local community and those known internationally, students identify values, attitudes, and approaches they can use to inspire change. Likewise they come to realize how the idea of being a *changemaker* is multifaceted and does not look the same in every context. The Story of Stuff Project (2017), for instance, breaks down the roles changemakers may take into categories: resister, networker, nurturer, investigator, communicator, and builder. By choosing to highlight changemakers in these different roles, students can connect their Passion Maps (p. 56) or Strengths Inventory (p. 247) to one of these areas. This strategy can also easily be modified to help students identify what solutions to issues may have already been developed.

How It Works:

There are many ways that we can use case studies of changemakers to support students in becoming local, national, and global citizens. Here are just a few ideas:

1. **Choose Changemakers:** Choose changemakers appropriate for the age and developmental stage of your learners. Where possible, include local changemakers, who can be interviewed in person. Picture books can also be used. If students are looking to develop solutions to a particular issue, such as homelessness, we can also focus our choice of changemakers on individuals looking to improve this.

2. **Research their Beliefs and Actions:** Invite students to research the chosen changemakers. What are their values, beliefs, and actions? How do these relate to each other? Use models such as the Iceberg Model (p. 110) or Ladder of Inference (p. 113) to look at relationships between these aspects of the changemaker.

3. **Consider Changemaker Barriers and Solutions:** A key aspect of developing a changemaker identity is recognizing how barriers to change are always present. These may influence what makes a successful solution in a particular context. Here we invite students to use the SWBST protocol to look at relationships between motivations, barriers, and solutions:

   - Somebody (individual)
   - Wanted (wish)
   - But (barriers)
   - So (possible solutions)
   - Then (what was done)

Figure 8.11

Changemaker Joshua Williams

Image shared with permission.

Scan this QR code to learn more about Joshua's story through a video created by Ashoka. Ashoka has a number of young changemaker stories, which act as powerful provocations for this strategy. You can also access the video at https://youtu.be/S2Elfg-13vk

Here is an example of the SWBST protocol in action using changemaker Joshua Williams:

- **Somebody:** Joshua Williams

- **Wanted:** He wanted to help homeless people in his community because he realized not everyone had access to food, water, and adequate shelter.

- **But:** He realized the complexity of the issue and had no idea where to start or what he could do to assist those around him in his community.

- **So:** He got his aunts and mother together to help him prepare and distribute food to homeless people in his community.

- **Then:** He ended up founding Joshua's Heart Foundation, which has delivered more than 3.2 million pounds of food since 2005 and has helped more than 500,000 individuals. His foundation helps other young people take an initiative to make a change and be their own changemaker. He now creates hope boxes with necessities and delivers food to those in need. He has raised over $2 million dollars for those in poverty and homelessness.

4. **Make Connections:** Using strategies such as those for generalizing in Chapter 7, ask students to make connections across case studies of changemakers (see Connect 4 strategy on p. 217). Likewise ask students to draw similarities between the changemakers researched and their own identities: How did you relate to the changemaker's story? What's similar or different? How might we continue to develop ourselves as changemakers?

STRATEGY FOR CITIZENSHIP IDENTITY
Circles of Compassion

Best for: Grades 4–8

Purpose: Circles of Compassion serves as a springboard for exploring compassion and introducing important social change issues to students. It supports learners in reflecting on their own identities as citizens and how compassion can spark action. It was developed by Nadia Erdolen, Sophia Seeramlal, Shannon Finch, Charley Korns, and Lynne Westmoreland. It has been modified and shared with permission from the Institute for Humane Education.

How It Works:

1. **Develop Stations and Create Charts (Preparation):** Create stations for students to visit, which can help them explore their circles of compassion. The number, type, and content of stations will depend on the age and developmental stage of students. These stations should include components of oppression, exploitation, or suffering, focusing on issues related to People, Planet, and Prosperity. For example, aspects of animal protection, human rights, environmental preservation, racial bias, and consumerism. Make sure to include facts that provide information about the issues introduced at each station.

2. **Introduce Compassion:** Let students know that they will explore their circle of compassion. Ask students to define compassion. Share a definition for compassion, and ask students to make connections to it. For example, "the feeling that arises when you are confronted with another's suffering and feel motivated to relieve that suffering" (Greater Good Magazine, n.d., para. 1).

3. **Create Circles of Compassion:** Provide each individual with a sheet of paper and have them draw a large circle and write their own name in the center of it. Ask them to write the names of everyone and everything included in their circle of compassion (e.g., family, friends, pets) inside the circle. Invite students to share who's included in their circle of compassion and why. Younger students can draw or collage the elements included in their circle of compassion.

4. **Reflect on Quotes:** Share quotes about compassion and encourage students to discuss their reactions to them. Examples might include

   - "Our task must be to free ourselves from this prison by widening our circle of compassion to embrace all living creatures and the whole of nature in its beauty." —Albert Einstein

   - "If you want others to be happy, practice compassion. If you want to be happy, practice compassion." —The Dalai Lama

Scan this QR codes to access a set of printable quotes, or visit **teachworldwise .com/resources**.

5. **Wander and Wonder at Stations:** Give participants time to walk through the stations, exploring the examples at each. For example:

- Have a small wire cage (like those used for dog kennels) just large enough for one to two students to fit into. Invite them to get into the cage and stay for a few minutes. Include information about factory farmed animals kept in such cramped conditions, such as battery hens, veal calves, and female pigs (who are kept in gestation crates), as well as dogs in puppy mills, and fur-bearing animals on fur farms.

- Have a station with large jugs filled with water. Invite participants to carry a jug around for a few minutes, imagining what it would be like to have to carry that heavy water for many miles each day. Include information about people who lack basic resources and how that may relate to our own consumerism.

6. **Return to Circles of Compassion:** Ask participants to return to their seats and draw another circle of compassion and write down who's included in it.

7. **Discuss:** Invite students to share: Has their circle of compassion changed? How? Why or why not? How can we continue to expand our circle of compassion? How might this connect to being a local, national, or global citizen? How might compassion connect to being a changemaker?

STRATEGY FOR CRITICAL LITERACY
Critical Questions

Best for: Grades K–8

Purpose: Reading high-interest picture books or other texts can foster empathy, perspective-taking, intercultural understanding, active listening, and critical thinking (Browett & Ashman, 2008). They can be used to explore global citizenship concepts, such as human rights and responsibilities, peace, equality, and interconnectedness. Because texts can reflect social and political structures, they also provide launch points for exploring issues such as racism and discrimination. Educators can build *critical questions* from read alouds that invite students to identify explicit and underlying messages of a text. These questions support learners in recognizing how texts can affirm or provide counterpoints to dominant perspectives.

How It Works:

1. **Select Appropriate Books:** Consider the purpose of the books and how you intend for students to engage with them. Analyze books for accuracy, authenticity, and representation (Short, 2019), such as by researching the author, origin of publication, and sociocultural and historical context. Engage in a *close reading* of each text, immersing oneself and reacting to it. When selecting global and multicultural texts, Kenyon and Christoff (2020) recommend asking questions, such as "Who has agency and power in the books?" and "Are stories about people from non-dominant groups always about the past?" (p. 406). Choose paired texts to allow students to make comparisons and go beyond *the single story* about a place, culture, or event (see p. 257).

2. **Write Critical Questions:** Identify the concepts and issues to be explored in the book. For example, in *The Paper Bag Princess* by Robert Munsch, the princess conquers a dragon and saves the prince, reversing traditional gender roles found in fairy tales. This book relates to concepts such as gender roles and societal norms. Next, draft questions that will engage students in interrogating the text. For instance, we may ask:

   - How do the princess's actions compare to princesses in other stories?

   - How does the author use the princess's clothing, words, and behaviors to show how she is different from other princesses?

   - What are some common differences between princes and princesses in stories? Why do we expect them to look and act differently?

   - Is it right for people to tell others how to look or act based on their gender?

As they consider such questions, invite students to make judgments using evidence from the text instead of asking for personal reactions. The Prindle Institute for Ethics, which has a focus on philosophy for children, has a database of picture books with a breakdown of related issues that can be explored. Each book is accompanied by sample critical questions.

Scan this QR code to access the Prindle Institute for Ethics database of picture books, or visit prindleinstitute.org/teaching-children-philosophy

3. **Foster Empathy:** While reading the book, help students connect to stories by identifying parallel experiences. This might be as simple as engaging students in a Think-Pair-Share using a question such as "What do you have in common with the story's protagonist?" or "How does the book reflect our common humanity?"

4. **Engage With Critical Questions:** During and after the reading, ask students to reflect on the critical questions. Student ideas can be recorded on chart paper or virtually. Likewise depending on the age of the student, we may ask them to reflect on questions individually or in pairs. What views have students found in the text that they would like to challenge?

Figure 8.12 shows students exploring the language of *human environment* in a unit about natural resource use. They were asked to consider how the term may show or hide our reliance on nature. After engaging with these questions, one student stated:

I think that the term human environment hides our reliance on nature because "human environment" means the environment that humans have made. That means that we made our cities on our own. "Human environment" doesn't acknowledge the nature that we get our materials from.

Figure 8.12

Using Critical Questions

5. **Encourage Students to Ask Questions:** When reading stories about real events and individuals, encourage students to ask questions they may investigate. Students then can investigate beyond the text, affording them to read more broadly and deepen their understanding. These questions may inspire case study choices within a unit.

STRATEGY FOR CRITICAL LITERACY
Close Read Analysis

Best for: Grades K–8

Purpose: In a Close Read Analysis, we slow down the process to deconstruct a text by inviting students to take part in multiple viewings or readings from different perspectives. A central goal of the Close Read Analysis protocol is to encourage students to separate what they are seeing from what they are thinking, feeling, or believing as they engage with a text. This strategy has been modified from the Center for Media Literacy (2011).

How It Works:

1. **Choose Text:** Choose a text related to the issue being studied, which can be read multiple times, once using visuals, and once using either sound or text. For this reason, we recommend multimodal texts that include sufficient visual content. For kindergarten to Grade 2 children, we recommend starting this strategy with short video clips (e.g., 30 seconds or less or a single page of a written text that includes visual elements).

2. **"Read" the Visuals:** This is the first of multiple readings of the text. Ask students to look only at the visual component at the text. What story do the visuals try to tell? What techniques do they use to do this? You may choose to ask students to record ideas on an individual or class chart, which can be built on during each read to facilitate answering the key questions in Step 4.

3. **"Read" the Audio or Text:** Now students engage in a second reading of the text. Either have students close their eyes and listen to the text (for texts with an audio component) or ask them to read written aspects of a text.

4. **Consider the Key Questions:** As students finish these two readings, ask them to consider the key questions found in Figure 8.13. Because some of these questions require a holistic interpretation of the text (e.g., the question about Content), students may benefit from small-group discussion to pull out important messages. The questions specific to Authorship and Format may be completed during the previous readings as they engage with the audio, visual, or written aspects of a text. An editable graphic organizer including these questions can be found here.

Scan this QR code to access an editable graphic organizer, or visit **teachworldwise .com/resources**.

Figure 8.13

Key Questions

Concept	Related Question
Authorship	Who created this message?
Format	What creative techniques are being used to attract and hold my attention?
Audience	How might different people understand this message differently?
Content	What values, lifestyles, voices, or perspectives are represented in, or omitted from, this message?
Purpose	Why is this message being sent?

5. **Review Insights:** Once students have jotted ideas for the key questions, invite a class discussion using the open-ended question, "What did you notice?" This question avoids leading the students to particular conclusions. Instead encourage students to share their opinions and back up their ideas with evidence from the text itself. These are some sentence frames we may provide our students to support their use of textual evidence:

- I think . . . because . . .
- In the text . . . this made me think . . .
- In the text I saw . . . this made me feel . . .
- I think _____'s perspective is included in the text because . . .
- I think _____'s perspective is not included in the text because . . .

STRATEGY FOR CRITICAL LITERACY
Paired Texts

Best for: Grades K–8

Purpose: By pairing texts, whether they be images, paragraphs, videos, or longer pieces of text, students can juxtapose multiple perspectives or messages shared by the authors. Because other texts act as points of comparison, pairing texts can make it easier for students to identify which perspectives are present or absent. When paired with Critical Questions (p. 253), students are able to develop new possibilities for understanding.

How It Works:

1. **Choose Texts to Pair:** Choose texts that have something connected to allow for an interesting comparison, such as the following:

   • Similar theme or issue

   • Different arguments on an issue

   • Same argument but different positions on an issue

   • Nonfiction texts with the same topic but varying focuses

   • Different genres with connecting aspect (e.g., topic, same problem)

   • Different modes (e.g., one written text and one video)

   • Different perspectives or voices

2. **Build Vocabulary and Background Knowledge:** Encourage students to preview the texts to build their vocabulary and background knowledge related to the article. For this purpose, you may choose to use a number of strategies. For example, we may invite students to read in pairs and allocate stopping points in a text (e.g., at the end of each paragraph). At the end of each section, students turn and talk to each other, sharing what they understood and connections they have already made to the text.

3. **Share Ideas with the Whole Class:** For a few minutes, invite students to share a few of their connections with the whole class. This provides us with information about students' prior knowledge as well as the opportunity to discuss any initial questions.

4. **Introduce the Critical Question(s):** Share the critical question(s) for the paired texts. These may come directly from the issue being studied, or students may use a protocol with more generic questions, such as those shared in the Close Read Analysis (p. 255). Learning for Justice (n.d.) also provides overarching categories within which we may choose to design questions specific to a text. Modified as reflective questions for educators, these are:

   • **Linguistic bias:** How might the text include culturally loaded terms or sexist language (e.g., "black sheep," or "fireman" instead of "firefighter")?

   • **Stereotyping:** How might the text perpetuate ethnic, gender, socioeconomic, religious, ability, or cultural stereotypes?

- **Invisibility:** How might the text exclude particular races, family types, socioeconomic class, or cultures? What is the effect of this?

- **Imbalance:** How might a text present an imbalanced representation of different groups (e.g., refugees)?

- **Unreality:** To what extent are sensitive or controversial issues (e.g., slavery, discrimination) glossed over with inaccurate or incomplete information?

5. **Text Analysis:** In pairs, invite students to read and analyze the paired texts. Each student takes one of the two texts then shares their ideas with each other. What's the same or different about the texts? Why might that be? Depending on the age and literacy level of students, we may ask them to highlight and annotate parts of the text or record their findings in a graphic organizer. To ensure students hear multiple perspectives on their paired texts, we can ask pairs to share with another partnership.

6. **Discuss:** Engage the whole class in a discussion about their readings. Their thoughts and opinions can be recorded on class charts, which can be returned to in a study. Prompt students to reflect on which voices were present or absent from the texts and why might this be. Might they need to read other texts to develop a more comprehensive understanding of an issue? Encourage students to consider action they could take to counter any of the messages that were uncovered in the texts.

Paired Texts in Action

INSECT REPRESENTATIONS

As part of their unit on Pollinators, kindergarteners went to a local supermarket to look at the different ways that insects are portrayed on consumer products. Why might insects be represented on the can of insecticide differently than on the jar of honey? What messages are the companies trying to convey? How do these representations connect to threats to pollinators? By thinking about why the same animal might be viewed as both a friend and a foe, students can develop more nuanced perspectives on the issue of protecting pollinators. During this analysis, one kindergartener remarked, "The company showed the insects on their backs, black, and dead to try to make us think that they should not be alive. The insects on the spraycan do not look friendly like the bees on the honey."

Figures 8.14 and 8.15

Paired Texts: Insects on Products

STRATEGY FOR CRITICAL LITERACY
Frames

Best for: Grades K–8

Purpose: Framing is an intentional technique that media producers use to convey a particular message. Frames provides an experiential, low-tech opportunity to discuss how the framing of an image changes its meaning. Students can use frames to analyze media messages or to help plan the creation of their own photographs and artwork. Because the frames in this strategy are paper, students can focus on the process of looking instead of being concerned with capturing images.

How It Works:

1. **Prepare the Frames:** Cut out the center square of the frame template (Figure 8.16) or cut a rectangle with no center for individual students or partnerships to use. We recommend using thick card stock paper so that the frames are stable and rigid. Frames should be a handheld size so students can hold the frame in one hand.

Figure 8.16

Frame Template

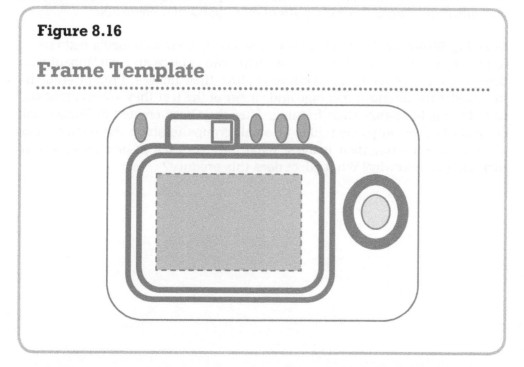

2. **Introduce the Concept of Framing and Driving Question:** Introduce the concept of *framing*. For example, show picture frames, cropped digital images, and so on. Children's books such as *Zoom* and *Re-Zoom* by Istvan Banyai are also excellent for this purpose. Ask students to consider the driving question for the lesson, such as "How might framing influence how we read images?" For use of frames within a specific case study or topic focus, we may ask a question such as "How might framing change the way to think about ___?"

Scan this QR code to access the frame template for your use, or visit **teachworldwise.com/resources**.

3. **Experiment with the Frame:** Invite students to experiment with the frame. For example, holding the frame at an arm's length, what happens when they move it closer to their eye? Ask students to consider how the image within the frame changes. Students can also walk around holding the frame relatively close to their face (e.g., six inches away). As they look at their classmates from different angles or at different heights, what do they notice? How does framing focus our attention yet leave out information?

4. **Analyze or Create Specific Media Texts:** Next, engage students in an opportunity to apply their initial understanding about framing to the analysis or creation of media texts:

Analyzing Media Texts: Provide media texts, such as magazines, newspapers, artwork, or photographs, for students to view using their frames. These can be around a particular issue or theme. How does seeing only part of an image shape the meaning we form? Invite students to explore how much of a person or object they can see by moving the frame closer to or farther from the subject. This process of "cutting out" is called *cropping*. By cropping or removing a part of the view, media producers change the meaning of a text. Give examples of how this has occurred, such as Black Ugandan climate activist Vanessa Nakate being cropped out of a photo with White climate activists at a conference in Davos. Analyze specific images in depth, comparing and contrasting how different framing draws our attention to particular elements.

Creating Media Texts: Students can also create their own media texts using frames as a scaffold. For instance, students can explore an environment with their frame before using a camera to capture their images. Prompt students to consider the intended message and viewer of the text they are creating and how this might change their framing. After they have created an image, ask students to meet in partnerships or small groups to share the choices they made in constructing their images. What have they left in or cropped out of their images, and why? What effect does this produce?

STRATEGY FOR DEVELOPING SOLUTIONS AND TAKING ACTION

Focused Observation

Best for: Grades K–8

Purpose: Focused Observation helps students gather data related to a specific focus and guiding question. Using the data gained through the process of observation, students can look for trends and patterns and develop informed ideas for action. Focused Observation is usually done by physically engaging in an environment (e.g., school, supermarket, park, river, etc.). Observation is coupled with tools to record data (e.g., tally chart, photography, etc.).

How It Works:

1. **Identify a Focus Question:** To create an effective environmental survey, develop a focus question. This should help students know what type of information they are looking for as they engage with the community. For example, as part of a process to enhance the linguistic diversity found on campus, students from UWC South East Asia's student council thought about the question, "What languages do we see on campus, and how well do these reflect the linguistic backgrounds of our students?" Students can co-construct the focus question with the teacher.

2. **Create the Survey Tool:** Next develop the survey tool that will provide data to answer that question. Students may need support in knowing which tools will help visualize the information sought, so teachers may make recommendations for the design of the tool. Figures 8.17 and 8.18 the student council using photography to record examples of the school's signage, which were stored and used in sorting activities later in the process.

3. **Collate and Analyze Data:** After students have engaged in their focused observation, invite them to look at the data for trends and patterns. This may be done on another day, if data needs to be organized by the teacher. During this step we help children both make observations and interpretations about the data. It is important to separate these steps, so students do not overgeneralize about the data or jump to conclusions. We may use sentence starters for children here to help them in making observations about the data before they interpret it:

   Observations:

   - In the data, I see . . .
   - I notice . . .
   - There are more/fewer . . .

Interpretations:

- I think . . .
- There is a pattern with . . .
- _____ is important, because . . .
- Overall . . .

Figures 8.17 and 8.18

Using Photography to Look for Linguistic Diversity

4. **Identify Needs and Recommend Actions:** Based on their interpretations, ask students to identify the needs of the community and recommend actions. Which needs seem the most important and why? What might we do to address them? How might we do this?

Modification: Community Mapping

Instead of physically exploring an environment to collect data, students can use their knowledge of a community to create a community map. Looking at a community using a bird's-eye view, the strategy seeks to have students identify interactions between the parts of a community and how they impact each other. By creating hand drawn or digital maps, students can recognize features of their communities relating to people, plants, animals, or the environment. Analyzing the features of their communities can enable students to brainstorm opportunities for action. See the full Community Mapping strategy, including modifications for 4 to 6 year olds on Jane Goodall's Roots and Shoots website using the QR code. Note that a version of this protocol for teachers to use in their planning can be found in Chapter 9.

Scan this QR code to access the full Community Mapping strategy, or visit rootsandshoots.org/our-model/four-step-formula/observe/

STRATEGY FOR DEVELOPING SOLUTIONS AND TAKING ACTION
Rapid Prototyping

Best for: Grades K–8

Purpose: Rapid Prototyping is an iterative process used to visualize what a solution may look like to get feedback, in particular from individuals or groups who are directly experiencing an issue. By getting feedback, students can adjust a solution to better address a need. To effectively engage in this strategy, students need to have identified a need. Rapid Prototyping can also be used in short focused projects, such as the SDG Projects in the Spotlight at the beginning of this chapter. The power of Rapid Prototyping is shared in the accompanying Spotlight on Design-a-thon Works projects.

How It Works:

1. **Prepare:** Collect various materials and tools that students can use to construct their prototypes. This may be as simple as paper and cardboard or could include other materials such as plasticine, clay, wire, blocks, and so on.

2. **Introduce:** Explain that the purpose of prototyping is to create a draft of our ideas, so that people can give feedback. Important is to stress that we do not go into prototyping with *final* thinking. Rather, we're open and flexible to changes in our solutions based on the feedback we receive.

3. **Identify Purpose and Parameters:** Ask students to confirm the need they are aiming to address, as well as the target population that would be served by this solution. This might be described by the geographical location (e.g., part of a community, city, country, etc.) or condition (e.g., those who have little access to play spaces). Co-planning strategies shared in Chapter 2 can also be used to identify questions that frame this step. Based on their need, invite students to consider what might be the requirements and constraints of a solution. Requirements are what the solution should do, whereas constraints are the limitations we have in developing them. We can give students sentence starters as scaffolds:

   Requirements:

   - To meet this need, our solution needs to . . .

   Constraints:

   - We have _____ to develop our solution. (time and resources)
   - _____ will limit how our solution looks because . . . (political, economic, environmental, and social factors)

4. **Create Prototypes:** Engage students in creating a visual representation of their solution. This can be annotated with writing on the material or using sticky notes to describe how parts of the solution connect and interact.

5. **Review Prototypes:** Feedback on prototypes can occur in a number of ways. First, we may ask student groups to swap prototypes, imagine they belonged to the community where that solution will be implemented and give feedback. In this case, we may ask groups to use a perspective-taking strategy such as the Think, Feel, Care thinking routine (p. 104). Likewise, we may share the prototype with affected individuals and ask them to evaluate how well it meets their needs and give feedback for improvement.

6. **Refine Prototypes:** Based on the feedback received, students identify areas to improve or clarify in their prototypes and iterate on them.

●●● SPOTLIGHT ON DESIGN-A-THON WORKS

"What if we radically reimagined the way we see children?

What if we listened to them seriously?"

—Emer Beamer, Founder and Designer at Design-a-thon Works

Design-a-thon Works is a Netherlands-based organization that nurtures creativity in children using design thinking. Design thinking integrates art and applied problem-solving where imagination, perspective-taking, and creation are at the center. Their mission to "empower children to design a better world" is pursued by offering professional development to educators, classroom and afterschool programs, and Design-a-thon challenges where children design, prototype, and present solutions to global issues aligned with the Sustainable Development Goals. To date, Design-a-thon Works has reached 75,000 children and youth in 45 countries located on all seven continents.

Essential to their mission, Design-a-thon Works believes that all children deserve the opportunity to use their voice and innate creativity to contribute to society. Emer Beamer, Founder and Designer at Design-a-thon Works, explains that traditional schooling can leave students uninspired. "We need more child-making work in the curriculum where children can cultivate their skills and attitudes as problem-solvers," she adds. To foster creative thinking, Emer recommends using open-ended questions and a neutral tone to glean children's perspectives. For example, one might ask, "What do you think of when you hear water? What do we use water for? Are there problems with water?" The adult presumes to not know the answers so the inquiry becomes child-led.

(Continued)

(Continued)

Scan this QR code to see the video of students presenting their prototype named D-RAIN, or visit https://youtu.be./0Sp329XmSWQ

Using a unique design thinking process, the Design-a-thon cycle culminates in students presenting their solutions to authentic audiences, such as at urban planning conferences. For example, in one session a group of children devised a prototype they named D-RAIN to solve city flooding in Amsterdam, Netherlands, exacerbated due to climate change. Scan the QR code to watch a video of the children presenting their innovation at the 2018 Co-Creating the City conference. The local mayor was actually keen to try the children's idea!

Design-a-thon Works research suggests that young people throughout the world are aware of and concerned about issues facing their generation, including poverty, climate change, and war. "Children really want to apply themselves on how to go about coming up with solutions; then they feel empowered by being allowed to tackle the material and come up with ideas," Emer adds. To learn more about Design-a-thon Works, please visit https://www.designathonworks.com/

STRATEGY FOR DEVELOPING SOLUTIONS AND TAKING ACTION

Artivism

Best for: Grades K–8

Purpose: Artivism is a powerful form of storytelling and activism, relating to both Direct Action and Advocacy as types of action. Using art as a visual prompt provokes an emotional response, inviting students to make connections, share perspectives, and engage in meaningful discussion around relevant and challenging issues. When exposed to effective examples of artivism, students become motivated to communicate their own concerns through art, unlocking their creativity and agency.

How It Works:

1. **Introduce the Concept of Activism:** Elicit students' prior knowledge of *activism*. Show examples from diverse places and times and ask, "What were these individuals and groups doing? What were they aiming to change?" Discuss how activism can take different forms, such as boycotts and marches, with the shared goal of bringing awareness and changing something that is unjust or harmful.

2. **Explore Artivism as a Form of Activism:** Display the word *artivism* and ask students what they notice and wonder about the term. Explain that artivism blends *art* with *activism*. While visual arts are commonly used, artivism may entail any artistic expression. As a class, discuss the question, "How can art be a form of activism?" Emphasize that artivism often aims to give a voice to the voiceless.

3. **Identify Key Messages:** With K–8 learners, it can be helpful to provide scaffolding as they prepare to create art. As artivism would likely occur within a unit with a clearly defined issue, we can collaboratively identify important messages to share in the art. Invite students to brainstorm key learning about the issue. We can then ask students to sort or prioritize these messages using Sort, Group, Name or Diamond Ranking strategies (p. 64). Ask students to choose a key message they would like to communicate and group them, where useful.

4. **Brainstorm Visual Elements:** Once individuals or small groups have their key message, invite them to consider visual elements that they may want to include in their artivism. For example, we may give students a Y-chart to jot ideas for what a piece of work might look, feel, and sound like (Figure 8.19). Note that this sample Y-chart only mentions certain elements and principles of visual arts. You may choose to modify this format for your students, for example, if they are creating work in a different mode. *Sounds like* has been repurposed to help students draw connections between visual and text-based aspects of an artwork.

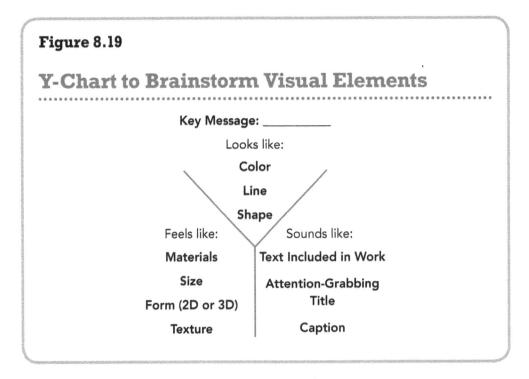

Figure 8.19

Y-Chart to Brainstorm Visual Elements

Key Message: _____

Looks like:

Color

Line

Shape

Feels like:

Materials

Size

Form (2D or 3D)

Texture

Sounds like:

Text Included in Work

Attention-Grabbing Title

Caption

5. **Create Art and Display:** Provide the space and resources for students to create work and use their voices to promote change. Decide on a location for display and how members of the community will engage with the work. It may be that a virtual space is used (e.g., photographs of the work plus captions are captured on slides). Where possible, design opportunities for students to have conversations about their pieces with individuals who come to view them. Students can even design questions, which can guide discussion with viewers.

Artivism in Action

Figure 8.20

Plastic Whale

At the end of a Grade 4 unit on sustainable businesses and consumer choices, students in Kris Leverton's class produced visual works to represent significant learning from the unit. This image by students Bea and Sofia, *Plastic Whale*, uses single-use plastics collected by students from their everyday experiences. While showing the ubiquitous nature of plastic waste, it also demonstrates the dire consequences for life below water and the lack of agency sea creatures have in advocating for their conditions.

STRATEGY FOR DEVELOPING SOLUTIONS AND TAKING ACTION
Reflection on Action

Best for: Grades K–8

Purpose: By reflecting on their action, students can determine how successful their solutions were in addressing an intended need. The learning gained from this reflection can transfer to students' future projects, when they design informed, purposeful action to address issues.

How It Works:

1. **Take Action:** A prerequisite to this strategy is that students have engaged in action that they helped design (e.g., through a rapid prototyping process).

2. **Reflect on Questions:** The checklist in Figure 8.21, modified from the Asia Society (2011), provides a range of areas for reflecting on action. We may choose to focus the range of reflective questions students consider, depending on what the action entailed and how co-constructed it was.

Figure 8.21

Reflective Questions Checklist

	Yes	No	Evidence for Thinking:
Relevance: Did the action address a need and relate to an issue that is important both locally and globally?			
Research: Did you use a variety of sources when conducting your own research (e.g., interviews or survey) to develop your action?			
Analysis: Was the action developed by thoroughly examining the issue as well as evaluating actions already taken on it?			
Perspective: Did the action consider the issue, and its possible solutions, from multiple perspectives?			
Implementation: Was the action collaborative, creative, and effective?			
Impact: Will the effects of the action sustain over time? Did the action inspire others to take action?			

Scan this QR code to access an editable version of this checklist, or visit **teachworldwise.com/ resources**.

With kindergarten to Grade 2 students, we may invite them to draw or paint the effects of their solutions directly or shortly after taking action, which can then be unpacked through short class discussions. Important is that students provide evidence for their thinking when completing the checklist. Having students initially engage in this thinking with a partner or small group often helps the quality of their reflections. An editable version of this checklist can be found here.

3. **Set Goals:** Ask students to identify one to two areas that could have been improved in their solution development and action. Give students a chance to write these down or record them, for example, using screencasting tools. Students can use the sentence frame, "Something I can improve next time when taking action is . . . "

4. **Discuss:** Provide students the opportunity to discuss their reflections. What commonalities exist across the class? What might this mean for the next time the class develops solutions and takes action? Record patterns and trends on a chart paper or slide to come back to in a future unit.

In this chapter, we've considered how developing our students' identities as local, national, and global citizens can empower them to take action in their communities. Looking at the role of critical literacy, we've established the importance of diving deep beneath the surface of texts to identify how particular perspectives and behaviors are promoted. Likewise we've explored how the democratic classroom advocates for student-led action, as we encourage our learners to design solutions that reflect their learning and their global competence. As we come to the end of this chapter, our exploration of the Act phase, and the Worldwise Learning Cycle more broadly, take a moment to pause, make connections, and reflect on your practice. In Chapter 9, which concludes the book, we explore how educators can bring together the Worldwise Learning Cycle in their personal and professional development, as well as in curriculum planning.

PAUSE AND REFLECT

- Think about yourself as a local, national, and global citizen. What experiences contributed to these identities? How might you foster citizenship at different scales in your classroom?

- How might your literacy instruction include opportunities for critical literacy? What are some of the benefits and challenges of asking students to identify perspectives, biases, or assumptions in texts?

- How much time do you allocate to student action? Would this be sufficient if students developed their own solutions and wanted to take action on them? Why or why not?

CHAPTER NINE
BEING A WORLDWISE EDUCATOR

GLOBAL COMPETENCE AS AN ONGOING JOURNEY

REIMAGINING POST-PANDEMIC LEARNING

UNDERSTAND PHASE FOR WORLDWISE EDUCATORS

CONNECT PHASE FOR WORLDWISE EDUCATORS

ACT PHASE FOR WORLDWISE EDUCATORS

BEING A WORLDWISE EDUCATOR

We began this book with an exploration of the various opportunities and implications of globalization on education today. With the backdrop of the COVID-19 pandemic—the first truly global event we have experienced in our lifetimes—we witnessed the transformation of the teacher's role and responsibilities. The sudden shift to remote learning demanded new knowledge and skills, from navigating online learning platforms to engaging learners at home. During this time of social isolation, teachers' abilities to remain emotionally connected with students also became paramount. Without question, the pandemic has served as a stark reminder that "teachers do much more than teach." It calls us to reimagine what post-pandemic learning could be.

The power of education to transform individual lives is well researched and documented. When children are valued and experience quality education, ripple effects occur throughout society: Citizens have greater economic opportunities and improved health and well-being. Countries are more secure and peaceful (United Nations Sustainable Development Goals, n.d.). More equitable societies with less poverty and social inequality also experience less conflict, more stability, and greater prosperity. Not surprisingly, education is considered vital to creating systemic changes to ensure a sustainable future (United Nations Educational, Scientific, and Cultural Organization, 2016). Such changes begin with individuals, and they happen through our relationships with them as educators.

By teaching to the heart, head, and hand of our learners, we contend that education can shape learners as global citizens who are committed to building a just, peaceful, and sustainable world. What kind of educator, then, does our current world demand?

Global Competence as an Ongoing Journey

As we have explored, global competence is a complex, multifaceted construct. It entails an interrelated set of knowledge, skills, understandings, and dispositions that, together, support informed action as global citizens. To nurture global competence in students, teachers must be committed to continuous personal growth and development as global citizens. In this way, global competence is also considered "an ongoing journey, not a one-time destination" for educators (Tichnor-Wagner, Parkhouse, Glazier, & Cain, 2019, p. 223). We call teachers who embrace this mindset **Worldwise Educators**.

Regardless of context, effective educators require specialized content and pedagogical knowledge and skills to facilitate learning in the classroom. Worldwise Educators, however, bring a unique lens to their planned curriculum. Boix Mansilla and Chua (2016) call this a "reinterpretation" of one's discipline. This entails thoughtfully bringing a global dimension to the standard curriculum, connecting key concepts and content with broader themes, perspectives, and an awareness of students' lives. It is an approach that views standards as opportunities for creating connected learning experiences around issues of significance to one's learners (Boix Mansilla & Jackson, 2011). Let's take a look at an example.

A second grade teacher in North Carolina follows a district-provided pacing guide for each discipline she teaches. In social studies, the standards include concepts like *goods and services*, *global trade*, *supply and demand*, and *location*. Instead of teaching concepts in an isolated manner, the Worldwise Educator reflects on how she could make these ideas connected, relevant, and meaningful for 8-year-olds. Noticing that her students bring a certain brand of chips to class for lunch, she realizes this *good* would be an engaging vehicle for learning her standard curriculum. And she was right: Her unit plan titled "Where in the World Did My Chips Come From?" was a success. Her students eagerly researched the ingredients on their chip bags, used map skills to locate where the crops are typically grown and the chips are produced, and determined how they, as consumers, are part of the global food trade system. Going further, they examined the *true cost* of the production, distribution, consumption, and disposal processes, such as human labor rights and the ecological impacts of packaging waste and corn cultivation on the soil and water systems. This integrated science concepts like *weather conditions*, *water cycle*, and the *needs of living organisms*. After learning how their consumer choices impact economic and ecological systems, some students decided to choose an alternative snack when going through the lunch line. Throughout such authentic experiences, students are not told *what* to think, but rather *how* to think, reflecting Paul's (1988) notion of "ethics without indoctrination." In short, Worldwise Educators offer students a locally rooted, globally oriented education that opens their hearts and minds to contemporary challenges and how they can make decisions to support healthier, fairer, and more sustainable systems.

Throughout this book, we have featured the voices of Worldwise Educators who live and teach in diverse contexts and countries around the world. This chapter brings key themes together by identifying educator competencies needed in our rapidly changing global society. Following are stories and words of wisdom to inspire you on your unique path. We frame these using the Worldwise Learning Cycle: Connect, Understand, Act. In this spirit, we invite you to reflect on your intentions for reading this book and where you wish to begin to make changes in your practice.

Connect Phase for Worldwise Educators

All meaningful and lasting change starts by looking inward. Recall from the Iceberg and Ladder of Inference tools (p.110 and p.113) that *who we are* and *how we think* act as filters that influence teaching and learning. The Connect phase entails widening one's awareness about interconnected issues and how we relate to them. Worldwise Educators see themselves as "cultural, political, and social beings situated in local and global contexts" (O'Connor & Zeichner, 2011, pp. 524–525). Because global challenges are complex and sometimes deeply personal, especially those that intersect race, culture, and identity, Worldwise Educators must be prepared to feel uncomfortable. Teacher leader and Director of the Leading Equity Center, Dr. Sheldon Eakins, explains why embracing such discomfort is integral to using equity-minded teaching practices:

> Many of us enjoy talking to our students about the latest movies we saw over the weekend, music, activities, and events in our communities. Yet, racial issues such as police brutality and xenophobia are avoided at all costs. Whether we address them in class or not, our students are thinking and talking about these issues. We cannot avoid these conversations because they make us uncomfortable. Get comfortable with your discomfort, and do not use it as an excuse to avoid engaging with people who are different from you. (personal communication, August 17, 2020)

Indeed, authentic connection builds the foundation for meaningful relationships and learning. In addition to being open to challenging conversations with students, Eakins recommends that educators analyze which sociocultural perspectives are included in or excluded from their curriculum. One way to do so is to listen and learn from diverse educators within and beyond your school context. Please visit our companion website for resources to connect globally for a variety of purposes. In the following story, we highlight one teacher's ongoing journey to strive to become anti-racist by learning alongside her colleagues.

Elementary educator Laura Montague models the value of looking inward as a commitment to her personal and professional growth. To step outside her

Worldwise Educators offer students a locally rooted, globally oriented education that opens their hearts and minds to contemporary challenges and how they can make decisions to support healthier, fairer, and more sustainable systems.

comfort zone as a White, middle-class woman, she has lived and taught in diverse sociocultural contexts in the United States, Kuwait, and the United Arab Emirates. These early teaching experiences involved collaborative planning with a group of inspiring international educators who continue to shape her worldview and teaching practices. "Anecdotes were shared, lofty ideas were considered, risks were taken, and we encouraged each other," she recalls.

Teaching using global lenses with a commitment to diversity, equity, and inclusion were also instilled as she became more acutely aware of social injustices and missing perspectives in the curriculum. Now as a New York-based educator, she and her colleagues leverage lenses from the Pollyanna Racial Literacy Curriculum, Learning for Justice's Framework for Social Justice Standards, and Multicultural Curriculum Reform to design units of inquiry. Head Teacher Staci Hyman crafted the following questions to guide her and her colleagues' self-reflection process:

- What opportunities does this lesson/experience lend to centering diversity, equity, inclusion, and justice?

- Whose voice or version of the story is being told, centered, and celebrated?

- What images am I showing students? Who is included? Who is not?

- How might my lesson design impact each student given their race, gender, ethnicity, culture, religion, home language, sexual orientation, and socioeconomic status?

- What language is being used? Who does it empower? Who does it marginalize or foster bias against?

In the quest to become an anti-racist educator, Laura explains:

> One never can truly *be* Anti-Racist. *Being* Anti-Racist constitutes a continual, ongoing, intentional force of naming, reflecting on, and revisiting our biases. Teachers can read *How to Be an Anti-Racist* by

Ibram X. Kendi, insert diverse windows, mirrors, and sliding glass doors into learning spaces, and attend the racial literacy workshops, but there is no end to this work. (personal communication, February 20, 2021)

Self-reflection is essential to moving forward on one's journey as a Worldwise Educator. As we learned in Laura's example, making progress does not necessarily imply acquiring new knowledge but rather "moving away from our existing mental structures towards a position which enables a fundamentally different way of seeing the world" (Laininen, 2019, p. 177). Numerous tools exist to guide looking inward, such as the Implicit Association Test and the Globally Competent Learning Continuum. See page 282 for examples of how you might use self-reflection and target areas for personal and professional growth.

Understand Phase for Worldwise Educators

The Understand phase for Worldwise Educators entails embracing the habits of a systems thinker: seeing the *big picture*, noticing interconnected elements, and finding connections. Worldwise Educators recognize that issues do not occur in a vacuum; they are part of complex webs of relationships occurring at multiple scales (see Chapter 6). To contextualize issues for learners, geographic knowledge is essential. In addition to foundational understanding of world geography, Tichnor-Wagner and colleagues (2019) recommend that teachers learn their local geography: "Begin at home. Come to understand the issues that most affect your students and local community" (p. 59). They suggest using maps to identify resources and better understand the communities where students live, reaching out to local organizations, and reading local news to find connections to the curriculum. Let's explore a powerful example from Washington state where educators have formed community learning partnerships with local organizations to strengthen their concept-based curriculum.

Worldwise Educators recognize that issues do not occur in a vacuum; they are part of complex webs of relationships occurring at multiple scales.

Situated in the Skagit Valley in coastal northern Washington, the Burlington-Edison School District is surrounded by diverse water ecosystems, from the Skagit River to the Salish Sea, offering an abundance of curricular connections. Learning partnerships and field experiences aligned with learning goals help contextualize and enrich student learning. They also provide new lenses through which to study concepts in context.

In Grade 5, for example, the science curriculum addresses concepts like *interdependence, human-environment interaction, conservation, energy, movement,* and *water system.* Educators identified related local issues that exemplify these concepts, such as water pollution, water sanitation, and water runoff. They considered the impact of these issues on living organisms like orca and salmon and Salish Sea residents. This is an example of *getting glocal,* where local places can be used to understand global patterns. Throughout the year, students follow the water system from the mountain to the ocean through multi-day field experiences supported by community partners. For example, they visit Mountain School facilitated by the North Cascades Institute to learn about the headwaters of the Skagit River. At Judy Reservoir, students learn how the Skagit Public Utility district turns the river water into drinkable water for the community's citizens. After learning about the impact of stormwater to non-point source pollution in partnership with the Skagit Watershed Council, students also explore solutions, such as how engineering can improve stormwater issues. The culminating experience includes a ferry ride to the Whale Museum located in the San Juan Island to learn about the impact of water pollution on whale populations (see Figure 9.1).

Not only do students acquire critical knowledge, skills, and understandings through these experiences, they also develop dispositions like the value of stewarding local habitats. District learning leaders Tiffanee Brown and Grant Burwash have witnessed the positive impacts of this place-based approach:

Figure 9.1

Headwaters of the Skagit to the Salish Sea

Headwaters of the Skagit to the Salish Sea:
Studying the Human Impact on our Environment through the water of our region.

5th Grade Science
Burlington-Edison School District

Field Experiences as Catalysts for Learning:

Judy Reservoir - Drain Rangers: This will support "Uncovering the Mysteries Around Us" as students learn about the tiny particles within water systems. Key phenomena can include water pollution, water sanitation, and water runoff.

Mountain School - Padilla Bay - Whale Museum: These will support "Energy's Epic Journey" as student learn about interactions between Earth's systems, the cycling of energy, interdependence and human impact. Key phenomena can include resident Orca, Salmon, and other Salish Sea residents.

"Together, the learning partnerships and field experiences help students to transfer their learning from the classroom to a critical issue in our community which brings relevance and personal meaning to the key unit generalizations" (personal communication, February 22, 2021).

Indeed, situating learning in the local community not only helps students form a special connection to place, it affords a meaningful interdisciplinary context through which to develop transferable understandings. To see an example of how to use Community Mapping in your setting, please see page 284.

Act Phase for Worldwise Educators

The Act phase supports the development of sustainable solutions and purposeful action. In Chapter 8, we explore how reflecting on one's identities as a changemaker provides clarity on how to participate meaningfully as a global citizen. To empower students as global citizens, educators themselves should "[assume] agency and responsibilities" in matters of local and global concern (Zhao, 2010, p. 427). When teachers emulate the belief that individuals can make a difference, they model what it means to contribute positively as global citizens. Educators can take purposeful, informed action in innumerable ways—both personally and professionally. Let's explore an example from North Carolina.

Shannon Hardy is a middle school educator and teacher leader in a collaborative learning community that engages students in a rigorous, relevant, and relationship-based education. Shannon serves in various leadership capacities within her school and community that connect to her personal passions and concerns. For example, she co-founded the Wake County Truth and Reconciliation Committee to bring awareness and promote healing to address systemic racism and violence in her community (see p. 34). Working alongside her students, Shannon has witnessed them transform into change agents. Years following this experience, 30 of her former students continued to advocate for social justice by initiating a movement called "Take Hate Down" directed at removing Confederate monuments throughout North Carolina. By leveraging community partners and communicating effectively via social media, her students demonstrate what it means to be a global citizen.

Shannon also serves as an Open Way Learning Ambassador to develop and sustain school cultures of innovation, particularly to support marginalized students. She is passionate about identifying and leveraging changes to address economic and social disparities. Shannon has taken action to build a statewide coalition of innovative teacher leaders and preservice teachers who use design thinking to solve complex, local problems through education. To date, she and colleagues have coached and connected more than 80 educators through professional development and online webinars through the Design for Change North Carolina cohort and North Carolina Service Learning Coalition. By creating a network of like-minded inquiry teachers who share resources and community partners, the ripple effects are magnified. Shannon explains:

> It's a duty to make the world better for the next generation. I was
> raised with this mindset and I had teachers who cultivated this belief
> in me. It's what we do now that will determine whether the arc of

Worldwise Educators nudge students to find their passions and determine how they can effect positive change within their spheres of influence.

the moral universe bends toward justice. I believe it can. (personal communication, February 12, 2021)

In another part of the world, Hanna Hjerppe is the Global Education Officer at Taksvärkki ry, a Helsinki-based NGO that guides educators throughout Finland to find practical solutions and support for the implementation of global citizenship education (GCE) in their curricula. As a former elementary school teacher, she became passionate about global injustices and how we can act to change existing norms and structures. In her current role, she designs teacher professional development centered on high-quality GCE, including opportunities for students to practice responsible global citizenship. Her over-arching aim is to create spaces for young people to understand and act on the structural cause-and-effect relationships within complex systems that impact sustainable development. Worldwise Educators nudge students to find their passions and determine how they can effect positive change within their spheres of influence.

To strengthen GCE throughout Finland, Hanna and her colleagues reflected on how they could better identify and support individuals to leverage changes in teacher practice. To do so, they adopted an outcome mapping (OM) approach to monitor and evaluate progress toward improving GCE in their organization and in Finnish schools. Hanna explains:

> OM is an actor-oriented way of thinking and working. It helps us carefully consider our vision for GCE. Because systems are complex, we can't, of course, anticipate and plan everything, but from a quality and effectiveness perspective, it's much more relevant to think about the behaviors of individual actors and how they can contribute to our GCE dreams rather than the number of individual projects or events. (personal communication, February 27, 2021)

Integral to OM is the participatory process that helps teams create a shared vision for change. To do so, they focus on their sphere of influence, or specific individuals and groups they aim to influence to create outcomes. See page 288 for a sample protocol applying the Sphere of Influence mapping tool in a school context.

By integrating systems thinking into teacher professional development, Hanna has witnessed positive changes in educators and students alike. Using a simplified Sphere of Influence Map (see p. 288), teachers, principals, and students can think together about their own school's vision: a global citizenship education dream. They reflect on what each individual's role is in school and what observable signs of progress show that change has taken place. Hanna adds, "Changes are not limited to increasing knowledge, but also changes in skills, attitudes, motivation, and relationships. Empowering learners to implement their own ideas as active actors is one of our key goals."

As Shannon Hardy and Hanna Hjerppe demonstrate, taking action as an educator will involve different goals and approaches. Yet what is common is the effectiveness of identifying leverage points that exist within your sphere of influence to effect long-lasting, systemic change.

Strategies for Worldwise Educators

The following strategies support Worldwise Educators as they continue to develop their globally competent teaching practice. Because each individual is on their own path, working in a unique context, these strategies are not intended to be prescriptive or linear. There is inherent flexibility in using self-reflection, visualization, community mapping, and strategic planning for different purposes and at different times. They can be implemented by individual educators to enhance personal and professional growth or as part of a team to leverage school- or system-wide change. Like diverse resources in a teacher toolbox, the strategies throughout this book offer new perspectives and approaches to nurture Worldwise Learning.

STRATEGIES FOR WORLDWISE EDUCATORS

Strategy	Description	Page Number
Self-Reflection	Educators self-assess strengths and set targeted goals for the development of global competence.	282
Community Mapping	Educators create a map to identify natural features and human resources in a community that may serve as contexts for authentic learning.	284
Visualization	Educators chart a vision using imagery and words to depict a student in the future and guide curricular decisions.	285
Sphere of Influence	Educators use strategic planning to identify with whom they might collaborate to effect positive change within their sphere of influence.	287

STRATEGY FOR WORLDWISE EDUCATORS
Self-Reflection

Purpose: Ongoing self-reflection is critical to developing global competence (Harshman, 2016). By reflecting on their knowledge, skills, and values, teachers can identify strengths and establish areas for growth to enhance their professional and personal development. This protocol uses the free, online tool, the Globally Competent Learning Continuum (http://globallearning.ascd.org/lp/editions/global-continuum/home.html).

How It Works:

1. **Review the Self-Reflection Tool:** First, become familiar with the 12 elements (organized by dispositions, knowledge, and skills) and their five developmental stages (nascent, beginning, progression, proficient, advanced) of the Globally Competent Learning Continuum (GCLC).

2. **Rate and Reflect:** For each element, rate your level along the continuum by reading the descriptions. Reflect on how your personal and professional experiences may demonstrate specific levels (strengths and areas for growth) and what evidence might support your rating.

3. **Establish SMART Goals:** Identify one or more SMART goals to target your growth. These goals are specific, measurable, attainable, relevant, and time-bound. Read the next highest level description to determine what is needed to move along the continuum. Note that goals may be more personal in nature or more specific to teaching. See Figure 9.2 for an example from an elementary educator teaching in a U.S. public school.

Figure 9.2

Sample Self-Reflection and Goal-Setting

GCLC Element	Rating and Explanation	Sample SMART Goals
# 10 Facilitate intercultural and international conversations that promote active listening, critical thinking, and perspective recognition	Beginning Being an immigrant I provide my students with opportunities to engage in cultural diversity, but I want to do more. I sincerely believe that if we expose our students to other cultures and give those cultures a voice, then our students will be less likely to discriminate or ostracize. It fosters empathy, which is critical in achieving the Sustainable Development Goals.	Join the Goals Project (https://www.goalsproject.org/) to partner with other classrooms on a shared Sustainable Development Goal for the duration of 6 weeks. Participate in an Out of Eden Learn Journey (https://learn.outofedenwalk.com/) aligned with my curriculum to promote storytelling and perspective-taking centered on local issues over the course of one semester.

4. **Take Action:** Use the resources provided on the tool's website, such as lesson plans and teacher videos, to support your SMART goals. You are also encouraged to network with other educators to share professional learning opportunities and other resources.

5. **Reflect:** Keep a journal or log to record and reflect on your progress. Review the GCLC levels again to rate your growth and ways you might continue to improve.

Self-Reflection in Action

As a Worldwise Educator, Grade 3 teacher Martina Croom-Schöfberger routinely practices self-reflection and goal-setting. Reflective of her commitment to diversity and inclusion in the curriculum, she often strives to improve her ability to recognize her own biases and the limitations of her perspectives. To do so, she has prioritized the building of her classroom library to include racially diverse literature. As a teacher at a Title I school in a standards-driven educational system in Florida, she sometimes struggles to provide the kind of education she desires. Despite constraints, she has had success engaging her students using diverse resources that show empowering stories of people who have experienced oppression. Martina advises:

> Carve out spots, no matter how small, where you can make a difference. Little things add up. Maybe I cannot do a big project, but I can still bring in big ideas and concepts through mentor texts that provide my kids with mirrors and windows to the world.

As her example shows, achieving small goals builds confidence and the motivation to continue the work.

STRATEGY FOR WORLDWISE EDUCATORS
Community Mapping

Purpose: Community mapping engages educators in noticing community assets that may serve as contexts for authentic learning. A community map includes elements like people, landmarks, physical structures, and institutions. By analyzing what and who live in the community and how they interact, including local human and ecological issues that may result, educators can design service learning projects, field trips, and community partnerships that enhance the relevance of students' learning. It can also support the identification of unit case studies (see pp. 83–86). This strategy can be used with students to locate community needs as part of solution prototyping. See page 264 for a short description.

How It Works:

1. **Define the Geographic Scope of the Community:** First determine how you will define your *community*. For example, one might *zoom in* on their school district region or a *zoom out* to include additional human or natural features (e.g., a body of water or mountain).

2. **Annotate the Map:** Use a digital geographic tool to annotate the map. This includes marking features and areas of interest, inserting captions with names and descriptions, and adding visuals.

3. **Seek Curricular Connections:** Analyze your community map for connections to your curriculum, including issues students might explore. For example, reflect on how your community features might provide an authentic context for unit knowledge, skills, and conceptual understandings. To guide the process, Vander Ark, Liebtag, and McClennen (2020) also recommend exploring questions like:

   - Who lives here now? Who lived here before?
   - What drives the economy of this place?
   - What are the ecological and geological systems at work in this place?
   - Who holds power in this community?
   - What are the current political issues?
   - Is there inequity in this place? (p. 119)

4. **Identify Potential Partners and Experiences:** Last, consider how students might learn about this place in meaningful ways, such as via guest speakers, field trips, and service learning. See the connected strategy of Interdisciplinary Contexts on pp. 87–91 for how these may be utilized in interdisciplinary experiences, projects, or units.

STRATEGY FOR WORLDWISE EDUCATORS
Visualization

Purpose: Visualization is a technique used to imagine and work toward the future we wish to create. For this application, educators chart a vision using imagery and words to depict a student in the future. Who will the child become, including the knowledge, skills, and attitudes they will possess? Once visualized, educators can create an action plan to guide their curricular decisions. This protocol is adapted from the Center for Collaborative Education (https://www.cce.org/). It can be led by a facilitator working with educator teams or followed by individual educators who wish to make positive changes to their practice.

How It Works:

1. **Anchor Your Imagination:** Choose a specific time frame for the visualization. For example, you might create a vision of your students at the end of elementary school or further into the future as high school graduates.

2. **Envision Your Students in the Future:** Next, imagine what competences students need to thrive in their future. Make a list of specific knowledge, skills, and dispositions that collectively support your students' well-being and readiness to contribute positively in their local communities and beyond. These might be outlined by Heart, Head, and Hand:

   - **Heart:** What dispositions, characteristics, or values should the student possess?

   - **Head:** What should the graduate know and understand? What kind of thinker will they be?

   - **Hand:** What skills should the graduate demonstrate? What should they be able to do?

3. **Create a Visualization:** Create a hand-drawn or digital visual of your *vision* including both imagery and text. For example, you might use chart paper to outline a large silhouette of a student and use the heart, head, and hand to guide your design. Use your creativity in this process! An example is featured in Figure 9.4.

4. **Develop an Action Plan:** Once you have established your vision, create a plan with actionable steps (see Figure 9.3) to support this desired future. Imagine there were no constraints (e.g., pacing guides and standardized testing). What would you do differently in your practice? Then, in light of any barriers, what is in your sphere of influence that you *can* change? Record *What, Why,* and *How* you will work toward your vision. This step can be elaborated using Sphere of Influence strategic planning on page 287.

Elementary educator Megan Gill created a vision of a passionate, confident, and happy high school graduate. This individual is an effective communicator, creator, "reader" of the word and the world, and global problem-solver. Her student possesses strong communication skills, like strategies for reading,

Figure 9.3

Action Plan Template

WHAT do you hope to achieve? Describe your desired outcomes.	WHY do you wish to achieve it? What is the purpose or value?	HOW will you get there? What strategies will you use to achieve your vision? List achievable action steps.

Figure 9.4

Example Vision of the Future Student

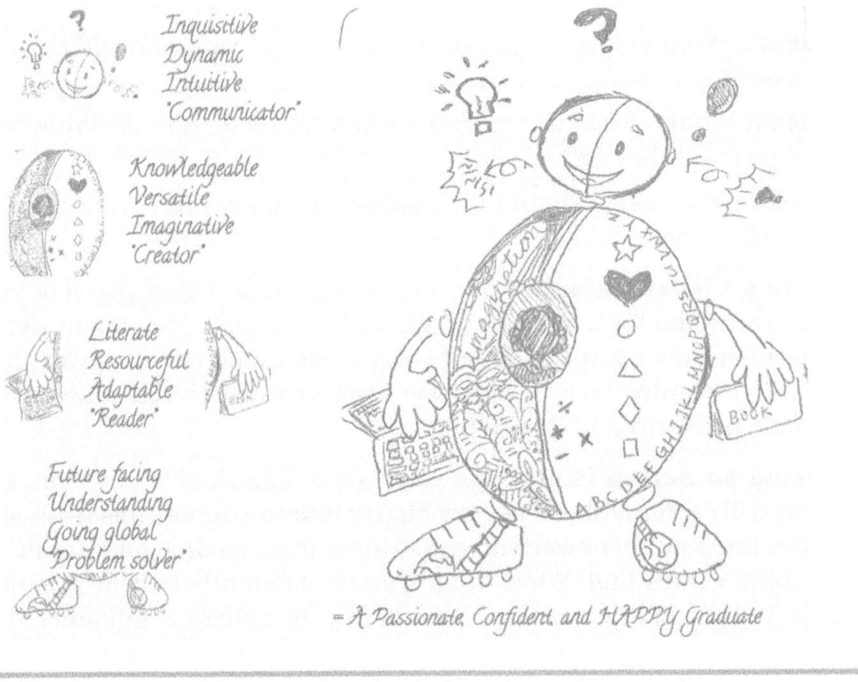

speaking, and communicating with people of different backgrounds. The graduate is also self-aware, knowing their own past, as well as the community's history and what we can learn from it. Versatility and resourcefulness were deemed critical to navigating a complex, uncertain future. To succeed and thrive, the graduate is curious, ready to explore, and eager to make new discoveries. They understand much remains unknown and uncreated.

STRATEGY FOR WORLDWISE EDUCATORS
Sphere of Influence

Purpose: This strategy works best for a team of educators and/or school leaders. Like all complex, adaptive systems, learning communities comprise multiple, dynamic interactions between actors, resulting in intended and unintended outcomes. Using strategic planning, educators identify who is in their sphere of influence, such as students, students' families, and community partners, that they may aim to influence to bring about desired outcomes. The following protocol is from Hanna Hjerppe, Global Education Officer at Taksvärkki ry (Finland), adapted from resources via the Outcome Mapping Virtual Learning Community (www.outcomemapping.ca). It is a simplified, accessible approach adapted for classroom teachers.

How It Works:

1. **Set the Vision:** In your team, reflect on your high-level *mission* or your desired outcomes as educators. What is your global education *utopia* or dream? For example, it might be:

   > Our school's vision aims to create "a just and sustainable school community for all." In our dream, teachers and students take initiative to promote their vision in various spheres. For example, students reach out to collaborate with teachers and youth in other spheres to offer mutual support and to resolve issues. All educators, students, school administration, and community members know that sustainable development is important and work together to achieve it. The dream is that eventually the decision-making structures promote and support sustainable development in teaching and the school's operational culture.

Note that the Visualization strategy on page 285 may help guide this process. Using chart paper or a digital tool, add these desired outcomes on the outer region labeled Sphere of Interest (Figure 9.5).

2. **Identify the Sphere of Control:** Next, consider what is in your sphere of control as an educator. These represent your main activities you can control, such as (a) designing your curriculum, (b) planning your daily schedule, and (c) building relationships with families. Add these to the core circle of your map.

3. **Identify the Sphere of Influence:** Afterward, identify individuals and groups with whom you might build coalitions. These are your *targets of change* to bring about your vision or desired outcomes. For example, to meet the global education vision, the Sphere of Influence for a team of educators planning and developing the school's global citizenship education curriculum might include: (a) the students they teach, (b) other teachers in the school, and (c) the school's PTA. The desired effects of targeting these groups are:

   - The school administration and all students are involved in changing the school's operating culture to take into account sustainable development.

- Through school leaders and parents, a broader opinion about sustainable development could be formed, resulting in consensus about the school's strategic direction and allocation of resources to promote sustainable development.

Place these in the inner circle of your map.

4. **Create Action Plan**: Determine how various actors in your Sphere of Influence might contribute to your global education vision. List specific, feasible steps you might take to promote changes in behavior for each actor. Reflect on these questions as you create a plan of action:

- What can key actors do together to achieve the global education dream?
- What specific steps will make the most difference toward our goals?
- What can we realistically do?
- Will we be able to sustain our work without funding, now or in the future?

5. **Check Assumptions:** Before implementation of the action plan, consider what assumptions might influence the outcomes. These include values, prior experiences, and capacity gaps. Checking assumptions is an opportunity to pause to ensure the desired outcomes and the sphere of influence are the best ones to target. The Iceberg Model (p. 110) might be useful for this process.

Figure 9.5

Example From Taksvärkki ry Partner Schools (Finland)

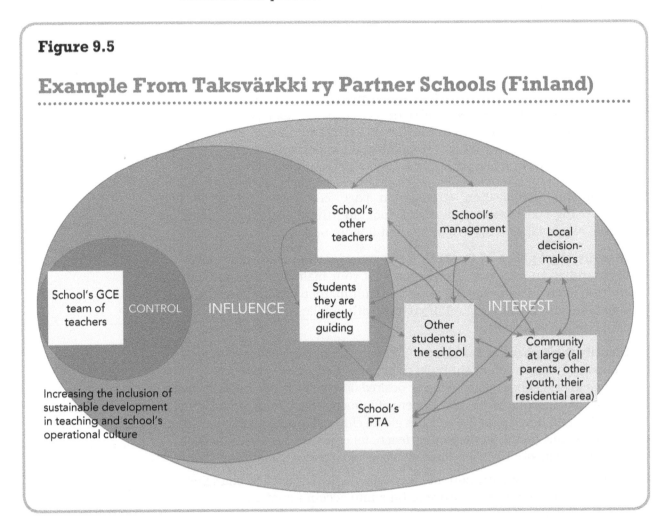

6. **Implement and Monitor:** Determine how you will monitor progress toward your desired outcomes. These might include participant monitoring (e.g., feedback surveys, individual or focus group interviews, etc.). As you implement your plan, review the results from these checkpoints to guide your strategy, making any needed changes.

7. **Evaluate and Reflect:** At the end of the time frame, evaluate what positive changes occurred and how you know. What was effective and why? What might you do differently next time?

Outcome mapping and the Sphere of Influence strategy can be used at any time for both short- and long-term planning. At Taksvärkki ry, partner schools use this approach to make a plan for global education for the upcoming academic year. Older students can also use it to plan and implement their own advocacy projects.

Closing Thoughts

In September 2019, it seemed the world was literally ablaze. Prolonged drought in Australia followed by months of catastrophic bushfires resulted in tragic loss at local and global scales. More than 18 million hectares burned, devastating among the most biodiverse habitats in the world upon which all life depends. Ash and soot from the fires turned beautiful beaches black and skies orange. The fires produced so much hazardous air pollution, the smoke made a full circuit around the entire globe (NASA, 2020). While devastating economic and ecological losses can be quantified, the emotional trauma of bearing witness to such an event is harder to measure.

In his photograph "Unsettling Evidence," Australian teenager Ned Henderson powerfully documented his experience of bearing witness up close (Figure 9.6). The statement accompanying his photo reads:

> This macro perspective of the inevitable devastation of our bushfire season was a message to the world . . . It is important to acknowledge the close connection between cities and the bush and the world's interconnectedness of ecosystems . . . To think that this is just one handful of ash and one small town upon thousands. (Global Oneness Project, 2020)

After more than 240 consecutive days of fire activity, 2 weeks of sustained, heavy rain fell. With the rain, signs that nature was beginning to regenerate emerged: Striking photographs appeared in the media of green shoots sprouting from the burnt woodland and on trunks of fire-ravaged trees. Plant species like the *Banksia* were particularly resilient, having adapted to

Figure 9.6

"Unsettling Evidence"

withstand high temperatures, only reproducing after fires stimulate the seed pods to open. Falling on newly fertilized soil, the seeds germinate and afford rapid regeneration. Once matured, banksias play an integral role in the ecosystem as heavy producers of nectar, providing food for a variety of birds and mammals (Huss, Fratzl, Dunlop, Merritt, Miller, & Eder, 2019). Such restoration in the face of widespread ecological loss reflects nature's will to live. As American poet Camille T. Dungy (2018) writes in her essay, *From Dirt*: "Where there appears to be only dirt, there may be the root system of some kind of insistent thriving" (para. 15).

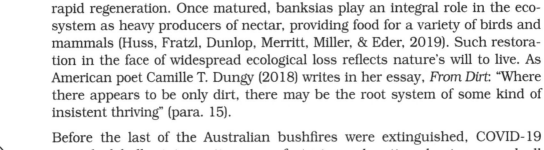

In this light, how might we see the global challenges we face as opportunities to rebuild better, together?

Before the last of the Australian bushfires were extinguished, COVID-19 spread globally, interrupting manufacturing, education, business, and all other facets of daily life. More wildfires erupted in Brazil, the United States, Turkey, Siberia, and other countries. Among their many lessons, contemporary global challenges like megafires and viruses highlight how inextricably interconnected they all are: climate change, the environment, government policy, economic systems, racial justice, and human health and well-being. Indeed, global issues have no borders; they impact all areas of life in direct and indirect ways. Crises also reveal the human capacity to come together for collective action in the face of adversity and challenge. During the bushfires, for example, international firefighters from numerous countries and cultures volunteered side-by-side, organizations coordinated efforts to rescue and treat impacted animals, and donations were collected throughout the world (World Economic Forum, 2020a). Acts of altruism and kindness are not uncommon during times of crisis; in fact, research suggests they are the norm (Schaffner, 2020). Co-Founder of the Gapminder Foundation, Ola Rosling explains that "[w]e humans have the exceptional ability to imagine a better world, even during crisis, and we are capable of collaborating globally to turn that imagination into reality" (Gapminder Foundation, 2020, 0:09). In this light, how might we see the global challenges we face as opportunities to rebuild better, together?

We believe that education can shape a better world where *people, planet, and prosperity* exist in harmony. To achieve this vision, we propose a pedagogy centered on significant issues that invites deep learning and compels our students to act. In building a culture of peace, inclusion, and sustainability in classrooms, teachers and students can transform schools, communities, and beyond. This must be a collective effort, but regardless of size, each of our individual actions as educators can contribute to shaping a just, sustainable future.

PAUSE AND REFLECT

- If you were to make one change to your practice, what might it be? What might be your leverage points for creating systemic change in your classroom?
- What systemic barriers do you face? Which obstacles can be removed?

- How might you tap into students' innate desire and capability to shape a better world?
- How might you create a sustainable future through education?

SAMPLE UNIT PLANNER
POLLINATOR POWER!

Unit Title: Pollinator Power!	**Grade:** Kindergarten (5–6 year olds)
Local, Global, or Intercultural Issues and/or Global Goals Explored: Pollinator Health, Food Production, Sustainable Farming	**Duration:** 8 Weeks (with yearlong engagement in pollinator garden)
Conceptual Lens: Interdependence	
Driving Concepts: Living Thing, Life Cycle, Pollinator, Habitat, Needs	

Unit Summary:

In this unit, kindergarteners explore the importance of pollinators to both habitats and farming (food production). Using local garden and park spaces as case studies, students come to recognize the interdependence of plants and animals within a habitat. They likewise learn about plant and animal life cycles, with a focus on bees and butterflies. Learners investigate how human activities can inhibit pollinators from meeting their needs. Specifically students look at pollinators' access to food and shelter (e.g., flowering plants, host plants) as well as modern farming techniques (e.g., monoculture, pesticides, etc.). Students are invited to take action on their knowledge in their local communities. The unit brings together learning from science, social studies, English language arts, and mathematics.

Learning Goals **(What is the intended learning?)**	**Guiding Questions** **(What questions will drive the learning?)**
Conceptual Understandings/Generalizations: *Students will understand that . . .*	**Guiding Questions (Factual, Conceptual, and Provocative):** F = Factual, C = Conceptual, P = Provocative
U1. In **living things**, **life cycles** contain stages for **growth** and **reproduction**.	1a. How are animal and plant life cycles similar and different? (F) 1b. How do young animals look similar to or different from the adults of a species? (F) 1c. How do flowering plants reproduce? (F) 1d. What is the life cycle of a butterfly? (F) 1e. What is the life cycle of a honey bee? (F) 1f. What stages occur in all life cycles? Why? (C)
U2. **Pollinators** help **plants** grow, breed, and produce **food**.	2a. What special features do bees, butterflies, and other pollinators have that support pollination? (F) 2b. How do pollinators and plants help each other? (C)

(Continued)

(Continued)

Learning Goals (What is the intended learning?)	Guiding Questions (What questions will drive the learning?)
U3. The way people farm can harm or help **pollinators** and their **habitats**.	3a. How does farming rely on pollinators? (C) 3b. How can farming harm pollinators and their habitats? (C) 3c. What are monocultures and why are they unhealthy habitats for pollinators? (F) 3d. What can farmers do to help pollinators in their fields? (C)
U4. **Habitats** enable **living things** to meet their **needs**.	4a. How are our garden plants and animals interdependent? (F) 4b. How does the food of caterpillars and butterflies differ? (F) 4c. What types of plants do gardens need to feed pollinators and their young? (F) 4d. How do habitats enable living things to meet their needs? (C) 4e. How are plants and animals interdependent in a habitat? (C)
U5. Humans can protect **pollinators** and restore their **habitats** through a number of **actions**.	5a. How can we take action to protect our local pollinators? (F) 5b. How can we show respect to living things in nature like pollinators? (F) 5c. What actions can humans take to protect pollinators? (C)
U6. Scientists use **observation** to identify **living things**, their **behaviors**, and **relationships** to other **plants** and **animals**.	6a. What observations can we make about how animals relate to each other in our local garden? (F) 6b. How can scientists use observation to make discoveries? (C) 6c. How do scientists use evidence to support their ideas? (C)
U7. Authors use a variety of **text features** to produce explanatory **information texts**.	7a. What is an information text? (F) 7b. What text features are common to information texts? How do they help us understand a topic? (F) 7c. Why might authors use text features in an information text? (C)
U8. By understanding their **properties**, mathematicians can use **two-dimensional** and **three-dimensional shapes** for a **purpose**.	8a. What 2D and 3D shapes can we find in our classroom? In our school? (F) 8b. What properties do different shapes have? How might these be useful for different purposes? (F) 8c. How can mathematicians use 2D and 3D shapes for a purpose? (C)

Critical Content (Knowledge and Skills)

(WHAT CRITICAL CONTENT IS REQUIRED TO DEVELOP THESE UNDERSTANDINGS?)

Knowledge: *Students will know . . .*	Skills (Disciplinary and Interdisciplinary): *Students will be able to . . .*
Next Generation Science Standards: K-LS1-1. All animals need food in order to live and grow. They obtain their food from plants or from other animals. Plants need water and light to live and grow. K-ESS2-2. Plants and animals can change their environment. • Pollinators include bees, butterflies, moths, wasps, flies, and beetles, but also a number of mammals, birds, reptiles, and amphibians. K-ESS3-1. Living things need water, air, and resources from the land, and they live in places that have the things they need. Humans use natural resources for everything they do. • Certain plants, such as milkweed for the monarch butterfly, act as host plants that butterflies rely on for food and reproduction. • Most plants rely on pollinators to fertilize them, for example by bringing pollen from one flower to another. K-ESS3-3. Things that people do to live comfortably can affect the world around them. But they can make choices that reduce their impacts on the land, water, air, and other living things. • Many of our fruits, vegetables, nuts, and grains rely on pollinators for fertilization and/or seed dispersal. • Without pollinators, pollination would need to be done by hand. • Planting natives or creating nesting places for pollinators can help bees and butterflies have food to eat and a place to live. **National Geographic Standards:** 14.3 The consequences of human modifications of the physical environment. Identify and describe the changes in local habitats that resulted from human activities.	**Next Generation Science Standards:** K-LS1-1. Use observations to describe patterns of what plants and animals (including humans) need to survive. K-ESS2-2. Construct an argument supported by evidence for how plants and animals (including humans) can change the environment to meet their needs. K-ESS3-1. Use a model to represent the relationship between the needs of different plants and animals (including humans) and the places they live. K-ESS3-3. Communicate solutions that will reduce the impact of humans on the land, water, air, and/or other living things in the local environment. **Common Core Literacy:** CCSS.ELA-Literacy.W.K.2. Use a combination of drawing, dictating, and writing to compose informative/explanatory texts in which they name what they are writing about and supply some information about the topic. CCSS.ELA-Literacy.W.K.6. With guidance and support from adults, explore a variety of digital tools to produce and publish writing, including in collaboration with peers. **Common Core Mathematics:** CCSS.Math.Content.K.G.A.2. Correctly name shapes regardless of their orientations or overall size. CCSS.Math.Content.K.G.A.3. Identify shapes as two-dimensional (lying in a plane, "flat") or three-dimensional ("solid"). CCSS.Math.Content.K.G.B.5 Model shapes in the world by building shapes from components (e.g., sticks and clay balls) and drawing shapes.

Connections to Dispositions and Social Emotional Learning

(WHAT CONNECTIONS WILL BE MADE IN THE UNIT TO DISPOSITIONS AND SOCIAL EMOTIONAL LEARNING?)

Students will show . . .

Curiosity as they investigate the local environment and interactions between living beings.

Empathy as they consider pollinator needs, including migrations.

Respect and Reverence for living things in nature.

Responsibility as they consider how human behaviors relate to pollinators, their habitats, and how we produce food.

Imagination as they develop local solutions to enhance pollinator habitats.

Assessment and Intended Student Action

(What connections will be made to prior learning? What evidence will reveal that the learners have met the learning goals? How might they take action?)

Understanding, Knowledge or Skill Assessed (e.g., U1.)	Pre-Assessment*, Formative or Summative Assessment. Assessing for Conceptual Understanding.
	*Pre-assess driving concepts as appropriate to the understandings being explored at the beginning of a unit. A unit may have multiple pre-assessments, which come at different points. Note and pre-assess any connections to prior learning.
U4. **Habitats** enable **living things** to meet their **needs**. U7. Scientists use **observation** to identify **living things**, their **behaviors,** and **relationships** to other **plants** and **animals**. K-LS1-1	**Pre-Assessment: Field Trip and See, Think, Wonder** After going on a walk to a local butterfly garden, students share what they noticed and how it connects to their prior knowledge using the See, Think, Wonder protocol. What did you see? What did you think? What did you wonder? The teacher takes anecdotal notes. This is followed by sorting activities, using photographs taken by students in the garden. Can they group photographs by type of living thing? What does each group of living things need to survive? What do living things in general need to survive? What is common across all living things?
U8. By understanding their **properties,** mathematicians can use **two-dimensional** and **three-dimensional shapes** for a **purpose**. CCSS.Math.Content.K.G.A.2 CCSS.Math.Content.K.G.A.3 CCSS.Math.Content.K.G.B.5	**Pre-Assessment: Classroom Shape Walk** Students take a classroom and/or school shape walk. What shapes can they see? What properties does each shape have? As students are working in small groups, recording shapes on a clipboard or photographing shapes with a tablet, listen for: • Accurate use of shape names • Students' understanding of 2D vs. 3D shapes • How students describe shapes (e.g., properties named) Use this experience to plan for appropriate mathematics investigations into 2D and 3D shape.

Assessment and Intended Student Action

(What connections will be made to prior learning? What evidence will reveal that the learners have met the learning goals? How might they take action?)

U1. In **living things**, **life cycles** contain stages for **growth** and **reproduction**.

U2. **Pollinators** help **plants** grow, breed, and produce **food**.

K-ESS2-2

K-ESS3-1

U7. Authors use a variety of **text features** to produce explanatory **information texts**.

CCSS.ELA-Literacy.W.K.2

CCSS.ELA-Literacy.W.K.6

Formative Assessment: Beehive Model Making

Students create model beehives to show:

- The parts of the bee life cycle
- How bees make food
- How bees and plants help each other
- Shapes used within the hive to maximize use of space

Students annotate their models with labels, photographs, arrows, and so forth and explain the parts of their hive, how they connect, and relationships with the local environment using a screencast.

U2. **Pollinators** help **plants** grow, breed, and produce **food**.

U4. **Habitats** enable **living things** to meet their **needs**.

U5. Humans can protect **pollinators** and restore their **habitats** through a number of **actions**.

K-ESS3-3

U7. Authors use a variety of **text features** to produce explanatory **information texts**.

CCSS.ELA-Literacy.W.K.2

CCSS.ELA-Literacy.W.K.6

Summative Assessment:

Design and create a pollinator garden:

Given a small plot in the school garden, students design and create a pollinator garden taking the following into consideration:

- Host plants for different insect young
- Flowering plants for pollinators, preferably those that bloom at different times
- Shelters for solitary bees and other pollinators
- Signs and/communication about how to protect pollinators in the garden (e.g., not using chemical pesticides, etc.)

Screencast:

As part of the design and creation process, students take photos, create a slide presentation, and do a voiceover (can also be done as a written book) using the following questions:

- How are our garden plants and animals interdependent?
- How do pollinators and plants help each other?
- What types of plants do gardens need to feed pollinators and their young?
- What actions can humans take to protect pollinators?

To do so, students use and show their understanding of various **text features**:

- Table of Contents (First slide of deck)
- Titles
- Photographs
- Captions
- Labels

Students are given feedback on their plans and actions based on:

- Integration of unit knowledge, skill, and understandings across the disciplines
- Feasibility and sustainability of their plans
- Display of unit dispositions during the planning and doing of the action

Inquiry Resources

(What sources of information are available? For example, relevant media, real-life experiences, creative use of technology, data collection opportunities, or interacting with people)

Resources for Teaching	Resources for Educators (Background Knowledge)
Local green spaces and gardens	U.S. Forest Service—Why is Pollination Important?
Local farms	Why are Pollinators so Important to the Planet? (NoMorePlanet)
Local botanic garden or national park staff	What is Monoculture? Michael Pollan
Media:	Marla Spivak: Why Bees are Disappearing
BBC Bitesize—Reproduction in Flowering Plants	Keep the Hives Alive Documentary
Story of Flowers	Pollinator Garden Design (Butterflies)
Time Lapse Video: Hatching Bees (National Geographic)	Pollinator Garden Design (Bees)
How Do Honeybees Get Their Jobs? (National Geographic)	
Honey Bees Make Honey and Bread (PBS / KQED)	
Why do Bees Love Hexagons? (TED-Ed)	
Monarch Butterfly Life Cycle (National Geographic)	
The Amazing Journey of the Monarch Butterfly (Facts in Motion)	
Go Into the Heart of a Kaleidoscope of Butterflies (Nat Geo Wild)	
What if All Bees Die? (ASAPScience)	
The Buzz about Pesticides (Nature)	
Why are Bees Dying (PBS—It's Okay to Be Smart)	
Farming and Biodiversity (Deutsche Welle)	
Forest Gardens (National Geographic)	
How to Create a Monarch Rest Stop (National Geographic)	
How to Help Pollinators in Cities (Nature)	
How to Plant a Butterfly Garden	This Old House	

Learning Plan

(What learning experiences will drive the inquiry and lead to the development of unit understandings?)

Learning Goals:	Phase of Worldwise Learning (Connect, Understand, Act)	Learning Experiences:
U1. In **living things**, **life cycles** contain stages for **growth** and **reproduction**. U4. **Habitats** enable **living things** to meet their **needs**. U6. Scientists use **observation** to identify **living things**, their **behaviors**, and **relationships** to other **plants** and **animals**. K-LS1-1	 **Connect**	**Introduction of Unit Dispositions:** What does it mean to be a scientist? What does it mean to be a changemaker? Before and after garden walks, students are encouraged to reflect on how they show Curiosity, Empathy, Responsibility, and Imagination during these walks and how these dispositions relate to being a scientist and changemaker. **Butterfly Garden Walks:** Students take multiple walks to a local butterfly garden, noticing what plants and animals they see and the relationships that exist between them. They are asked to consider: What do you see? What do you think? What do you wonder? How does it feel to be in nature? What are the benefits to self and others? These trips go across multiple weeks, helping students see the complete butterfly life cycle as well as the ways that butterflies interact with other animals within the garden, such as bees, flies, beetles, snails, lizards, and birds. Where possible, visiting the garden multiple times a week will enable students to hone their skills of observation and make connections to aspects such as weather and time of day that might affect what they see in the garden (Slow Looking strategy Set a Schedule p. **80**). Students can take photos of flora and fauna they observe, such as with tablets, learning how to carefully and respectfully approach animals. In particular, encourage students to reflect on these four questions over the course of their multiple visits: • 4a. How are our garden plants and animals interdependent? (F) • 4b. How does the food of caterpillars and butterflies differ? (F) • 4c. What types of plants do gardens need to feed pollinators and their young? (F) • 4d. How do habitats enable living things to meet their needs? (C) **Living Thing Categorizing:** What living things do we see in this garden? How can we put these in groups? Students take photos of different species, which are used later in the unit to look for interconnections between them. Students are invited to sort their photos into groups based on the type of plants and animals found (e.g., flowering plants, insects, birds, reptiles, etc.).

(Continued)

(Continued)

Learning Goals:	Phase of Worldwise Learning (Connect, Understand, Act)	Learning Experiences:
U1. In **living things, life cycles** contain stages for **growth** and **reproduction**.	**Understand**	**Understanding Living Things:** Engage students in the Is/Is Not strategy (p. 208) to differentiate between living and nonliving things. Provide the characteristics of living things prior to the sort. Note any naive conceptions students may hold about living things (e.g., a car is living because it moves). **Animal Parent and Young Sort:** Match the parent to its young. What do you notice? How can we group these? Students use their sorting to answer the question: How do young animals look similar to or different from the adults of a species? Encourage students to recognize which animals are likely to go through metamorphosis (e.g., insects and amphibians) and which look more like their adult parents (e.g., mammals, birds, and reptiles). This prepares students for the life cycle investigations into pollinators and flowering plants.
U1. In **living things, life cycles** contain stages for **growth** and **reproduction**. U2. **Pollinators** help **plants** grow, breed, and produce **food**. U7. Authors use a variety of **text features** to produce explanatory **information texts**. U8. By understanding their **properties**, mathematicians can use **two-dimensional** and **three-dimensional shapes** for a **purpose**.	**Connect** **Act**	**Pollination Frayer** **Model:** What is pollination? How do flowering plants reproduce? (1c) Watch BBC Bitesize—Reproduction in Flowering Plants to introduce the concept of pollination and how flowering plants reproduce. Use a wall Frayer Model to collect thinking about pollination over time (p. 206). Add to the wall chart during the unit, showing examples and non-examples. Photograph flowering plants on a garden walk, in particular those which are being pollinated by insects or birds, and add them to the chart. **Immersive Storytelling—Flowering Plant Reproduction:** Watch Story of Flowers twice as part of Immersive Storytelling (p. 147). **First Watch—Connection:** What is happening? What connections can you make to what you learned about how flowering plants reproduce? To your lives? Have a short discussion after the first viewing, giving students the following frames to support the conversation: • Connection: ○ *I connected to _____ in the story because . . .* ○ *This story is similar/different to _____ because . . .*

Learning Goals:	Phase of Worldwise Learning (Connect, Understand, Act)	Learning Experiences:

		Second Watch—Importance of Flowers:
		
		As students engage in the second viewing, encourage them to think about why flowers/flowering plants might be important to habitats. Who interacts with the flowers both above and below ground? Why? What might this tell us about the important role flowers play? Students can use the following frame to construct their ideas:
		
		• Argument:
		
		    ○ *I think this story shows us flowers are important because . . .*
		
		    ○ *_____ relies on flowers in this story . . . for example . . .*
		
		    ○ *In a habitat, flowers . . .*
		
		Mini-Action—Advocate for Flowers: Provide students with a mini-opportunity for action by allowing them to advocate for flowers with their families and the school community. Using learning from the Immersive Storytelling experience, students create a short Flipgrid to share why flowers are important, who depends on them, and how we should treat them as a result.
		
		Bee Life Cycle and Investigation: Using garden visit experiences and media resources, students investigate the questions:
		
		• 1e. What is the life cycle of a honey bee? (F)
		
		Time Lapse Video: Hatching Bees (National Geographic)
		
		How Do Honeybees Get Their Jobs? (National Geographic)
		
		• 2a. What special features do bees, butterflies, and other pollinators have that support pollination? (F)
		
		Honey Bees Make Honey and Bread (PBS / KQED) (features that support pollination)
		
		How Bees Can See the Invisible (PBS)
		
		• 8b. What properties do different shapes have? How might these be useful for different purposes? (F)
		
		Why do Bees Love Hexagons? (TED-Ed)
		
		As students watch these videos, provide students with sketch pads to take visual notes. Choose stopping points for creating quick sketches of life cycles, annotated pictures of bees, and so on. Before viewing, hold mini-lessons related to text features, encouraging students to use them during the viewing experience. If needed, show the videos in small groups to scaffold the note-taking skills for students' varying skill levels.

(Continued)

Learning Goals:	Phase of Worldwise Learning (Connect, Understand, Act)	Learning Experiences:
U1. In **living things, life cycles** contain stages for **growth** and **reproduction**. U2. **Pollinators** help **plants** grow, breed, and produce **food**. U7. Authors use a variety of **text features** to produce explanatory **information texts**. U8. By understanding their **properties**, mathematicians can use **two-dimensional** and **three-dimensional shapes** for a **purpose**.	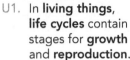 **Understand**	**Model Bee Hive:** Students create system models (p. 25) of a beehive to show: • The parts of the bee life cycle (1e) • How bees make food (2a and 2b) • How bees and plants help each other (2b) • Shapes used within the hive to maximize use of space (8b) Students annotate their models with labels, photographs, captions, arrows, and so on and explain the parts of their hive, how they connect, and relationships with the local environment using a screencast. Provide a checklist of relevant text features to include (as explored in literacy instruction). This formative assessment gives the chance to see how well students are applying these text features to their writing. Teach mini-lessons on junk modeling techniques (e.g., joining using cuts, ways to tape, etc.), if necessary.
U1. In **living things, life cycles** contain stages for **growth** and **reproduction**. U2. **Pollinators** help **plants** grow, breed, and produce **food**.	 **Connect** **Understand**	**Monarch Butterfly Life Cycle and Migration Investigation:** Using garden visit experiences and media resources, students investigate the question: • 1d. What is the life cycle of a butterfly? (F) Monarch Butterfly Life Cycle (National Geographic) The Amazing Journey of the Monarch Butterfly (Facts in Motion) Go Into the Heart of a Kaleidoscope of Butterflies (Nat Geo Wild) **Storytelling about Monarch Butterflies:** Using their learning from the monarch investigation, students are invited to create a StoryMap (p. 153) that charts a monarch's migration. Where does it travel and why? What challenges does the butterfly face? How does it overcome them? After creating their Story Maps, students can either write their stories or record them as voiceovers, while showing the journey on the map. **Generalizing About Life Cycles:** Students are invited to think about what stages occur in all life cycles they have explored (including human life cycle) and the importance of these various stages (in particular the role of growth and reproduction) using the Connect 4 strategy.

Learning Goals:	Phase of Worldwise Learning (Connect, Understand, Act)	Learning Experiences:
		Use diagrams of the flowering plant, bee, butterfly, and human life cycles, each in one quadrant of the Connect 4 placemat. This can be done on a classroom wall or whiteboard. Students think about the following questions: • What is the same across all four life cycles? • Why are these stages or aspects the same? (purpose) • Why might all life cycles share certain stages? To answer this last question as a generalization, students can be given the sentence starter: *All life cycles share . . . because . . .*
U2. **Pollinators** help **plants** grow, breed, and produce **food**. U7. Authors use a variety of **text features** to produce explanatory **information texts**.	**Connect**	**Farming Investigation:** Having learned about pollination and life cycles, now it is time for students to connect this learning to farming and food production. In this investigation, students explore the following questions using the linked media resources. If farms are nearby, take students to visit one to learn about this through hands-on experience and interviewing instead: 3a. How does farming rely on pollinators? (C) What if All Bees Die? (ASAPScience) 3b. How can farming harm pollinators and their habitats? (C) (e.g., monoculture agriculture, pesticides, lack of flowers, etc.) What is Monoculture? Michael Pollan (pre-watching for educators) The Buzz about Pesticides (Nature) Why are Bees Dying (PBS—It's Okay to Be Smart) 3d. What can farmers do to help pollinators in their fields? (C) Farming and Biodiversity (DW) Forest Gardens (National Geographic) How to Create a Monarch Rest Stop (National Geographic) Information related to these questions can be kept on a class chart and added to during or after each video. **Jigsaw Poster Challenge:** In small groups, students create a poster to show learning from the investigation about one of the following areas: • Foods Produced through Pollination

(Continued)

(Continued)

Learning Goals:	Phase of Worldwise Learning (Connect, Understand, Act)	Learning Experiences:
		• Ways Farming Can Harm Pollinators (e.g., use of monoculture agriculture, pesticides, not having enough flower diversity) • How People can Help Pollinators Encourage students to use text features explored earlier in the unit in their poster design.
U2. **Pollinators** help **plants** grow, breed, and produce **food**. U3. The way people farm can harm or help **pollinators** and their **habitats**.	**Understand**	**Making Connections:** Looking across the various posters that students have created, what connections can they make between them? In this game, students will need to connect two or more posters. First engage students in a Think-Pair so they can gather ideas. Then invite sharing. As students say their connections, write each on a sticky note and place it on one of the posters being connected. Students can use the following sentence frame to support them: • _____ connects to _____ because . . . **Critical Literacy—Paired Texts Strategy (p. 257):** How are insects portrayed on supermarket products, and how does this affect how we view them? Visit a local supermarket (or invite students to do so with their parents). Photograph any images of insects found on products. Back at school, reflect on these questions together using two dissimilar representations: • Why might insects be represented on these products differently? • What messages are the companies trying to convey with these images? • How do these representations connect to threats to pollinators and to insects in general?
U4. **Habitats** enable **living things** to meet their **needs**.	**Understand**	**Butterfly Garden Walks:** After having done Slow Looking in a local garden or park, invite students to make connections. Using photos taken by students showing the different living creatures they found in the garden (plants, animals, fungi, etc.) do Connected Circles (p. 180) and Causal Maps (p. 183). The goal of these two experiences is to explore the following questions: • 4a. How are our garden plants and animals interdependent? (F) • 4b. How does the food of caterpillars and butterflies differ? (F) • 4c. What types of plants do gardens need to feed pollinators and their young? (F)

Learning Goals:	Phase of Worldwise Learning (Connect, Understand, Act)	Learning Experiences:
		Generalizing about Habitats: After students have done Systems Mapping and Causal Mapping, engage them in a conversation to reflect on the conceptual question: • 4d. How do habitats enable living things to meet their needs? (C) Using the Corner Connections strategy (p. 221) students make connections between the words Habitat, Needs (Food, Water, Shelter), and Living Thing. 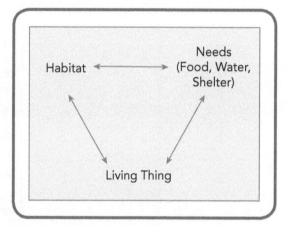 **Reflection on Scientific Behaviors:** In each students' learning journal, ask them to reflect on the scientific behaviors they showed throughout the unit, in particular in outdoor experiences. Use the following questions to support student reflection: • 6a. What observations can we make about how animals relate to each other in our local garden? (F) • 6b. How can scientists use observation to make discoveries? (C) • 6c. How do scientists use evidence to support their ideas? (C)
U5. Humans can protect **pollinators** and restore their **habitats** through a number of **actions**.	 **Connect**	**Local Pollinator Actions:** Invite students to learn more about the needs of local pollinators. Who are they (what species)? What plants to do they like? This connects to question 5a above. They can engage in this through interviews with local parks staff or other knowledgeable gardeners. Make a T-chart for the classroom wall showing different pollinators and their plant needs as research continues:

(Continued)

(Continued)

Learning Goals:	Phase of Worldwise Learning (Connect, Understand, Act)	Learning Experiences:

Pollinator	Plant Needs
Monarch Butterfly, for example	Milkweed for laying eggs/caterpillar food
	Flowering plants such as zinnia, Mexican sunflowers, and Brazilian verbena

Improving Local Environments: Next use a number of resources, such as these videos to learn about ways that the local environment can be improved to support pollinators (question 5c).

How to Help Pollinators in Cities (Nature)

How to Plant a Butterfly Garden | This Old House

How to Create a Monarch Rest Stop (National Geographic)

Help students pull out key ideas from these videos such as:

- Planting wildflowers

- Creating gardens that flower all year long

- Creating gardens that include butterfly host plants as well as flowering plants

Ask students to make connections to these key ideas and how they connect to student generalizations about:

- Life cycles

- Habitats that provide for the needs of living things

U5. Humans can protect **pollinators** and restore their **habitats** through a number of **actions**.

Act

Take Action: Provide the time for students to plan and take action.

Design and create a pollinator garden:

Given a small plot in the school garden, students design and create a pollinator garden taking the following into consideration:

- Host plants for different insect young

- Flowering plants for pollinators, preferably those that bloom at different times

Learning Goals:	Phase of Worldwise Learning (Connect, Understand, Act)	Learning Experiences:
		• Shelters for solitary bees and other pollinators • Signs and/communication about how to protect pollinators in the garden (e.g., not using chemical pesticides, etc.) **Screencast:** As part of the design and creation process, students take photos, create a slide presentation, and do a voiceover (can also be done as a written book) using the following questions: • How are our garden plants and animals interdependent? • How do pollinators and plants help each other? • What types of plants do gardens need to feed pollinators and their young? • What actions can humans take to protect pollinators? To do so, students use and show their understanding of various **text features:** • Table of Contents (First slide of deck) • Titles • Photographs • Captions • Labels Students are given feedback on their plans and actions based on: • Integration of unit knowledge, skill, and understandings across the disciplines • Feasibility and sustainability of their plans • Display of unit dispositions during the planning and doing of the action **Reflection on Unit Dispositions:** Return to the unit dispositions (e.g., Curiosity, Empathy, Responsibility, and Imagination). How have they developed these over the unit? How might these dispositions help the class as they plan their unit actions? Why?

Reflection

Reflect on the outcome of the inquiry. To what extent did students develop the unit knowledge, skills, and understandings? How was this demonstrated? How did students transfer understanding? What changes would you recommend if this unit were taught again?

(Continued)

(Continued)

Learning Goals:	Phase of Worldwise Learning (Connect, Understand, Act)	Learning Experiences:

Over the course of the unit, students deepened their understanding of pollinators and their importance to both ecosystems and our food. In Slow Looking experiences, students showed curiosity about caterpillars, butterflies, nectar-drinking birds, and bees. Over these repeated experiences, they made connections between living things and how they rely on each other. Students were able to use these real-life experiences to generalize about how habitats allow living things to meet their needs. Students were also able to take this understanding and transfer it to their pollinator garden design, recognizing that they were in essence creating a habitat for these creatures. This connected to students' sense of personal responsibility. They wanted to create a garden that our pollinators would enjoy spending time in. Regarding recommendations, many video resources are made for older children and so need scaffolding and slowing down for learners to pull out key ideas. Pre-teaching note-taking skills and then having clear stopping points throughout a video for learners to write down or sketch ideas was imperative for student comprehension. That said they were able to understand key ideas once the pace of information was slowed down for them.

Assets: Each child's thoughts, culture, and traits, viewed as strengths that contribute to the richness and diversity of classroom learning.

Changemakers: Agents of change who can question, think deeply, and problem solve to take meaningful action in their communities both now and in the future.

Character Strengths: Positive personality traits that encompass one's thoughts, feelings, and behaviors, such as kindness and humility, that have been recognized and valued throughout time and cultures.

Classroom Climate: The academic and social dimensions of the learning environment, including interactions, norms, and instructional practices, that holistically influence students' sense of belonging and connectedness with peers and educators. A **positive classroom climate** is characterized as feeling safe, inclusive, and supportive.

Competency: A set of interrelated knowledge, skills, and attitudes that demonstrate readiness and the motivation to act, such as to solve an authentic challenge.

Concept Formation: The process by which one acquires an individual concept through analyzing, classifying, and labeling examples and non-examples of the concept.

Concepts: Abstract mental organizers that transfer *across* time, place, and situation.

Conceptual Questions: Guiding questions that explore the relationship between two or more concepts, are transferable across contexts, and guide learners to develop conceptual understandings.

Conceptual Understanding: A statement of relationship between two or more concepts. It may also be referred to as a generalization or *big idea*.

Conflict: A difference between the needs and interests of two parties, which can be either positive or negative.

Critical Consciousness: Students' awareness of the social and political systems that shape society and how it functions.

Critical Literacy: The practice of deconstructing a text to uncover and question embedded messages that may perpetuate social and/or environmental inequities and power structures.

Deductive Approach: A more teacher-centered instructional practice, where the teacher introduces concepts and conceptual understandings to students followed by examples, which aim to validate those conceptual understandings.

Democratic Classroom: A safe environment, where students actively practice democratic values, understand their rights, and take responsibility for their behavior as both individuals and members of a community.

Disciplinary Learning: An approach that divides content into separate and distinct subjects or disciplines, such as science, mathematics, and social studies. This term covers the full range of subjects, both those more traditional such as language arts and newer areas of study, such as media education.

Dispositions: Characteristic patterns of behavior and ways of thinking that are relatively enduring, meaning that students display them in different contexts and situations, such as open-mindedness, empathy, curiosity.

Empathy: The capacity to sense and understand others' thoughts and emotions. Empathy can be categorized as *affective* (feeling another's feelings) or *cognitive* (imagining what another is feeling or thinking, also known as **perspective-taking**).

Facts: Discrete information that relates to a topic locked in time, place, and situation. Unlike conceptual understanding, factual knowledge does *not* transfer.

Feedback Loop: A naturally occurring process that reflects the interconnectedness of system elements. Feedback loops can be **balancing** (stabilizing systems) or **reinforcing** (accelerating changes, such as the growth or decline of system conditions).

Flows: The elements that go into (**inflows**) and come out of (**outflows**) a system that are produced from interactions within that system.

Geo-Literacy: A skill coined by the National Geographic Society that integrates geographic understanding with geographic reasoning to help individuals make critical, far-reaching decisions in an interconnected, multicultural world.

Generalization: See **Conceptual Understanding**.

Global Challenge: Situations where multiple factors interrelate to produce intended and unintended outcomes, often at various scales. They are persistent, borderless, large in scale, and complex.

Global Citizenship: An overarching term for citizenship that transcends a single nationality and political or geographic borders with emphasis on global interconnectedness and a shared humanity.

Global Competence: The knowledge, skills, and dispositions needed to understand and act on local, global, and intercultural issues.

Globalization: The increased interaction and interdependence of people and places across borders.

Identity: A set of socially and independently constructed, multifaceted, and fluid characteristics that we use to describe ourselves and others, such as gender, race, and religion, that affect interactions and one's sense of belonging within social groups.

Inductive Approach: An instructional practice where students explore factual examples, look for patterns across them, and then form conceptual understandings to synthesize their thinking.

Integrated Approach: A teaching and learning lens that brings together the self, social, and cognitive dimensions of students, viewing their backgrounds as assets, the social environment as a space to form trusting relationships, and the disciplines as resources to foster deep understanding about issues.

Intercultural Understanding: The interrelated knowledge of one's own and other cultures and attitudes of compassion, respect, and open-mindedness essential to living peacefully and in harmony with diverse peoples and nature.

Interdisciplinary Learning: An integrated curriculum approach that explores a topic, theme, or issue holistically, synthesizing disciplinary perspectives into a unique whole.

Local, Global, and Intercultural Issues: Complex issues that manifest within and across geographical and cultural contexts resulting from human and ecological interactions, often with far-reaching impacts.

Mental Models: Deeply held beliefs, assumptions, and stories individuals hold about themselves, others, and the world that influence human perspectives.

Mindful Awareness: The conscious act of focusing attention to present experiences without judgment to respond more thoughtfully and compassionately to oneself and others.

Multidisciplinary Learning: An integrated curriculum approach that explores a topic, theme, or issue through the distinct perspectives of two or more disciplines.

Peace: Composed of both *negative* peace (the absence of war and conflict) and *positive* peace (attitudes, institutions and structures that create and sustain peaceful societies).

Pedagogy for People, Planet, and Prosperity: An approach that seeks to teach for a sustainable future with the goal of shaping Worldwise Learners (See Teaching for a Sustainable Future; Worldwise Learner).

Perspective Consciousness: The awareness that one's perspective and interpretation of events are unique, shaped by one's cultural beliefs, values, and lived experiences.

Perspective-Getting: The deliberate act of seeking an individual's perspective by gathering information via questioning, active listening, and observation.

Perspective-Taking: The psychological process of inferring and understanding another's beliefs, values, and viewpoints.

Racial Trauma: The mental, physical, and emotional injuries resulting from systemic racism, racial bias, and discrimination, making Black, Indigenous, and People of Color particularly vulnerable in schools.

Responsibilities: Duties associated with actions and attitudes within one's power or control.

Rights: Legal, social, or ethical principles that frame what individuals are allowed to be, to do, or to have, categorized as **absolute** (cannot be limited or restricted for any reason) and **non-absolute** (may be limited in certain circumstances).

Self-Awareness: The ability to recognize and understand one's feelings, thoughts, and behaviors through self-examination and reflection.

Slow Looking: Coined by Project Zero researcher Shari Tishman, the practice of close observation of an object, text, or idea, over time to notice details, interrelationships, and complexities beyond initial impressions.

Social-Emotional Learning (SEL): The process of acquiring and applying the knowledge, skills, and dispositions needed to nurture individual and collective well-being; to establish caring, supportive relationships; and to participate in responsible decision-making in classroom and school communities.

Student Agency: A student's capacity and motivation to influence their own learning processes, including setting goals, acting to achieve those goals, and reflecting to inform future actions based on feedback from teachers.

Sustainable Development: A holistic approach to development that balances economic growth with social and environmental justice.

Synergistic Thinking: Derived from the Greek word for synergy (meaning working together), a type of thinking coined by Lynn Erickson that involves the interplay between factual and conceptual levels of thinking needed for deeper understanding.

System: A group of interconnected elements that are organized for a function or a purpose.

Teaching for a Sustainable Future: An educational approach centered on nurturing students' knowledge, understanding, skills, and motivation to promote a sustainable world where economic prosperity is in balance with the carrying capacity of the planet.

Topic: A specific, narrow focus for learning such as an event or issue that is framed by facts and locked in time, place, and situation.

Transfer: The application of conceptual understandings and skills to a new context or situation, accelerating the rate and/or depth of new learning. Transfer can occur in near (similar) or far (dissimilar) contexts.

Visual Storytelling: Using art, data, or maps to contextualize complex issues and perspectives.

VUCA: An acronym that refers to the volatility, uncertainty, complexity, and ambiguity of current world conditions.

Worldwise Educators: Teachers who are committed to continuous personal and professional growth as global citizens so they may, in turn, nurture global competence in their students.

Worldwise Learners: Globally competent students and engaged citizens who care about, investigate, and take action on significant local, global, and intercultural issues.

REFERENCES

Adichie, C. N. (2009, October 7). *The danger of the single story* [Video]. TED Conferences. https://www.ted.com/talks/chimamanda_ngozi_adichie_the_danger_of_a_single_story

Agency by Design. (n.d.). JusticexDesign: Developing a sensitivity to designed injustices. http://agencybydesign.org/node/466

Alim, H. S., & Paris, D. (2017). What is culturally sustaining pedagogy and why does it matter? In D. Paris & H. S. Alim (Eds.), *Culturally sustaining pedagogies: Teaching and learning for justice in a changing world* (pp. 1–24). Teachers College Press.

Asia Society. (2011). Considering what it means to "take action." http://asiasociety.org/files/afterschool-ehtrainers-workshop-takingaction.pdf

Asia Society. (2005). *What is global competence?* https://asiasociety.org/education/what-global-competence

Associated Press. (2019). *NC school's slavery role-playing game prompts investigation.* https://apnews.com/article/1b97a219815 64df5acf9d87fb7c8b35d

Bandura, A. (1997). *Self-efficacy: The exercise of control* (1st ed.). W. H. Freeman & Company.

Beane, J. A. (1997). *Curriculum integration. Designing the core of democratic education.* Teachers College Press.

Bennis, W. G., & Nanus, B. (1986). *Leaders: The strategies for taking charge.* Harper & Row.

Berger Kaye, C. (2010). *The complete guide to service learning: Proven, practical ways to engage students in civic responsibility, academic curriculum, & social action* (2nd ed.). Free Spirit.

Bishop, R. S. (1990). Mirrors, windows, and sliding glass doors. *Perspectives: Choosing and Using Books for the Classroom, 6*(3).

Black, M. (2016). *The fall of Flint.* https://www.globalonenessproject.org/library/photo-essays/fall-flint

Boix Mansilla, V. (2016). How to be a global thinker. *Educational Leadership, 74*(4), 10–16.

Boix Mansilla, V. (2015). *Finding our way into each other's worlds: Musings on cultural perspective taking.* https://pz.harvard.edu/resources/finding-our-way-into-each-others-worlds-musings-on-cultural-perspective-taking

Boix Mansilla, V., & Chua, F. (2016). *Signature pedagogies in global competence education: Understanding quality teaching practice.* Harvard.

Boix Mansilla, V., & Jackson, A. (2011). *Educating for global competence: Preparing our youth to engage the world.* The Asia Society.

Boix Mansilla, V., Miller, C. M., & Gardner, H. (2000). On disciplinary lenses and inter-disciplinary work. In Wineburg, S., & Grossman, P. (Eds.), *Interdisciplinary curriculum: Challenges to implementation.* Teachers College Press.

Boudreau, E. (2020). *The art of slow looking in the classroom: The cross-disciplinary learning benefits of paying close attention.* https://www.gse.harvard.edu/news/uk/20/01/art-slow-looking-classroom

Browett, J., & Ashman, G. (2008). *Thinking globally: Global perspectives in the early years classroom.* Curriculum Corporation.

Brown, B. (2010, October 6). *The power of vulnerability* [Video]. TED Conferences. https://www.ted.com/talks/brene_brown_the_power_of_vulnerability

Bruner, J. S. (1987). *Actual minds, possible worlds.* Harvard U.P.

Camarota, S. A., Griffith, B., & Zeigler, K. (2017, January 9). *Mapping the impact of immigration on public schools.* https://cis.org/Report/Mapping-Impact-Immigration-Public-Schools

Campbell-Patton, C., & Mortenson, D. (2011). *WorldSavvyglobalcompetencematrix.* https://www.worldsavvy.org/our-approach/global-competence/

Centers for Disease Control and Prevention. (n.d.). *Adverse childhood experiences: Behavioral risk factor surveillance system ACE data.* https://www.cdc.gov/violenceprevention/acestudy/ace-brfss.html

Center for Media Literacy (2011). *A recipe for action: Deconstructing food advertising educator guide.* http://www.medialit.org/sites/default/files/Recipe%20for%20Action%20Educator%20Guide.pdf

Clapp, E. P., Solis, S. L., Ho, C. K. N., & Laguzza, K. (2020). *Maker-centered learning playbook for early childhood education.* Project Zero at the Harvard Graduate School of Education.

Clark, A. (2005). Ways of seeing: Using the Mosaic approach to listen to young children's perspectives. In A. Clark, A. T. Kjørholt, & P. Moss (Eds.), *Beyond listening: Children's perspectives on early childhood services* (pp. 29–49). Policy Press.

Cole, B., & McGuire, M. (2012). Real-world problems: Engaging young learners in critical thinking. *Social Studies and the Young Learner, 24*(4), 15–17.

Collaborative for Academic, Social, and Emotional Learning. (2020). *SEL: What are the core competence areas and where are they promoted?* https://casel.org/sel-framework/

Commoner, B. (1971). *The closing circle: Nature, man, and technology.* Alfred A. Knopf.

Compass Education. (2017). *A guide to Atkisson accelerator and systems thinking tools and methods.* https://www.compasseducation.org/

Cook, A., & Beer, T. (2018). Planting citizenship: Lessons for invoking sustainability via children's civic voice. Architecture MPS Conference Proceedings.

Costa, A. L., & Kallick, B. (Eds.). (2008). *Learning and leading with habits of mind: 16 essential characteristics of success.* ASCD.

Crawford, E.O., & Shelit, D. (2012). *Peaceful communities for all: An early childhood unit.* U.S. Fund for UNICEF.

Dack, H., van Hover, S., & Hicks, D. (2016). "Try not to giggle if you can help it": The implementation of experiential instructional techniques in social studies classrooms. *Journal of Social Studies Research, 40*(1), 39–52.

Dalmases, F. B., & Albarenga, P. (2020). *Lilia: Preserving the Amazon River's fauna is preserving planet Earth.* Pulitzer Center. https://pulitzercenter.org/reporting/lilia-preserving-amazon-rivers-fauna-preserving-planet-earth

Demetriou, H. (2018). *Empathy, emotion, and education.* Palgrave Macmillan.

DeSilver, D. (2020). *In past elections, U.S. trailed most developed countries in voter turnout.* Pew Research Center. https://www.pewresearch.org/fact-tank/2020/11/03/in-past-elections-u-s-trailed-most-developed-countries-in-voter-turnout/

Dewey, J. (1916). *Democracy and education: An introduction to the philosophy of education.* MacMillan.

Dias, M. (2018). *Marley Dias gets it done: And so can you!* Scholastic Press.

Doman, F. (2018). *True you: Authentic strengths for kids.* Next Century.

Djikic, M., & Oatley, K. (2014). The art in fiction: From indirect communication to changes of the self. *Psychology of Aesthetics, Creativity, and the Arts, 8,* 498–505.

Dungy, C. T. (2018). *From dirt.* https://emergencemagazine.org/story/from-dirt/

Easton, F. (1997). Educating the whole child, "Head, Hearts, and Hands": Learning from the Waldorf experience. *Theory into Practice, 36*(2), 87–94.

Epley, N. (2014). *Mindwise: How we understand what others think, believe, feel, and want.* Knopf.

Erickson, H. L., & Lanning, L. (2014). *Transitioning to concept-based curriculum and instruction: How to bring content and process together.* Corwin.

Erickson, H. L., Lanning, L., & French, R. (2017). *Concept-based curriculum and instruction for the thinking classroom* (2nd ed.). Corwin.

Farber, M. (2019). *The benefits of constructionist gaming.* Edutopia. https://www.edutopia.org/article/benefits-constructionist-gaming

Feng, L. (2012). Teacher and student responses to interdisciplinary aspects of sustainability education: What do we really know? *Environmental Education Research, 18*(1), 31–43.

Frank, T. (2020, June 2). Flooding disproportionately harms black neighborhoods. *E&E News.* https://www.scientificamerican.com/article/flooding-disproportionately-harms-black-neighborhoods/

Freire, P. (2000). *Pedagogy of the oppressed.* Continuum.

Freire, P. (1998). *Pedagogy of freedom: Ethics, democracy, and civic courage.* Rowman & Littlefield.

Freire, P. (1970). *Pedagogy of the oppressed.* Bloomsbury.

Gagné, R. M. (1965). *The conditions of learning and theory of instruction* (1st ed.). Holt, Rinehart & Winston.

Gapminder Foundation. (2020). *The SDGs aren't the same old same old* [Video file]. https://youtu.be/v7WUpgPZzpI

Gee, J. (2007). Learning and games. In K. Salen (Ed.), *The ecology of games: Connecting youth, games, and learning* (pp. 21–40). MIT Press.

Gleeson, A. M., & D'Souza, L. A. (2016). Expanding local to global through ESRI Story Maps. *Social Studies and the Young Learner, 29*(2), 14–16.

Global Oneness Project. (2020). *Winners of our first student photography contest: Document your place on the planet.* https://www.globalonenessproject.org/student-projects/winners-our-first-student-photography-contest

Goleman, D., & Senge, P. (2014). *The triple focus: A new approach to education.* More Than Sound.

Gollob, R., Krapf, P., Ólafsdóttir, O., & Weidinger, W. (2010). *Educating for democracy: Background materials on democratic citizenship and human rights education for teachers.* Council of Europe.

Gottschall, J. (2013). *The storytelling animal: How stories make us human.* Mariner Books.

Greater Good Magazine. (n.d.). *Compassion: Defined.* https://greatergood.berkeley.edu/topic/compassion/definition

Greene, M. (2005). Teaching in a moment of crisis: The spaces of imagination. *New Educator, 1*, 77–80.

Haidt, J. (2006). *The happiness hypothesis: Finding modern truth in ancient wisdom.* Basic Books.

Hammond, Z. (2014). *Culturally responsive teaching and the brain: Promoting authentic engagement and rigor among culturally and linguistically diverse students.* Corwin.

Hanvey, R. G. (1982). An attainable global perspective. *Theory Into Practice, 21*(3), 162–167.

Harshman, J. (2016). Critical global competence and the C3 in social studies education. *Social Studies, 107*(5), 160–164.

Heafner, T. L. (2020). Agency, advocacy, activism: Action for social studies. *Social Education, 84*(1), 4–12.

Health, C., & Heath, D. (2010). *Switch: How to change things when change is hard.* Broadway Books.

Hedefalk, M., Almqvist, J., Östman, L. (2015). Education for sustainable development in early childhood education: A review of the research literature. *Environmental Education Research, 21*(7), 975–990.

Hill, M., & Beraza, S. (2010). *Bag it: Is your life too plastic?* Reel Thing Production Films.

Hinton, A. (2011). *Amar* [film]. Pilgrim Films.

Horowitz, S. S. (2012). *The universal sense: How hearing shapes the mind.* Bloomsbury.

HundrED. (2017). *Sir Ken Robinson compares human organisations to organisms: Education is a dynamic system.* https://hundred.org/en/articles/5-sir-ken-robinson-compares-human-organisations-to-organisms-education-is-a-dynamic-system

Huss, J. C., Fratzl, P., Dunlop, J. W., Merritt, D. J., Miller, B. P., & Eder, M. (2019). Protecting offspring against fire: Lessons from *Banksia* seed pods. *Frontiers in Plant Science, 10*, 1–12. https://doi.org/10.3389/fpls.2019.00283

IDEO. (2012). *Design thinking for educators.* http://designthinkingforeducators.com

Institute for Humane Education. (2020). *The solutionary guidebook.* https://humaneeducation.org/solutionary-hub/educate-solutionary-generation/solutionary-guidebook/

International Society for Technology in Education. (2020). *ISTE standards.* https://www.iste.org/standards

Jenks, C. E. (2010). Using oral history in the elementary school classroom. *Social Studies and the Young Learner, 23*(1), 31–32.

Jones, S. P. (2020). *Ending curriculum violence.* https://www.learningforjustice.org/magazine/spring-2020/ending-curriculum-violence

Jordan, C. (n.d.). *Running the numbers: An American self-portrait.* http://www.chrisjordan.com/gallery/rtn

Katz, C. (2017). *Small pests, big problems: The global spread of bark beetles.* Yale Environment 360. https://e360.yale.edu/features/small-pests-big-problems-the-global-spread-of-bark-beetles

Kenyon, E., & Christoff, A. (2020). Global citizenship education through global children's literature: An analysis of the NCSS Notable Trade Books. *Journal of Social Studies Research, 44*(4), 397–408.

Kohlberg, L. (1980). High school democracy and educating for a just society. In R. Mosher (Ed.), *Moral education: A first generation of research and development.* Praeger.

Laininen, E. (2019). Transforming our worldview towards a sustainable future. In J. W. Cook (Ed.), *Sustainability, human well-being, and the future of education* (pp. 161–200). Palgrave Macmillan. https://doi.org/10.1007/978-3-319-78580-6_5

Learning for Justice. (n.d.). *Creating questions to engage critically with texts.* https://www.tolerance.org/classroom-resources/teaching-strategies/exploring-texts-through-read-alouds/creating-questions-to

Lewison, M., Leland, C., & Harste, J. C. (2015). *Creating critical classrooms: Reading and writing with an edge* (2nd ed.). Routledge.

Loften, A. (Director), & Vaughan-Lee, E. (Co-Director). (2019). *The atomic tree* [Film]. GoProjectFilms.

Mar, R. A., Oatley, K., Djikic, M., & Mullin, J. (2011). Emotion and narrative in fiction: Interactive influences before, during, and after reading. *Cognition and Emotion, 25*, 818–833. https://doi.org/10.1080/02699931.2010.515151

Marschall, C., & French, R. L. (2018). *Concept-based inquiry in action: Strategies to promote transferable understanding.* Corwin.

Marzano, R. J. (2010). The art and science of teaching / Representing knowledge nonlinguistically. *Educational Leadership, 67*(8), 84–86.

Meadows, D. H. (2008). *Thinking in systems: A primer.* Chelsea Green.

Merryfield, M. (2004). Elementary students in substantive culture learning. *Social Education, 68*(4), 270–273.

Migration Policy Institute. (2020, February 14). *Frequently requested statistics on immigrants and immigration in the United States.* https://www.migrationpolicy.org/article/frequently-requested-statistics-immigrants-and-immigration-united-states

Murdoch, K., & Hornsby, D. (1997). *Planning curriculum connections: Whole-school planning for integrated curriculum.* Eleanor Curtain.

Myers, J. P., & Zaman, H. A. (2009). Negotiating the global and national: Immigrant and dominant culture adolescents' vocabularies of citizenship in a transnational world. *Teachers College Record, 111*(11), 2589–2625.

National Aeronautics and Space Administration. (2021). *Climate change: How do we know?* https://climate.nasa.gov/evidence/

NASA. (2020). *From smoke going round the world to aerosol levels, NASA observes Australia's bushfires.* https://www.nasa.gov/feature/goddard/2020/from-smoke-going-round-the-world-to-aerosol-levels-nasa-observes-australias-bushfires

National Geographic Society. (1996–2020). *What is geo-literacy?* https://www.nationalgeographic.org/media/what-is-geo-literacy/

National Geographic Society. (2017). *Geo-inquiry process: Educator guide.* https://media.nationalgeographic.org/assets/file/Educator_Guide_Geo_Inquiry_Final_1.pdf

Next Generation Science Standards. (2013). *The standards.* https://www.nextgenscience.org/search-standards

Nissani, M. (1995). Fruits, salads, and smoothies: A working definition of interdisciplinarity. *Journal of Educational Thought, 29*(2), 121–128.

O'Bryne, W. I., Houser, K., Stone, R., & White, M. (2018). Digital storytelling in early childhood: Student illustrations shaping social interactions. *Frontiers in Psychology, 9,* 1800. https://doi.org/10.3389/fpsyg.2018.02749

O'Connor, K., & Zeichner, K. (2011). Preparing US teachers for critical global education. *Globalisation, Societies and Education, 9*(3–4), 521–536.

Organisation for Economic Co-operation and Development (OECD). (2018a). PISA: Preparing our youth for an inclusive and sustainable world. *The OECD global competence framework.* Retrieved from https://www.oecd.org/pisa/Handbook-PISA-2018-Global-Competence.pdf

Organisation for Economic Co-operation and Development (OECD). (2018b). *The future of education and skills: Education 2030.* https://www.oecd.org/education/2030-project/

Orr, D. W. (2004). *Earth in mind: On education, environment, and the human prospect* (2nd ed.). Island Press.

Osorio, S. L. (2018). Multicultural literature as a classroom tool. *Multicultural Perspectives, 20*(1), 47–52.

Out of Eden Learn. (n.d.). *About us.* https://learn.outofedenwalk.com/about/

OXFAM. (2008). *Education for global citizenship.* https://www.oxfam.org.uk/education/who-we-are/global-citizenship-guides/

Paris, D. (2012). Culturally sustaining pedagogy: A needed change in stance, terminology, and practice. *Educational Researcher, 41*(3), 93–97.

Paul, R. W. (1988). Ethics without indoctrination. *Educational Leadership, 45*(8), 10–19.

Paul, R., & Elder, L. (2006). *The miniature guide to critical thinking concepts and tools.* Foundation for Critical Thinking Press.

PBL Works. (n.d.). *What is PBL?* https://www.pblworks.org/what-is-pbl

Population Connection. (2016). *World population history.* https://worldpopulationhistory.org/

Rakel, D. (2018). *The compassionate connection: The healing power of empathy and mindful listening.* W. W. Norton & Company.

Rapoport, A. (2020). Development of global identity in the social studies classroom. *Journal of Social Studies Education Research, 11*(1), 1–20.

Raygorodetsky, G. (2018). *Indigenous people defend Earth's biodiversity—but they're in danger.* https://www.nationalgeographic.com/environment/article/can-indigenous-land-stewardship-protect-biodiversity-

Resnick, I., Newcombe, N. S., & Shipley, T. F. (2016). Dealing with big numbers: Representation and understanding of magnitudes outside of human experience. *Cognitive Science, 41*(4), 1020–1041.

Richardson, C., Henriksen, D., & Mishra, P. (2017). The courage to be creative: An interview with Dr. Yong Zhao. *TechTrends, 61,* 515–519.

Sarangapani, P. (2003). *Constructing school knowledge: An ethnography of learning in an Indian village.* SAGE.

Schaffner, A. K. (2020). *The power of altruism: Why it matters even more in times of crisis.* https://www.psychologytoday.com/us/blog/the-art-self-improvement/202004/the-power-altruism

Schank, R. C., & Abelson, R. P. (1995). Knowledge and memory: The real story. In R. S. Wyer (Ed.), *Advances in social cognition, Vol. 8. Knowledge and memory: The real story* (pp. 1–85). Lawrence Erlbaum Associates.

Schaul, K., Rabinowitz, K., & Mellnik, T. (2020). Elections: 2020 turnout is the highest in over a century. *Washington Post.* https://www.washingtonpost.com/graphics/2020/elections/voter-turnout/

Schmidt, J. C., Manson, P. A., & Windschitl, T. A. (Eds.). (2000). *Our world, our rights: Teaching about rights and responsibilities in elementary schools.* Amnesty International USA.

Schweber, S. A. (2003). Simulating survival. *Curriculum Inquiry, 33*(2), 139–188.

Seligman, M. (2002). *Authentic happiness.* Atria Paperback.

Senge, P. M., Kleiner, A., Roberts, C., Ross, R. B., & Smith, B. J. (1994). *The fifth discipline fieldbook: Strategies and tools for building a learning organization.* Doubleday.

Short, K. G. (2019). The dangers of reading globally. *Bookbird: A Journal of International Children's Literature, 57*(2), 1–11.

Siegel, D. (2012). *The developing mind: How relationships and the brain interact to shape who we are* (2nd ed.). Guilford Press.

Simmons, D. (2021). Why SEL alone isn't enough. *Equity in Action, 78*(6), 30–34. http://www.ascd.org/publications/educational-leadership/mar21/vol78/num06/Why-SEL-Alone-Isn't-Enough.aspx

Singh, N. C., & Duraiappah, A. (Eds.). (2020). *Rethinking learning: A review of social and* emotional learning for education systems. United Nations Educational, Scientific and Cultural Organization Mahatma Gandhi Institute of Education.

Sobel, D. (2004). *Place-based education: Connecting classrooms and communities* (2nd ed.). Orion Society.

Stanford dSchool. (2020). *Tools for taking action.* https://dschool.stanford.edu/resources

The Story of Stuff Project. (2017). *What kind of changemaker are you?* https://action.story ofstuff.org/survey/changemaker-quiz/

Sweeney, L. B. (2017). All systems go! Developing a generation of "systems-smart" kids. In The Worldwatch Institute (Ed.), *EarthEd (state of the world): Rethinking education on a changing planet* (pp. 141–154). Island Press.

Sweeney, L. B. (2015, July 1). Why "think about systems"? *Talking about systems: Looking for systems in everyday life.* https://www.lindaboothsweeney.net/blog/?tag=systems-literacy

Taba, H. (1965). The teaching of thinking. *Elementary English, 42*(5), 534–542.

Tichnor-Wagner, A., Parkhouse, H., Glazier, J., & Cain, J. M. (2019). *Becoming a globally competent teacher.* ASCD.

Tishman, S. (2018). *Slow looking: The art and practice of learning through observation.* Routledge.

UNICEF Canada. (n.d.). *Classroom charters.* https://www.unicef.ca/sites/default/files/legacy/imce_uploads/UTILITY%20NAV/TEACHERS/DOCS/GC/Classroom_Charters_Instructions.pdf

United Nations. (2020). *Policy brief: Education during COVID-19 and beyond.* https://www.un.org/development/desa/dspd/wp-content/uploads/sites/22/2020/08/sg_policy_brief_covid-19_and_education_august_2020.pdf

United Nations Department of Economic and Social Affairs. (2019). *The number of international migrants reaches 272 million, continuing an upward trend in all world regions, says UN.* https://www.un.org/development/desa/en/news/population/international-migrant-stock-2019.html

United Nations Educational, Scientific, and Cultural Organization. (2020). *Manual for developing intercultural competencies.* Author.

United Nations Educational, Scientific, and Cultural Organization. (2018). *Issues and trends in education for sustainable development.* https://unesdoc.unesco.org/ark:/48223/pf0000261954

United Nations Educational, Scientific, and Cultural Organization. (2016). *Education for people & planet: Creating sustainable futures for all.* https://en.unesco.org/gem-report/report/2016/education-people-and-planet-creating-sustainable-futures-all

United Nations Educational, Scientific, and Cultural Organization. (2014). *Global citizenship education: Preparing learners for the challenges of the twenty-first century.* https://unesdoc.unesco.org/ark:/48223/pf0000227729

United Nations Educational, Scientific, and Cultural Organization. (2010). *Education for intercultural understanding. Reorienting teacher education to address sustainable development: Guidelines and tools.* https://unesdoc.unesco.org/ark:/48223/pf0000189051/PDF/189051eng.pdf.multi

United Nations Educational, Scientific, and Cultural Organization International Bureau for Education. (2020). *Glossary of curriculum-related terms.* http://www.ibe.unesco.org/en/news/ibe-unesco-global-consultation-revised-curriculum-glossary

United Nations Environment Programme. (2020). *How to feed 10 billion people.* https://www.unenvironment.org/news-and-stories/story/how-feed-10-billion-people

United Nations General Assembly. (2015). *Transforming our world: The 2030 Agenda for Sustainable Development.* https://www.refworld.org/docid/57b6e3e44.html

United Nations High Commission for Refugees. (2020). *Figures at a glance.* https://www.unhcr.org/asia/figures-at-a-glance.html

United Nations Sustainable Development Goals. (n.d.). *Goals: 4 Quality education.* https://www.un.org/sustainabledevelopment/education/

United States Census Bureau. (2017). *Voting in America: A look at the 2016 presidential election.* https://www.census.gov/newsroom/blogs/random-samplings/2017/05/voting_in_america.html

United States Environmental Protection Agency. (n.d.). *Climate change indicators: Oceans.* https://www.epa.gov/climate-indicators/oceans

van Klink, R., Bowler, D. E., Gongalsky, K. B., Swengel, A. B., Gentile, A., & Chase, J. M.

(2020). Meta-analysis reveals declines in terrestrial but increased in freshwater insect abundances. *Science, 368*(6489), 417–420.

Vander Ark, T., Liebtag, E., & McClennen, N. (2020). *The power of place: Authentic learning through place-based education.* ASCD.

Vasquez, V. M., Janks, H., & Comber, B. (2019). Critical literacy as a way of being and doing. *Language Arts, 96*(5), 300–311.

Vaughan-Lee, C. (2019). The power of immersive storytelling: A tool for transformative learning. *Childhood Education, 95*(3), 23–31.

VIA Institute on Character. (2020). *Professionals working with youth: Inspire children to celebrate their unique gifts.* https://www.viacharacter.org/professionals/youth

Vidili, M. (2018). *Why we must engage women and children in disaster risk management.* https://blogs.worldbank.org/sustainablecities/why-engaging-women-and-children-disaster-risk-management-matters-and-how-it-makes-difference

Waters Center for Systems Thinking. (2020). *Habits of a systems thinker.* https://waterscenterst.org/systems-thinking-tools-and-strategies/habits-of-a-systems-thinker/

Weil, Z. (2011, January 14). The world becomes what you teach. https://youtu.be/t5HEV96dIuY

Wilson, E. O. (1999). *The diversity of life.* W. W. Norton & Company.

World Commission on Environment and Development. (1987). *Our common future.* Oxford University Press.

World Economic Forum. (2020a). *5 global efforts to tackle Australian bushfires.* https://www.weforum.org/agenda/2020/01/ways-to-help-australia-bushfires-volunteer-firefighters-fundraisers/

World Economic Forum. (2020b). *Reports: A decade left. Confronting runaway climate threat.* https://reports.weforum.org/global-risks-report-2020/a-decade-left/

World Economic Forum. (2019). *How much data is generated each day?* https://www.weforum.org/agenda/2019/04/how-much-data-is-generated-each-day-cf4bddf29f/

World Economic Forum. (2013). *Digital wildfires in a hyperconnected world.* http://reports.weforum.org/global-risks-2013/risk-case-1/digital-wildfires-in-a-hyperconnected-world/?doing_wp_cron=1551866882.2552580833435058593750#read

World Health Organization. (2020). *Pneumonia of unknown cause – China.* https://www.who.int/csr/don/05-january-2020-pneumonia-of-unkown-cause-china/en/

World Health Organization. (2017). *Diarrhoeal disease: Key facts.* https://www.who.int/news-room/fact-sheets/detail/diarrhoeal-disease

World Innovation Summit for Education. (2020, January 24). *WISE global education barometer: Youth perceptions on their education and their future.* https://www.ipsos.com/sites/default/files/ct/publication/documents/2020-01/wise-global-education-barometer-2020-ipsos.pdf

Zak, P. (2015). Why inspiring stories make us react: The neuroscience of narrative. *Cerebrum, 2.*

Zhao, Y. (2010). Preparing globally competent teachers: A new imperative for teacher education. *Journal of Teacher Education, 61*(5), 422–431.

Confident Teachers, Inspired Learners

CAROL PELLETIER RADFORD

This vivid and inspirational guide offers educators practical strategies to promote their well-being and balance. Readers will find wisdom for a fulfilling career in education through teachers' stories of resilience, tips for mindful living, and podcast interviews with inspiring teachers and leaders.

JULIE STERN, KRISTA FERRARO, KAYLA DUNCAN, TREVOR ALEO

This step-by-step guide walks educators through the process of identifying curricular goals, establishing assessment targets, and planning curriculum and instruction that facilitates the transfer of learning to new and challenging situations.

STEPAN MEKHITARIAN

Transition back to school by leveraging the best of distance learning and classroom instruction. Learn how to create a blended learning experience that fosters learning, collaboration, and engagement.

SHIRLEY CLARKE

Learning intentions and success criteria expert Shirley Clarke shows how to phrase learning intentions for students, create success criteria to match, and adapt and implement them across disciplines.

No matter where you are in your professional journey, Corwin aims to ease the many demands teachers face on a daily basis with accessible strategies that benefit ALL learners. Through research-based, high-quality content, we offer practical guidance on a wide range of topics, including curriculum planning, learning frameworks, classroom design and management, and much more. Our resources are developed by renowned educators and designed for easy implementation in order to provide tangible results for you and your students.

WARREN BERGER, ELISE FOSTER

Written to be both inspirational and practical, *Beautiful Questions in the Classroom* shows educators how they can transform their classrooms into cultures of curiosity.

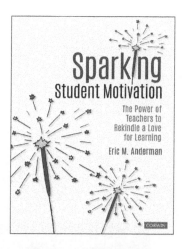

ERIC M. ANDERMAN

Delve into the what, why, and how of motivation, its effects on learning, and your ability to spark that motivation using practical strategies to improve academic outcomes.

SERENA PARISER, EDWARD F. DEROCHE

Gain time in each day, reduce stress, and improve your classroom learning environment with 35 practical, teacher-proven strategies for managing time and setting personal boundaries.

CATLIN R. TUCKER

Balance With Blended Learning provides teachers with practical strategies to actively engage students in setting goals, monitoring development, reflecting on growth, using feedback, assessing work quality, and communicating their progress with parents.

CORWIN

A SAGE Publishing Company

Helping educators make the greatest impact

CORWIN HAS ONE MISSION: to enhance education through intentional professional learning.

We build long-term relationships with our authors, educators, clients, and associations who partner with us to develop and continuously improve the best evidence-based practices that establish and support lifelong learning.